CIVIL WAR PRISONS

AMERICAN CLASSICS

CIVIL WAR PRISONS

A Study
in War Psychology

WILLIAM BEST HESSELTINE

FREDERICK UNGAR PUBLISHING CO.
NEW YORK

Republished 1964
in the American Classics series

Third Printing, 1977

Printed in the United States of America

ISBN 0-8044-1382-7

Library of Congress Catalog Card No. 64-25556

TO
KATHERINE LOUISE HESSELTINE

PREFACE

"Why did he pick such a controversial subject?" asked a Quaker friend of the writer's mother as she learned the subject of this study. Writing in the *New Englander* in 1880 Professor Rufus B. Richardson answered this question:

> It will be a long time, then, before anyone will need to apologize for treating of a dead subject when he treats of Andersonville. It is not dead; at the most it only sleepeth. . . . Perhaps a sufficiently worthy excuse for not letting the subject sleep may be a conviction that the facts which have hitherto been treated polemically may be treated pacifically. There would be a satisfaction in not merely proving that humanity had not yet been capable of such a national crime as that charged upon the South, but also in finding a more rational explanation of Andersonville than the deliberate intention to destroy the prisoners.

Since Professor Richardson's apology for writing on the subject, the hatreds of those war times have been cooled by half a century of peace. Within that half century two wars have arisen to test the firmness with which the union was re-welded by 1865. Increased facilities of transportation and communication have added to that welding to make the United States an organic whole. It is possible now, more possible than at the time of Professor Richardson's article, to examine the prisoners and prisons of the Civil War in a scientific spirit.

In addition to the fact that the war has been placed by the passage of time in a position where it may be dealt with in a more proper perspective, the materials which relate to the subject may be said to have been completed. These materials are of two classes. *The Official Records of the Union and Confederate Armies* devote the eight volumes of the second series to the publication of all of the important documents relating to the subject of prisoners of war and military prisons on the two sides. The other class of materials consists of the personal narratives of those who were connected with the prisons of the North and South either as officials or as prisoners. Neither of these sources was available in its entirety to Professor Richardson. In addition to these classes of materials, the more influential newspapers of the two sections have been used.

The materials of the second class are indeed polemical; the prisoners were thoroughly convinced that they had been subjected to treatment by their captors, whether Federal or Confederate, designed to reduce their ranks by starvation and disease. It is for this reason that the subject of prisoners of war appears to be a controversial one. It has been the purpose of the writer to examine, without being swayed by these accounts, the true conditions in regard to prisons and prisoners of the Civil War. In doing this it had been necessary to devote a large amount of space to the matters relating to the exchange of prisoners. An understanding of the issues, the events, and the personalities involved in the technical questions growing out of the execution of the cartel is indispensable to a comprehension of the conditions not only within the prisons but in the minds of the people in the two parts of the country. Two chapters on prisons in North and South in the years 1861-62 reveal that the prisoners were well treated by their captors in the early days of the war. But after the cessation of exchanges under the cartel, the prisons of the South became crowded, and the poverty of the Confederacy resulted in excessive suffering among those unfortunates who were confined in the stockades of Andersonville, Florence, Millen, Macon, and Columbia, or spent dreary days in the famed Libby prison or on Belle Isle. These conditions being reported in the North created the belief that the prisoners were ill treated through a deliberate purpose; the inevitable hatred engendered by the war made such a belief readily credible. The result of this psychosis was that prisoners in the Northern prisons were forced to suffer in retaliation for the alleged Southern cruelty. This feeling did not die with the close of the war but remained to bring about the farcical trial and execution of Henry Wirz, the Andersonville jailor. The same spirit also gave the urge to

the production of a voluminous polemical literature by former prisoners.

A disproportionate amount of space in this study is devoted
to the Southern prisons. This has been made necessary by
two things; a greater amount of material exists on the Southern prisons, and the prison system of the South was less
worthy of the name than that of the North. On the one side,
the prisons came into being as a result of definite plans and
were administered by officers experienced in military administration. In the South, on the other hand, the prison system
was the result of a series of accidents. It was not until the
last months of the war that a commissary-general of prisoners
was appointed in the Confederacy. Prisons came into existence, without definite plans, to meet the exigencies of the
moment.

To Professors Arthur C. Cole, Homer C. Hockett, and
Carl Wittke, of the Ohio State University, the thanks of the
writer are due for their helpful criticisms, constant inspira-
tion, and kindly interest in this study. Miss Isobel Griscom
of the Department of English, University of Chattanooga,
has rendered valuable assistance in preparing the manuscript.

W. B. Hesseltine.

Chattanooga, Tenn., 1930.

CONTENTS

CHAPTER I

THE FIRST PRISONERS

The vicissitudes of warfare render it inevitable that some portion of the armed forces involved in the conflict should fall captive to their opponents. Any person in arms or attached to the hostile army who falls into the hands of the enemy, regardless of his social or military standing, his physical or mental state, is a prisoner of war.[1] As such, he is, of course, entitled upon capture to all of the privileges and subject to all of the inconveniences which the usages of civilized nations impose upon prisoners of war.

The greatest inconvenience to which the prisoner of war is subjected is the loss of liberty, which may take either of two forms: first, it may require the prisoner to give a parole to the effect that he will bear no arms against the captor, will not visit certain localities, or will not give aid and comfort to the enemy; second, it may mean indefinite confinement in a prison under the control of the military authorities of the capturing party. Further punishment than the necessary curtailment of liberty is proscribed by custom. Modern usage requires that prisoners of war shall be treated with humanity, and that they shall not be punished for the crime of belonging to the armed force of the enemy. On the other hand, the prisoners must be supported at the expense of the captor; they must receive the same care in respect to food and clothing as that accorded to the soldiers of the capturing army. The usages of war permit each belligerent to force the other to comply with these rules by retaliation in kind upon the persons of such prisoners as may be held by the aggrieved party. This insistence upon the principles of humanity toward prisoners is peculiar to modern warfare. Savage peoples killed their captives; the civilized states of

[1] See General Orders No. 100, U. S. War Department, 1863, *Official Records of the Union and Confederate Armies in the War of the Rebellion,* series 2, V., 674.

1

Greece and Rome enslaved theirs; the Crusaders held their prisoners for ransom. From this precedent developed the custom of exchanging captives, grade for grade, and man for man. Hence, by the time of the American Revolution, this principle of exchange was universally accepted, and during the War of 1812 was actively practiced. Since its inception, it has been the prisoner's only means, aside from escape or recapture, of regaining liberty.[2]

During the Civil War in America prisoners were duly taken and held by each side. The United States held approximately 220,000; the Confederacy, about 200,000.[3]

As long as two months before the opening guns were fired at Fort Sumpter, the question of prisoners of war arose in Texas, where the Civil War might have first broken out had not Brevet Major General David E. Twiggs, commanding the department of Texas, been a Southerner. Under the command of Twiggs, scattered in frontier posts from San Antonio along the Rio Grande to the borders of New Mexico Territory, were 2,648 officers and men of the regular army of the United States.[4] When the state of Texas decided on secession from the Union, the convention called for that purpose faced the problem of relieving the state of the presence of these troops of the United States. The Committee of Public Safety deputed four commissioners to make the necessary arrangements with Twiggs to remove the troops immediately from the department. In case Twiggs should not be disposed to surrender his troops and the public property under his command, the committee ordered one Ben McCulloch to so display his volunteer "minute men" as to convince Twiggs of the wisdom lying in nonresistance.[5] When the commissioners came to Twiggs, he assured them of his favorable sentiments toward the rights of the South,

---

[2] Cf., Lawrence, *Principles of International Law*. Also *Treatment of Prisoners of War by the Rebel Authorities*, 27-53.

[3] Rhodes, *History of the United States*, V, 506-8.

[4] *Official Records of the Union and Confederate Armies*, series 2, I, 7-8. Schwartz, *Twenty-Two Months a Prisoner of War*, 80.

[5] *Official Records*, series 2, I, 25, 26. February 5, 1861.

but he refused to withdraw immediately from the state and surrender the property under his control; he orally agreed, however, to await the coming of March 2 and to surrender all under his command at that time if the people of the state ratified the ordinance of secession. But the general declared it his "fixed determination" to march his troops with their arms out of the state. The commissioners were not satisfied with this attitude, failing to appreciate the ethics involved in the soldier's pride in his command, and demanded that the general place his acquiescence in writing. Upon Twiggs' refusal to comply, the commissioners decided to resort to the display of force which had been provided, and called upon Colonel McCulloch to advance with the troops under his command.[6]

On February 16 McCulloch marched into the city at four o'clock in the morning with about nine hundred volunteers and militia. The guards on the Alamo were withdrawn on the approach of the Texas forces, who took command of the historic building and stationed themselves in positions to command the Federal troops. In this setting the rising sun found the commissioners again stating their demands to General Twiggs, who finally agreed to the surrender of the public property on condition that his troops be permitted to keep their side arms and equipment and be allowed to march out of the state. To this the commissioners agreed, with the requirement that the troops go by way of the coast, lest in passing through New Mexico or Kansas they "fix freesoilism on the one, or be the nucleus of a Northern army on the other, to menace our frontier in the future."[7]

The commissioners guaranteed to the troops freedom from molestation and assured the officers that every facility would be given to the troops in moving to the coast. "They are our friends," read a circular to the people, "they have heretofore afforded to our people all the protection in their power, and we owe them every consideration."[8] But among

---

[6] *Ibid.*, 3, 26-32.
[7] *Ibid.*, 32-34. Twiggs' report, pages 1-6.
[8] *Ibid.*, 6, 12.

the facilities which were guaranteed to the troops, promptness was not included. Ships and transports arrived on the coast at Indianola; but Colonel Waite, successor to Twiggs who had been removed for discreditable surrender, complained that he had been subjected to delays in obtaining the necessary transportation. The delay caused Waite some unpleasant moments since he feared that the outbreak of hostilities would result in the troops being seized by the Confederacy as prisoners of war. In order to prevent this possibility he concentrated his forces rapidly near Indianola.[9]

This concentration of the troops became a subject of much concern to the Confederate leaders who foresaw that such action prevented their enlistment in the Southern ranks. When Texans called the matter to the attention of the Richmond authorities[10] the war department ordered Colonel Earl Van Dorn to proceed to Texas to procure the troops for the Confederacy. Van Dorn was not eminently successful in his efforts in regard to numbers, but he gained the adherence to his cause of a Major E. Kirby Smith, whose value to the South was to prove equal to numerous men.[11]

Not only did the South desire the services of these veteran troops but they feared the assistance such troops could give to the North. Postmaster-General Reagan was warned that Lincoln might use these troops in an attack on Pensacola "and by a brilliant stroke arouse Northern enthusiasm in favor of coercion."[12] Whatever the considerations involved, April 11 Van Dorn was ordered to assume command in Texas and prevent the further embarkation of the troops.

[9] Ibid., 14, 15. Twiggs was removed from command January 28, 1861 and was dismissed from the service for treachery to the flag March 1. Cf., Ibid., 7, 9-10.

[10] The matter of the enlistment of the troops in the Confederate service was the subject of much concern. McCulloch pointed out to Postmaster-General J. H. Reagan that the officers were unwilling to do anything to help the South. He cited the fact that Twiggs had ordered his men to take their arms and equipment with them. The officers were willing to resign, he declared, after they had arrived in Washington, but "what good will their resignations do the South after they have kept their commands embodied and turn them over with their arms in their hands to Lincoln . . .? This force ought to be disorganized before it leaves this state." Ibid., 36.

[11] Ibid., 37, 38.

[12] H. W. Hawes to Reagan, Ibid., 28.

"Officers and men," he was instructed, "must be regarded as prisoners of war." Those willing to enter the service of the Confederacy might be received and the others were to be confined or paroled.[13] News came to the Confederate authorities that there were still sixteen companies in Texas, nine at Indianola and the others enroute for that point, and Van Dorn received emphatic orders to prevent their escape. The war department authorized Colonel Henry McCulloch to take prisoners the troops in San Antonio, accepting his representations that the change in conditions since Twiggs' surrender justified this action.[14]

From April 23 to May 13 the various detachments on the way to the coast were met by Confederate troops and forced to surrender. Steamers sailed into the channel to block the exit from Indianola and prevented the escape of the troops ready to embark.[15] Waite and his officers, though protesting the legality of the action, signed paroles presented to them by a former associate who had accepted a Confederate commission.[16] These paroles allowed the officers to return to the United States, but confined the men to the limits of the county of Bexar, Texas.[17]

The capture of the United States troops in Texas was counterbalanced, though not numerically, in a short time by the capture of a brigade of the Missouri State militia, assembled for their annual drill at Camp Jackson in St. Louis. Captain Nathaniel Lyon, commanding the United States troops in the city, acted under a proclamation of President Lincoln calling upon all armed rebels to disperse. Since Lyon believed that the state militia was composed of ardent secessionists, and since it was evident that they acted under the orders of a governor who was in favor of taking Missouri out of the Union, he felt himself justified in the precau-

[13] Ibid., 56-57.　　　　[15] Ibid., 39, 40.
[14] Ibid., 58.　　　　　　[16] Ibid., 23, 48.

[17] These officers became the objects of special exchanges in later negotiations between Generals Wool and Huger, facing each other before Richmond (Ibid., 61-103), while the men remained in prison camps in Texas until released under the cartel in February, 1863. Cf., Schwartz, op. cit., 149-206.

tionary measure of surrounding the brigade and calling upon
General D. M. Frost for their surrender. Frost indignantly
protested that Lyon's action was illegal and declared that the
Missouri troops were not in the service of the Confederacy,
that they had taken oaths to support the constitutions of the
state and of the United States. Nevertheless, he surrendered
the men, 669 in number, into the hands of the Federal captain. These prisoners were released on paroles and oaths
not to bear arms against the United States during the existing
conflict.[18]

These two captures—that in Texas in April by the Confederacy, and this in Missouri in May by the United States—
preceded the beginning of armed conflict between the North
and the South. In each case the ethics was questionable.
After promises of free passage North to the troops, the South
took the Texas veterans as prisoners of war. After merely
suspecting the loyalty of the Missouri militia, the North
made captive these men.

Though of little importance in the later development of
the subject of prisoners of war, these early captures served
to bring the question to the attention of both governments.
It became necessary for some policy to be adopted to meet
future developments.

[18] *Official Records*, series 2, I, 106, 116. Bell, "Camp Jackson Prisoners" *Confederate Veteran*, XXXI, 260-61.

CHAPTER II

EXCHANGE PRIOR TO THE CARTEL OF 1862

Before the Texas and Missouri captures, the dominant issue before the United States Government was the theoretical one of the legal status of the seceded states. For a half century one of the dominant schools of political thought and constitutional interpretation had been teaching that there was an inherent right in the structure of the American Union for a state to sever its connection with the Union. However, in opposition to this view flourished the one that held the union indivisible. These theories were forced into the field of practical policy when the South seceded. Had the right of secession been recognized, then the Civil War would have been one of conquest and not, as the administration contended, "a war for the Union."

Since the Lincoln government refused to admit the right of secession, they declared the attempt to secede, rebellion; they regarded all adherents to the Southern cause, traitors, and the army an insurgent force. Although the administration foresaw the possibility of complete recognition, they cautiously avoided any act which might be interpreted as a recognition of the South. Throughout the war, the United States held captive men of the South and treated them as prisoners of war, rather than as traitors, but they refused to admit that their captives were other than traitors. The Southern states, alert, and eager to entrap the United States into recognizing their rights, became interested in inducing the North to exchange prisoners which had been captured.

The question of the recognition of the South, in so far as prisoners of war were concerned, came to an issue in connection with the commissioning of privateers by the Confederacy. On April 17, 1861, President Davis by a proclamation offered to issue letters of marque and reprisal to any men who desired to engage privately their vessels against the United States. This action was legal, for the United States had failed with characteristic slowness to accede to the proposal of the Conference of Paris of 1856, to outlaw privateering. Now, however, in 1861 the United States felt that the time had come to remedy this failure of the preceding administration; so Lincoln issued, on April 19, a counter proclamation that all vessels and their crews taken while acting under the letters of marque and reprisal, issued by Davis, would be considered engaged in piracy and dealt with according to the municipal law of the United States.[1]

June 3, a small schooner, the "Savannah," formerly a pilot boat in the harbor of Charleston, having taken out letters of marque and reprisal, was captured with a prize by the United States brig "Perry." The members of the "Savannah" crew were placed in irons and sent into New York harbor. It was evident the authorities of the United States intended to carry out Lincoln's proclamation.[2]

Immediately after the news of the capture of the "Savannah" was received, Davis ordered the officials at Charleston to arrange for an exchange of the privateersmen. To the overtures the commanding officer of the blockading squadron replied that the men were no longer under his control. On July 6, Davis wrote to Lincoln stating the case:

> It is the desire of this Government so to conduct the war now existing as to mitigate the horrors as far as may be possible, and with this intent its treatment of the prisoners captured by its forces has been marked by the greatest humanity and leniency consistent with public obligation. Some have been permitted to return home on parole, others to remain at large under similar condition within this Confederacy, and all have been furnished with rations for their subsistence such as are allowed to our own troops. It is only since the news has been received of the treatment of the privateers taken on the "Savannah" that I have been compelled to withdraw these indulgences and to hold the prisoners taken by us in strict confinement.

[1] Davis, *Rise and Fall of the Confederate States*, II, 582.
[2] *Ibid.*, 11 ff. *Official Records*, series 2, III, 1-6.

Further, Davis threatened to retaliate in kind if any of the officers or crew of the "Savannah" should be executed.[3]

The retaliation threatened in this letter to Lincoln had already been prepared for, as Davis had stated, by an order of General Lee to General Winder, in charge of matters connected with prisoners in Richmond, to recall the paroles of a colonel and two captains and place them in confinement.[4]

In the North Lincoln received support for his policy. "It is merely a question of nerve," declared one supporter, with the added assurance that Davis would not dare to retaliate.[5] "It seems to us that, in view of the complications . . . it becomes very necessary to try conclusions at once with his braggart rebel bands," another staunch supporter of the administration urged.[6] And with such support the administration decided to ignore Davis' letter, and the prosecution of the privateers for piracy proceeded. But the complexion of affairs changed with the defeat of the Northern arms at the battle of Manassas.

The battle of Bull Run brought into the possession of the Confederates about fifty officers and approximately a thousand enlisted men, who were carried to Richmond and there confined in accordance with the policy announced by Davis in his letter on the "Savannah" prisoners.[7] The possession of these prisoners by the South shook the North from its lofty, theoretical perch. Davis now held prisoners, the Northern press reminded Lincoln, upon whom he could retaliate in case the privateers were hanged. "Let us have war, if war we must have, conducted according to civilized usages—not a savage struggle," demanded the Democratic press.[8]

---

[3] *Ibid.*, 5-6. Several other ships were captured before the matter of the privateers was finally settled. In the following pages the statements in regard to the "Savannah" are not restricted to or necessarily true of that particular ship. The case of the "Savannah" was typical and contemporary documents make little attempt to insure accuracy, the term *Savannah* being used to apply to all the privateersmen. The attempt to unravel the various ships would be tedious and confusing while it would add nothing to the understanding of the general principles involved.

[4] *Ibid.*, 689.

[5] *Harper's Weekly*, June 29, 402.

[6] New York *Times*, July 13.

[7] Ely, *Journal of Alfred Ely*, 23 ff.

[8] New York *News*, July 24.

Even the administration papers changed their tone. No longer complacent, they rather excitedly urged Lincoln to proceed with caution and not to take a position which would increase the horrors of war; they pointed out that the mere taking of prisoners was as much a recognition of belligerency as flags of truce; they sustained their point by citing European precedents. Even the staunchest administration papers declared that it would be unpolitic to hold prisoners until the end of the war and expressed the hope that the government would alter its announced policy. The opinion was that "even he [Lincoln] must be tolerably well satisfied by this time that we are at war with somebody."[9] The democratic papers added their voice to these protestations and smugly proclaimed "absurd" the idea that exchange would mean recognition, suggesting at the same time that the administration "condescend" to adopt the usages of civilized warfare.[10]

The prisoners from Bull Run had anticipated that they would be released on parole from Richmond as had been the practice on both sides up to that time. When they found that an indefinite confinement faced them, the officers drew up a petition addressed to President Lincoln stating that forty officers and some nine hundred men were held in captivity and requesting that some action should be taken which would release them.[11] But the petition met with no response from the government. In the minds of the prisoners, the attitude taken by their government was unfair and the Honorable Alfred Ely, Representative in Congress from the Rochester district of New York, captured while playing the role of spectator on the day of the battle, pointed out in his diary that paroles which McClellan had accepted in western Virginia were recognized by the government and were certainly as near recognition of the Confederacy as would be an arrangement for the exchange of the prisoners. The only hope for the prisoners was that public sentiment, already moving in their favor, would force the administration to

[9] New York *Times*, August 1.   [10] New York *News*, August 2, 19.
[11] Ely, *Journal*, 25. Jeffrey, *Richmond Prisons 1861-62*, 10.

enter into an exchange. "The question does not attract the attention of our Government with the solicitude which belongs to its importance," bewailed Mr. Ely, voicing the sentiments of his fellow unfortunates who had lost relish for the limited view of Richmond that they obtained from the windows of Liggon's quondam tobacco warehouse.[12]

In the field exchanges took place between generals with but slight consideration for the technical question of recognition. In Missouri, after considerable negotiation, three prisoners of the Missouri State Guard were exchanged in September for a like number of Union soldiers by Generals Gideon Pillow and W. H. L. Wallace.[13] This exchange formed the basis for arrangements between Grant and Polk, facing each other at Cairo, Illinois. Grant's early refusal to negotiate on the grounds that he did not recognize the Confederate government was overcome by placing the arrangements on the basis of humanity. From October, 1861, to the fall of the Mississippi forts exchanges continued on this front.[14]

Meantime the government at Washington remained firm in the apparent intention to do nothing to exchange the prisoners. Despite the actions of generals in the West no move was made at Washington, and the Confederacy, having made overtures before Bull Run, now felt "that it would be inconsistent with the dignity and self respect of this government" to attempt further negotiations.[15] Military events of the last of August gave to the Federal government prisoners taken at the fall of Cape Hatteras, some of whom were released on parole, but the majority of whom were confined in Fort Lafayette.[16] No longer could the plea be made that it was impossible to relieve the Richmond prisoners, and public opinion again demanded that something be done for them.[17]

[12] Ely, op. cit., 50, 68.
[13] Official Records, series 2, I, 504-510.
[14] Ibid., 511, 547.
[15] Ibid., series 2, III, 714-15.
[16] Ibid., 32-33.
[17] New York Herald, September 3. The Herald suggested that since the South had not lost prisoners of similar rank to Ely they should be allowed to retain him, while the North would retain Captain Barron, taken at Hatteras. Ely, according to the Herald, was a member of the party which had caused the war and was not worth a drummer boy in exchange.

The prisoners, likewise, felt that if the president and cabinet could see the destitution existing at Richmond and Charleston they would set aside all technical difficulties. They were all persuaded that the conduct of their government was neither wise nor humane and they found hope in the insistent tone of the Northern press,[18] which, even including the stoutest administration organs, began to decry the government's policy of letting men die in prison rather than run the risk of recognizing the Confederacy.[19]

An act of humanity on the part of the Confederacy failed to bring about the hoped-for change in the Northern position. Fifty-seven wounded prisoners in Richmond, convalescing from wounds received in the battle of Bull Run and other engagements, were released on parole and sent north under a flag of truce. This act was reciprocated by President Lincoln who ordered General Scott to release an equal number upon their taking an oath not to bear arms—or, preferably, the oath of allegiance.[20] This was reciprocal humanity, but if the South had any hopes that they would be able to use this action as an opening wedge they were frustrated by the guarded conduct of the Federal authorities.

Another hope for the South came in a proposal from Flag Officer Goldsborough, in command of the blockading squadron off Norfolk, who addressed to General Benjamin Huger, in command of the Confederates before Richmond, a proposition to exchange two lieutenants of their respective navies. Goldsborough, however, was careful to state that he had "no specific authority on the subject of exchanging prisoners" and based his action on the grounds of his friendship for the Federal lieutenant involved. Secretary of War Benjamin welcomed the proposition and gave General Huger permission to make the proposed exchange, suggesting the necessity of making a formal arrangement before transferring the men. But Goldsborough insisted that the arrangement was to be

[18] Ely, *Journal*, 35 ff.

[19] New York *Times*, September 30. Cf. also *National Intelligencer*, October 5 and 12.

[20] Davis, *Rise and Fall of the Confederate Government*, II, 585.

informal, and it was finally carried out on that basis. Again there was no relaxation in the position taken by the North.[21]

Meantime the privateersmen were being tried in Philadelphia for piracy. On October 25 a verdict of guilty was rendered by the jury in the case of Walter W. Smith, Captain of the Confederate brig "Jeff Davis." Thirteen other members of the crew faced trial; three of whom were found guilty three days later; the others awaited proceedings.[22] Meantime the crew of the "Savannah" was tried in New York, but the jury was unable to come to any agreement (October 31).[23]

Already the Confederate congress had passed an act authorizing the president to resort to retaliation for these prisoners.[24] November 9, General Winder was ordered to select by lot from the highest ranking prisoners in his custody one to be confined in a felon's cell and given a felon's treatment while waiting to be executed in the same way as was Smith. Thirteen others of the highest rank were to be selected to await the verdict of the courts in the case of those privateersmen yet to be sentenced. These too were to be confined and treated as though prisoners accused of infamous crimes.[25] The next day the general proceeded to carry out his instructions, and, reading the order of the secretary of war to the assembled officers, he called upon Congressman Ely to draw the slip bearing the name of the fated man. Ely drew and the lot fell upon Colonel Michael Corcoran of the 69th New York militia [Irish]. The selection of the other officers resulted in five colonels, two lieutenant colonels, three majors —all of these grades held as prisoners—and two captains selected by lot, being chosen to await the decision of the Northern court.[26] The hostages were removed, such of them as were in Richmond, to the Henrico county jail; and others,

[21] *Ibid.*, 51-52, 728-29.
[22] *Ibid.*, series 2, III, 58-121.
[23] *Ibid.*, 20, note.
[24] *Statutes at Large, Provisional Congress*, C. S. A.
[25] *Official Records*, series 2, III, 738-39.
[26] Ely, *Journal*, 210-16. Jeffrey, *Richmond Prisons*, 39-42.

who had been sent to Charleston, were confined in the jail at that place.[27]

By this time sentiment in the North was becoming aroused to the extent of open denunciation of the government for its exchange policy. The people were beginning to feel that "If you can crush the rebellion, the acknowledgment of the Confederacy so as to get an exchange of prisoners would amount to nothing; on the other hand if you cannot whip them your refusal to exchange would none the less prevent them from obtaining the end sought—their separation from the Union."[28] It was reported in the press that Secretary of War Stanton approved of exchange and thought that it was demanded by considerations of policy and humanity.[29] Among the few of the more important journals that upheld the administration policy, *Harper's Weekly* declared that the prisoners themselves should not wish the recognition of the Confederacy.[30] But the prisoners were more interested in release than in supporting the government on a technical point which was causing them so much inconvenience. Prisoners in Richmond wrote letters to the Northern papers—the letters were duly passed through the lines by the Confederates—asking querulously when the government was going to exchange them, and expressing the pious wish that Ely were in Congress where he could do something for them. Prisoners importuned Representatives in Congress and the wives of the prisoners added their pleas to the letters of their husbands.[31] To aid this rising tide in favor of exchange came a statement from General Halleck, a writer and recognized authority on international law, who wrote to McClellan, "After full consideration of the subject I am of the opinion that prisoners ought to be exchanged. This exchange is a mere military convention. A prisoner exchanged under the laws of war is not thereby exempted from trial and punish-

[27] *Official Records,* series 2, III, 132. Corcoran, *Captivity of General Corcoran,* 86.

[28] William Irvin to Cameron, *Official Records,* series 2, III, 126-27.

[29] Cincinnati *Daily Commercial,* November 11.

[30] *Harper's Weekly,* November 30, 754. Jeffrey, *op. cit.,* 44-46.

[31] *Official Records,* series 2, III, 152-53, 160-61. *Congressional Globe,* Dec. 17, 1861.

ment as a traitor. Treason is a state or civil offense punishable by the civil courts—the exchange of prisoners of war is only a part of the ordinary *Commercia belli*."[32]

Added to these considerations of humanity and theory, was an ethical and psychological force influencing, pressing the administration to abandon its stand. The government, of necessity, had to consider the attitude of the soldiers; for each man who goes into battle does so under the tacit understanding that his government will care for him in case of mishap. Failure to do so tends to diminish the efficiency of the individual soldier, and to deter others from entering the ranks. Early in the contest the government's course was branded unjust and prophecies of decreased enlistments were made.[33] "It is hard," admitted one paper, "for men going into battle to think that if captured, they cannot be exchanged."[34]

Finally on December 11, Congress came to the point of action. A joint resolution was passed declaring that since exchange had already been practiced indirectly, and since such a course would tend to increase enlistments, to serve the interests of humanity, "and such exchange does not involve a recognition of the rebels as a government," the president was called upon to "inaugurate systematic measures for the exchange of prisoners in the present rebellion."[35]

The "indirect exchanges" in this resolution referred to a system which had developed in the east. Here a plan had been worked out for special exchanges. Following the

[32] *Official Records, loc. cit.*, 150-51. Revolutionary precedents were cited as having a bearing on the existing situation. New York *Times*, December 11; cf. also *National Intelligencer*, December 3. The Massachusetts Historical Society appointed a committee to investigate the extent to which exchanges were carried on during the Revolutionary War. Their report, made December 19, 1861, concluded that exchanges could be carried on in civil war as well as in warfare with a foreign power. No recognition was involved in such exchanges. *National Intelligencer*, January 7, 1862.

[33] New York *News*, August 2, 20. New York *Times*, October 3.

[34] *Harper's Weekly*, November 30, 754.

[35] *Official Records*, series 2, III, 157. The *National Intelligencer*, Devember 13, stated that a committee from New York interviewed the President, General McClellan, and the military committees of both houses. The joint resolution resulted from these interviews.

prompt acceptance of his former offer for an informal mutual release of naval prisoners, Flag Officer Goldsborough again offered to exchange for a Federal lieutenant a prisoner who had resigned his commission in the United States navy.[36] The resigned officer, not in the Confederate service, stood, therefore, in the position of a citizen. Benjamin thought, however, that the Confederacy had a sufficient surplus of prisoners to spare a few for desirable personages, regardless of their status at the moment,[37] and Huger accepted the proposition, though he protested that the action was not in accordance with the usages of war. Goldsborough took pains this second time to point out that the offer originated with him and was in no sense the action of his government.[38] Huger, on the other hand, lost no opportunity to impress on his correspondent that the Confederate States were willing at any time to enter negotiations for a general exchange.[39] Benjamin, however, was disgusted with the small returns in the way of recognition which such negotiations as these were producing. He wrote:

The puerility and tergiversation that marks the whole conduct of the enemy on this subject merit contempt, and it is scarcely consistent with self-respect to continue any intercourse with them in relation to exchange of prisoners until some semblance of regard for civilized usages is displayed by them.[40]

But the Confederate secretary, unwilling to lose this opportunity, let negotiations for special exchanges continue between the two commanders.[41]

Another form of special exchange was put into operation by the adoption of the practice of releasing men from prison on parole to proceed to the enemy capital and there obtain the release of officers of equal rank, generally specified by name, upon which they were to be absolved from their paroles. Failing to accomplish the desired exchange the men so released pledged themselves to return to the prison within

[36] *Official Records*, series 2, III, 155-56.
[37] *Ibid.*, 742.   [39] *Ibid.*, 53.
[38] *Ibid.*, 137.   [40] *Ibid.*, 746.
[41] *Ibid.*, 155, 752, 164, 168 *passim* for others.

a specified time.[42] Two hundred and forty-nine of the North Carolina captives were released from Fort Warren to proceed south to procure releases for themselves.[43] The commander at Fort Warren was ordered to prepare a list of persons to be released including the "most feeble and infirm" and those having families to support.[44] The object of this, of course, was to give the enemy as little reinforcement as possible as well as to relieve the government of the additional expense of caring for such prisoners. But this policy was matched in the South where the commander of one of the Richmond prisons submitted a list of prisoners whom he recommended for exchange; ". . . from my personal knowledge of all the prisoners I think those names are those least likely to be efficient for harm to the Confederacy in the event, not probable, that they again enter the service of the United States."[45] The Fort Warren releases were sent through General Wool, facing General Huger at Norfolk, and were passed through the lines from the one general to the other.[46]

About the same time Generals Wool and Huger had found it convenient to exchange prisoners with each other, Huger assured Wool that the Confederacy was willing to comply with the customs of civilized nations and hence accepted Wool's proposals for individuals. He seldom failed to impress upon Wool as he did upon Goldsborough that the cause of humanity would be served to a much greater extent by making the exchange general rather than special.[47]

The system of special exchanges was eminently satisfactory to the administration. They planned to continue the system, for it afforded the prisoners a needed relief from confinement and it rendered unnecessary the dangerous practice of negotiations which might result in the inadvertent recognition of the Confederacy. The union commanders constantly insisted that the arrangements which they made with Huger were special arrangements made on their own responsibility,

[42] Ibid., 166, 170, 263, 463, 782, 698, 841.
[43] Ibid., 161, 162, 163.   [45] Ibid., 753.
[44] Ibid., 128.   [46] Ibid., 158, 162, 167.
[47] Ibid., 165. See also 170, 171, 173, 175, 176, 188, 189, 195-98.

and they consistently refused to allow the practice to develop into a general system.[48]   In accordance with the administration's plan to continue the practice of releasing the prisoners to procure exchanges for themselves in the South, Secretary Seward ordered General McClellan to release 500 of the Hatteras prisoners as soon as the 250 already released had secured their exchanges.[49]

Indications of a weakening in the administration's position came in two cases.   McClellan instructed Burnside, preparing for an expedition against Roanoke Island in Hatteras Inlet, to exchange for any prisoners which might be taken from his army in the engagement,[50] and the war department instructed Halleck in Missouri to obtain the release of the Texas prisoners in such a way as not to "commit the United States."[51]   Halleck was unable to understand this limitation until it was explained that he was not to recognize that there was a Confederate government.[52]   These two cases, while adding nothing to actual practice, were a weakening of the theory since exchanges in the field heretofore had never enjoyed the official cognizance of the war department.

Another step in the breakdown of the United States position came in a decision to regard the privateersmen as prisoners of war.   The hand of fate, acting through Congressman Ely, had been particularly kind to the Confederacy in the selection of a hostage for the pirate Smith.   Colonel Corcoran was an Irishman, who had emigrated to New York in 1849.   Here he had gained wealth as the proprietor of the "Hibernia" Hotel, had attained prominence in the affairs of the Irish 69th regiment of the state militia of which he had been elected colonel, and finally had won undying fame as an Irishman by refusing to order his regiment out in a special

[48] *Ibid.*, 173-74.   The *National Intelligencer*, January 21, 1862, declared that all "questions may be regarded as solved by the arrangements into which our government has entered . . . . conducted as they are through direct negotiations between the commanding Generals, ... all ends of military justice and humanity are fully subserved, while no political admission is made or gained on either side."

[49] *Official Records*, series 2, III, 175.   [51] *Ibid.*, series 2, I, 69-70.

[50] *Ibid.*, series 1, IX, 353.   [52] *Ibid.*, 74.

parade in honor of the Prince of Wales. Proceedings to courtmartial him for this act of racial chauvinism were estopped at the outbreak of the war, and his regiment was ordered to the front, where the gallant colonel fell into the hands of the enemy in his first battle at Bull Run.[53] His selection as a hostage aroused his fellow countrymen to protestations in his favor, and in February a monster mass meeting in Faneuil Hall demanded his immediate release.[54]

By January, 1862, the administration realized that it could not retain the support of the people in its intention to regard privateersmen as pirates. Secretary Seward ordered General Wool to inquire whether Corcoran could be exchanged for Smith.[55] "This," declared Huger, "is a complete giving away of the principle hitherto asserted"; and he thought that the North ought to go a step further and begin the principle of general exchanges.[56] Benjamin instructed Huger to reply that no such proposition would be considered until there was "an unconditional abandonment of the pretext that they [the privateersmen] are pirates and until they are released from the position of felons and placed in the same condition as other prisoners of war."[57]

At the same time the business of the special exchanges had grown to unwieldy proportions, involving a great deal of clerical work in receiving the propositions for exchange and transmitting them to the secretary of war, who, in turn, sent to General Winder for the prisoners. The prisoners were then sent to the secretary of war and by him to Huger who passed them through the lines to Wool. Huger demanded that he should be relieved from the duties attendant on this business in order that he might devote some of his time to the military affairs under his control.[58] He further suggested to Wool that, since the business of exchange had become established, it would save trouble if the two governments should appoint commissioners to attend to such matters, add-

[53] Ely, *Journal*, 219-222.   [56] *Ibid.*, 774.
[54] New York *Times*, February 6.   [57] *Ibid.*, 776.
[55] *Official Records*, series 2, III, 197.   [58] *Ibid.*, 774. Huger to Benjamin.

ing the assurance that the Confederate States were willing to make any arrangements which would facilitate matters. Wool concurred in this suggestion and recommended to the war department that some such system should be adopted.[59]

Well aware of the sentiment in the North in favor of exchange, the Confederate authorities lost no opportunity to promulgate the idea that the entire odium for failure to participate in a general system should rest upon the Lincoln administration. In pursuing this idea, they informed the prisoners that their government "has so far ignored your existence," while Huger wrote to the commander of Fort Warren suggesting mutual cooperation in releases to meet the demands of humanity and civilization. State legislatures swelled the chorus seeking the release of the prisoners and the abandonment of the theory of piracy in connection with the privateers.[60]

In the hope of quieting Northern opinion, Secretary of War Stanton issued an order, January 20, declaring that his department recognized as its first duty the care of the prisoners in the South, and that he, therefore, appointed two commissioners who were to proceed south "and there take such measures as may be needful to provide for the wants and contribute to the comfort of such prisoners at the expense of the United States." The Reverend Bishop Ames of the Methodist Episcopal Church and the Honorable Hamilton Fish of New York were appointed as the commissioners, and orders were given to the quartermaster-general, the surgeon-general, and General Wool to establish a depot for the reception of food, clothing, and medical supplies subject to the requisitions of the commissioners. Twenty thousand dollars were deposited to their credit in New York banks.[61]

The selection of these two men did not meet with approval. Mr. Ely, who had been released from Richmond in the latter part of December, was considered to be the proper

[59] *Ibid.*, 192, 212, 213.

[60] *Ibid.*, 706, August 20, 1861. *Ibid.*, 199-200. Action of the Michigan legislature *Ibid.*, 211. *National Intelligencer*, January 21, 1862.

[61] *Official Records*, series 2, III, 192, 213, 221-24, 230.

person for the mission. He knew the prisoners better than anyone else could. It was also a disappointment that the relief and not the release of the prisoners was contemplated, but there was some consolation to be obtained from the hope that the existing system of special exchanges would eventually secure the release of all.[62]

But, however satisfied the North might be with the existing arrangements, the South was looking for something more definite than informal and partial exchanges. Secretary Benjamin found himself as impatient as Huger in regard to the time required to deal with the numerous applications for individual exchanges. Further, the system of individual exchange, while it served the ends of humanity in releasing those prisoners who needed it most, did not meet the need of the Confederacy for a formal system, for it depended too much on the individual whims of the officers having the release of the prisoners in charge.[63] In order to remedy matters in a direction more in accordance with the wishes of the Confederacy, Benjamin instructed General Joseph E. Johnston, the ranking officer of the Southern army, to enter into negotiations with General McClellan for a general exchange. This was to be an ultimatum: "We regret to be forced to decline making further exchanges on the anomalous system which now exists and which experience has satisfied us must prove impracticable."[64] Johnston readily undertook this mission, and made the proposed overture to McClellan. Receiving no answer to his communication, Johnston reported, February 11, his information that a cabinet meeting in Washington had considered the matter and that he therefore expected no reply; adding, "Under such circumstance permit me to suggest the propriety of at least suspending the un-

[62] New York *Times*, January 25, 28.

[63] The Richmond *Dispatch*, June 7 and 10. Three-months volunteers whose terms had expired while in prison were released in preference to soldiers of the regular army or those who had volunteered for the war. The *Dispatch* recommended that foreigners, with whom Yankees would gladly dispense, be sent in exchange while native Americans be held to increase pressure on the Northern government.

[64] *Official Records*, series 2, III, 778-79.

precedented mode of exchange now practiced."[65] Just at this
time Benjamin learned of the mission of Ames and Fish from
the newspapers. Such a mission was the antithesis of his
plans and he ordered Huger to detain the bishop and his
associate and forward their instructions to Richmond.[66]

The commissioners arrived at Fort Monroe on February
4th, and Wool asked Huger to receive them; Huger delayed
meeting them until he sent their instructions to Richmond
where they became the subject of a cabinet meeting. The
result of the meeting was a letter, written by Benjamin for
Huger to sign, which welcomed Ames and Fish on behalf of
the Confederate States. But the Confederacy desired to save
the gentlemen the trouble and the expense of making a trip
to Richmond and therefore appointed two commissioners to
meet with the representatives of the United States. Messrs.
James A. Seddon and Charles M. Conrad were designated
commissioners and they had instructions to agree to an immediate exchange and release of all prisoners in Confederate
and Federal prisons.[67] Benjamin could evidently conceive of
no relief for the prisoners comparable to an exchange. Ames
and Fish were quite bewildered by this turn of events and
hastily asked Stanton for instructions to cover the situation.
Stanton ordered them to return to Washington.[68]

[65] *Ibid.*, 231, 784, 794.

[66] *Ibid.*, 217, 783-84. The Richmond *Dispatch*, February 1, 1862, declared the
"prison inspecting committee" to be an insult to the South and hoped that the government would refuse to receive Ames and Fish. February 7th, it was declared that the invaders who had been captured had not been treated as they deserved but had been
accorded the best of treatment.

[67] *Official Records*, series 2, III, 790-91.

[68] *Ibid.*, 248, 250. Ames and Fish were able, however, to give the Confederacy
some valuable information while they awaited the desired permission to pass through
the lines. They bore the official confirmation of the news that the privateersmen were
now treated as prisoners of war. Huger had refused Wool's offer to exchange Smith
for Corcoran (the difference in rank of the two would prevent this) until the North
gave up the pretext that the privateersmen were pirates and treated them as prisoners
of war. Benjamin, however, was willing to overlook their case if the proposed
Johnston-McClellan convention should mature. "We can force them on that point
simply by retaining the hostages and refusing to exchange them," he declared, relying
on the agitation in the North to secure the release of Corcoran and the other colonels.
Ibid., 785. During the Ames-Fish correspondence Wool transmitted Seward's order

The failure of the Ames-Fish mission was final proof that nothing but a general exchange would be acceptable to the South, and it was evident that Northern public opinion could no longer be put off with half-way measures. When he recalled Ames and Fish, Stanton informed Wool that he could tell Huger that he (Wool) alone was clothed with full power to arrange the exchange of prisoners. Wool was authorized to confer with Seddon and Conrad, Huger or anyone else who might be sent to make an exchange. In the instructions to Seddon and Conrad had been the provision that in arranging for a general exchange and a permanent system it should be provided that if one or the other of the parties should hold an excess of prisoners, those were to be released on parole, and sent to their own country. When more prisoners were captured by the side to which these paroled prisoners belonged, upon the release of these captives, that side could declare exchanged a number of their paroled soldiers equal to the number of prisoners so released by them. This provision was embodied in the instructions which Wool received from Stanton.[69] This result was naively hailed as a glorious success for the mission of Ames and Fish[70] and the commissioners themselves took occasion to congratulate the government on finding a means to liberate the prisoners which, at the same time, enabled the government to "vindicate its authority and to maintain its National existence."[71]

Wool, on February 16, offered suggestions to Huger as a basis for a cartel between the two armies. He repeated the

of January 31, placing the privateersmen in the same condition as prisoners of war. *Ibid.*, 229. The North welcomed this decision, looking forward to a general exchange of prisoners. The New York *Times* branded the technical question of recognition as "senseless red-tape" and called for results. New York *Times*, February 3, 1862.

[69] *Official Records*, series 2, III, 88-90, 254.

[70] New York *Times*, February 15. Cf. also the *National Intelligencer*, February 18, 1862. "Our commissioners opened negotiations which resulted in perfect success. An equal exchange was agreed on, but the Confederates had three hundred more prisoners than our Government; but, with commendable magnanimity they proposed to release those also on parole if our Government would agree to release three hundred of their men that hereafter fall into our hands. This noble commission of Secretary Stanton, therefore, has its ample reward."

[71] *Official Records*, series 2, III, 261.

proposition that the excess of prisoners should be released on parole to await exchange and offered a scheme for the evaluation of officers of different ranks.[72] Huger was relieved from the necessity of carrying on the negotiations and Brigadier General Howell Cobb was selected, since, Wool having accepted the major principle of releasing the excess on parole, there remained "only the military details" to be completed. These details involved the delivery of the prisoners on parole to the "frontier" of their country at the expense of the captor, the choosing by each party of the prisoners to be released from parole when a number of the enemy's forces had been discharged—thus obviating the pernicious system of having the choices made by the enemy—and, finally, the scale of equivalents for officers of unequal rank. Above all, Cobb was instructed to make no rule which could possibly cause disputes. The system of special exchanges was suspended to await developments.[73]

On February 23, Wool and Cobb met and discussed the cartel of exchange. It was agreed that exchange should be based on the cartel which had been drawn up during the War of 1812 between the United States and Great Britain, especially such features as provided for the evaluation of the different grades of officers. It was agreed that prisoners in excess should be delivered on parole and that each party should have the right to release such of its prisoners as it wished on discharging a like number of the enemy. One proposition submitted by Cobb was rejected by Wool until he could obtain instructions from Washington: "that prisoners be discharged or paroled within ten days of their capture, and to be delivered on the frontier of their own country free of expense to the prisoners and at the expense of the capturing party." Wool agreed to accept this, leaving out the

[72] Ibid., 266. Wool's scheme was a complicated one which would have proven unworkable as the officers were finally counted in exchange. He suggested that a colonel should be equal to a lieutenant colonel and one major, or three majors or seven captains; a lieutenant colonel to be equal to two majors, or four captains or six first lieutenants; a major to two captains, or four first lieutenants, etc.

[73] Ibid., 800-801; series 2, I, 87.

word "frontier" until he could obtain further instructions.[74]

Down to the time of the negotiations between Wool and Cobb the Confederacy had held the majority of the prisoners. Hence the acceptance of the proposal to release this excess on parole gave the advantage to the North. But events just preceding the negotiations had changed the relative situation. The Burnside expedition against Roanoke Island resulted in the capture of 2,500 prisoners, while on February 16, General Grant captured Fort Donelson, and 15,000 prisoners were sent north to prison camps in Ohio, Indiana, and Illinois. The acceptance of the proposition to deliver the excess of the prisoners on parole would be expensive to the North while all of the advantage of the arrangement would accrue to the South. As was natural under such conditions Wool's arrangements were subjected to the closest scrutiny, and in the moment of victory it was not to be expected that such unusual favors to the enemy would be shown. Wool was informed by Stanton that "the proposition is obnoxious in its terms and import and wholly inadmissible, and as the terms you were authorized to offer have not been accepted you will make no arrangement except for actual exchanges."[75]

While these negotiations were in progress, the Confederate authorities had issued orders for the release of 400 prisoners to balance a number coming from Fort Warren in response to a proposition which General Huger had made to the commander of that prison. An arrangement with Burnside had led to orders being given also for the release of all of the prisoners held in Richmond—about 3,500.[76] But Cobb had become suspicious when Wool had referred the arrangement to Washington and he advised retarding the removal of the

[74] *Ibid.*, series 2, III, 301-9. The equivalents fixed by this cartel and taken from the cartel of 1813 valued a general-in-chief at 60 enlisted men; lieutenant general, 40; major general, 30; brigadier general, 20; colonel, 15; lieutenant colonel, 10; major, 8; captain, 6; lieutenant, 4; second lieutenant, 3; non-commissioned officers, 2.

[75] *Ibid.*, 322.

[76] Richmond *Enquirer*, February 19. New York *Times*, February 25. Harris, *Prison Life in the Tobacco Warehouse at Richmond*, 163.

prisoners until Stanton's reply had been received. He had also made arrangements for the release on parole of the privateersmen and the hostages held for them, and these especially he advised retaining.[77]

When Wool learned of Stanton's decision, he called Cobb for another meeting, telling him that his instructions were strictly limited to the specifications in his letter to Huger. It was useless for Cobb to point out that Wool had had the fullest power at that time; and, despite the fact that Cobb offered a cartel providing for the delivery of prisoners "to the frontier of the line of hostilities," he was forced to write to Benjamin that the North had "backed down from their own proposition."[78]

The reasons for the sudden change of the administration was the subject of misunderstanding at the time. The use of the word "frontier" was later claimed as the reason for changing Wool's instructions, for such a statement implied that the North recognized a territorial boundary of the South.[79] But at the time Wool declared that the question at issue was really the matter of expense attached to transporting the captives. He said that as the matter involved an expenditure he was not authorized to provide, he was therefore obliged to submit the proposition to his government.[80] The more likely interpretation, however, is that the war department did not base its action on any well-defined issue; but, since the North now held the excess of prisoners, it took advantage of a doubtful provision in the proposed cartel to reject the entire settlement.[81]

The system of special exchanges was satisfactory to the North and Wool was instructed to continue this arrangement, but the South was unwilling that such exchanges be continued. Huger was instructed to enter into no more such arrangements; and Stanton, upon receiving the news, piously

[77] Official Records, series 2, III, 806-8.
[78] Ibid., 333, 338, 809, 812.
[79] Treatment of Prisoners of War, 294-95.
[80] Official Records, series 2, III, 347.
[81] See Cobb's Report, Ibid., 812.

stated that since the department had "exhausted all the means in a fruitless effort to establish a just and liberal system of exchange with the enemy" there was nothing to do but abide the enemy's reopening of the question. In the same spirit he was able to inform Congress a month later that the rebels had disregarded the arrangements which Cobb had made with Wool.[82]

After the failure of the Wool-Cobb negotiations there still remained the problem of the privateersmen and the hostages held for them. There had been an understanding that they were to be the first released and it was their failure to arrive, on the advice of Cobb, which caused the failure of the negotiations to be particularly felt. The House of Representatives passed a resolution demanding that the war department make no more exchanges until Corcoran and a Colonel Wilcox were released.[83] Accordingly, the efforts of the United States centered in the effort to obtain this release. There was one opening in the Confederate position which gave some hope of accomplishing the end; Huger believed that the negotiations pending at the time of the meeting between Wool and Cobb should be carried out.[84] Wool agreed that this was true and added that he saw no reasons why they should not continue exchanges. A correspondence continued between these two generals, while the Confederate authorities insisted that they would no longer consider propositions for individual and special exchanges. But the economics of the situation began to be pressing and Huger, April 15, suggested to Wool that each side appoint a commissary to care for the needs of their own prisoners in the hands of the enemy. Wool

[82] *Ibid.*, 376, 460-61, 811.

[83] *Ibid.*, 401. Some of the hostages had been already passed through the lines in accordance with the understanding between Wool and Cobb. These had been sent out before Cobb stopped the release. The colonels, particularly Corcoran, were still held. Corcoran, according to the New York *Times* of March 10, was held as a spy for having had in his possession maps of the defenses of Richmond which he was attempting to take through the lines. This report was incorrect but aided the sentiment in his favor and may have been responsible for the resolution of Congress.

[84] *Ibid.*, 406. Huger had especial reference to the exchange of Colonel William Hoffman, taken in Texas and commissary-general of the Northern prisons, for Captain Barron, taken at Hatteras.

felt that "the proposition would have been tantamount to a recognition of their Government and independence as a nation" and refused, but took occasion to suggest, as the Confederacy had hastily done when a similar proposition had been made by Ames and Fish, that the best way to relieve the prisoners was to exchange them, and reiterated his willingness to accept propositions of exchange.[85]

Since this accorded with the desires of the Confederates, Huger was authorized to make arrangements for a fair and honorable exchange.[86] The new negotiations began auspiciously with Wool declaring "I have no doubt that you and myself could agree upon a cartel for a general exchange that could be as I believe satisfactory to all parties interested."[87] In the same spirit Huger suggested to Randolph, the new secretary of war, that the noncommissioned officers and privates, about whom there could be no controversy, should be released and sent down the river to Fort Monroe. To Wool, Huger suggested that the new arrangements should start with the mutual release on parole of the privateersmen and the hostages. These were then to be exchanged for each other so far as their assimilated ranks would allow, and the remainder of the hostages might be exchanged for those prisoners who had been longest in captivity.[88]

Stanton approved the proposition and told Wool that the privateersmen were at Fort Lafayette and ready to be exchanged.[89] Huger's suggestion to release the noncommissioned officers and privates was acted upon, and May 15 the first of 800 released men arrived at Fort Monroe.[90] Wool sent for the privateersmen while Huger asked Randolph to have the hostages forwarded to him at City Point and the two generals prepared to pass them through the lines.[91] Randolph, however, replied that the hostages were at Salisbury, and that they would be delivered when a cartel was made according to the cartel of 1813 which Wool and Huger had

[85] *Ibid.*, 407, 456, 458.   [88] *Ibid.*, 510, 860.
[86] *Ibid.*, 846.   [89] *Ibid.*, 514-15.
[87] *Ibid.*, 504-5.   [90] New York *Times*, May 15.
[91] *Official Records*, series 2, III, 561, 877 *et seq.*

agreed was to be made the basis of the exchange. Huger asked authority to wire Salisbury to have the hostages sent immediately but Randolph declared that he would have to know the number and the rank of the privateersmen before he could fix the equivalents for them.[92] Huger now perceived that Randolph was playing a double game. It was his plan to receive the privateersmen and declare that they were exchanged for a portion of the hostages who had already been sent through the lines in February. Such a scheme would have effectively blocked the way for any exchange. Huger indignantly protested that while it would probably fulfill the letter it would certainly not meet the spirit of his offer to Wool.

I must comply with the terms of my letter. . . . or I shall be guilty of similar conduct to that pursued by General Wool, to which I cannot consent. I repeat my request that I have authority granted me to send for and deliver over on parole, all officers once held as hostages provided General Wool delivers to me all the privateersmen.[93]

On June 1, a lieutenant colonel appeared before the Confederate troops at Petersburg with the privateersmen. He was armed with copies of the cartel of 1813 and the letters which had formed the basis of the agreement. Since Huger had been removed from the control of the business under Randolph's plea that Wool had overreached him,[94] the colonel was detained until word could be sent to Richmond. On June 4, having refused to deliver the privateersmen without receiving the hostages, he was informed that there had been a misunderstanding of Huger's promise and that the Confederate authorities were willing to confer with the commander at Fort Monroe in regard to an exchange.[95] The privateersmen were returned to Fort Lafayette and the hopes for the relief of the hostages sank again. Randolph evidently

---

[92] Ibid., 881-85.   [93] Ibid., 886.

[94] Ibid., 650. Wool had been removed from the command at Fort Monroe and succeeded by Dix before the completion of these negotiations . The matter was of so much interest to him that he had asked for and received permission to remain until a settlement was made.

[95] Ibid., 654-56. Huger wrote to Wool explaining the entire proceedings and stated that he was not in Petersburg on the day the privateersmen arrived.

thought that the Irish hero was too valuable to surrender
for anything so intangible as Wool's promise that a system
of general exchanges would be inaugurated.

This new failure to effect any plan of exchange left the
question unsolved, and added the obstacle that each side now
had the basis for a well-founded distrust of any proposition
which came from the other. Fortunately this feeling did not
extend to the army, and on June 8 General McClellan
offered to send a staff officer to meet a representative of General Lee for the purpose of arranging a general exchange.
McClellan received authority for this action, after it was
taken, but was permitted to arrange only for an exchange
between his and Lee's armies. He was told of the "perfidy"
of the South in overruling Huger. Preliminary courtesies
passed between the commanders in the mutual release of
medical officers taken in the battles then in progress before
Richmond.[96] Lee appointed General Cobb to represent him
in an endeavor to retrieve his former lack of success, and gave
him instructions to conclude any arrangement which provided
for exchange on the basis of equality.[97] Colonel Key was
appointed to meet Cobb on behalf of the federal commander
and for two hours the two held an enjoyable conversation,
during which Key learned that Cobb had plenary powers and
concluded that there was "no disposition to overreach me in
this conference" but failed to conclude any arrangement
about exchanges. He made a long report on his conversation
in regard to the course and conduct of the war, a report which
earned him a reprimand from Stanton for not confining his
intercourse with the enemy to the matter in hand, and Mc-
Clellan was informed that "The President's instructions re-
specting any further effort at exchange will be speedily communicated to you."[98] With this curt notice the subject of
exchange resumed its wonted status.

Nevertheless, the subject was not to be permitted to lie
dormant. The South still refused individual exchanges,

[96] *Ibid.*, 663, 666, 670-71.   [98] *Ibid.*, series 2, IV, 31, 48.
[97] *Ibid.*, 773.

while an ever increasing number of prisoners were confined in Richmond, or released on paroles which prohibited their becoming anything but a burden on the government. On June 23, Congress in a joint resolution called upon Stanton for information as to the progress of the negotiations,[99] while the battles before Richmond continued to pour prisoners into the South. The feeling grew that the government was at fault and popular imagination was stirred with pictures of the crowded warehouses of Richmond, with their brutal keepers, cruel guards, and rotten food. "Political necessity should yield to humanity," thought the people who joined in the cries, "our government must change its policy!" "our prisoners must be exchanged!"[100]

While Northern opinion demanded exchange on the grounds of humanity, more practical considerations prevailed in the South. General Lee called the attention of the war department to the necessity for providing for the greatly increased number of prisoners and suggested that General Cobb again be appointed to deal with Wool, who still retained his full authority over the subject. At the same time he made arrangements to send the wounded home on parole. General Winder reported to Randolph on July 3 that 2,000 prisoners had been released on parole at Chattanooga.[101] Randolph realized the embarrassment due to the increasing number of prisoners and authorized Lee to appoint Cobb, and to hasten the arrangements as much as possible.

The release of the wounded prisoners served to increase the already friendly relations between McClellan and Lee, causing McClellan to commend to Stanton the humane spirit which Lee had evinced and to join his voice to the public demand by recommending mutual releases and the exchange of those on parole.[102]

With such spirit on both sides the new negotiations promised some satisfactory plan for the release of the prisoners.

[99] *Ibid.*, 53.
[100] New York *Times*, July 9, 17.
[101] *Official Records*, series 2, IV, 197 ff., 797, 811.
[102] *Ibid.*, 168.

July 12, Dix was notified that Lincoln wanted him to undertake the negotiations, observing caution, however, to avoid any recognition of the Confederacy. A personal interview convinced Dix that this was really the desire of the president. Because of the illness of Cobb, the Confederate appointee to meet Dix was General D. H. Hill, who was clothed with full authority for the occasion. Dix and Hill met on July 18 and drew up a tentative cartel which was submitted to their respective chiefs, both of whom approved the arrangement. Four days later the cartel was formally signed and ratified by the commissioners.[103] In no essential features did the document which now actually went into effect differ from the

[103] *Ibid.*, 174 ff., 210, 239, 266-67. The Cartel read as follows: The undersigned having been commissioned by the authorities they respectively represent to make arrangements for a general exchange of prisoners of war have agreed to the following articles:
Article 1. It is hereby agreed and stipulated that all prisoners of war held by either party including those taken on private armed vessels known as privateers shall be discharged upon the conditions and terms following: (Here follows a schedule of ranks of officers in terms of privates. See note 74.)
Article 2. Local State, civil and militia rank held by persons not in actual military service will not be recognized, the basis of exchange being the grade actually held in the naval and military service of the respective parties.
Article 3. If citizens, held by either party on charges of disloyalty or any alleged civil offense are exchanged it shall only be for citizens. Captured sutlers, teamsters and all civilians in the actual service of either party to be exchanged for persons in similar positions.
Article 4. All prisoners of war to be discharged on parole in ten days after their capture, and the prisoners now held and those hereafter taken to be transported to the points mutually agreed upon at the expense of the capturing party. The surplus prisoners not exchanged shall not be permitted to take up arms again, nor to serve as military police or constabulary force in any fort, garrison or field work held by either of the respective parties, nor as guards of prisons, depots or stores, nor to discharge any duty usually performed by soldiers, until exchanged under the provisions of this cartel. The exchange is not to be considered complete until the officer or soldier exchanged for has been actually restored to the lines to which he belongs.
Article 5. Each party upon the discharge of prisoners of the other party is authorized to discharge an equal number of their own officers or men, from parole, furnishing at the same time to the other party a list of their prisoners discharged and of their own officers and men relieved from parole, thus enabling each party to relieve from parole such of their own officers and men as the party may choose. The list thus mutually furnished will keep both parties advised of the true condition of the exchange of prisoners.
Article 6. The stipulations and provisions above mentioned to be of binding obligation during the continuance of the war, it matters not which party may have the surplus of prisoners, the great principles involved being, first, an equitable exchange of prisoners,

agreement made by Wool and Cobb, nor did it contain provisions which were in any way new to the discussion. It was designed for permanence, for Article 9 provided that no disputes which might arise should affect the exchanges provided for by the document. The New York *Times* promised that the exchange of prisoners would be good for a hundred thousand recruits.[104]

man for man, officer for officer, or officers of higher grade exchanged for officers of lower grade or for privates, according to the scale of equivalents; second, that privateers and officers and men of different services may be exchanged according to the same scale of equivalents; third, that all prisoners, of whatever arm of service, are to be exchanged or paroled in ten days from the time of their capture, if it be practicable to transfer them to their own lines in that time; if not, as soon thereafter as practicable; fourth, that no officer, soldier or employee, in the service of either party, is to be considered as exchanged and absolved from his parole until his equivalent has actually reached the lines of his friends; fifth, that the parole forbids the performance of field, garrison, police, or guard, or constabulary duty.

D. H. HILL,   JOHN A. DIX,
Major General C. S. Army   Major General

Supplementary Articles

Article 7. All prisoners of war now held on either side and all prisoners hereafter taken shall be sent with all reasonable dispatch to A. M. Aiken's, below Dutch Gap, on the James River, Va., or to Vicksburg, on the Mississippi River, in the state of Mississippi, and there exchanged or paroled until such exchange can be effected, notice being previously given by each party of the number of prisoners it will send and the time when they will be delivered at those points respectively; and in case the vicissitudes of war shall change the military relations of the places designated in this article to the contending parties so as to render the same inconvenient for the delivery and exchange of prisoners, other places bearing as nearly as may be the present local relations of said places to the lines of said parties shall be by mutual agreement substituted. But nothing in this article contained shall prevent the commanders of two opposing armies from exchanging prisoners or releasing them on parole from other points mutually agreed on by said commanders.

Article 8. For the purpose of carrying into effect the foregoing articles of agreement each party will appoint two agents, to be called agents for the exchange of prisoners of war, whose duty it shall be to communicate with each other by correspondence and otherwise, to prepare the lists of prisoners, to attend to the delivery of the prisoners at the places agreed on and to carry out promptly, effectually, and in good faith all the details and provisions of the said articles of agreement.

Article 9. And in case any misunderstanding shall arise in regard to any clause or stipulation in the foregoing articles it is mutually agreed that such misunderstanding shall not interrupt the release of prisoners on parole, as herein provided, but shall be made the subject of friendly explanations in order that the object of this agreement may neither be defeated nor postponed.

D. H. HILL,   JOHN A. DIX,
Major General C. S. Army   Major General

[104] New York *Times*, July 13. Cf. *National Intelligencer*, July 24, 1862.

CHAPTER III

NORTHERN PRISONS 1861—1862

The beginning of armed conflict in the Civil War found both belligerents without an organization for the care of prisoners of war. The outbreak of the war revealed that there was no one to care for the prisoners, as a prison system with its commissary-general, prisons, clerks, commanding officers, and guards had been unnecessary in times of peace. A system of paroling the troops captured in battle was the obvious solution of the problem. With the exception of Twiggs' command in Texas, where the enlisted men were confined in hastily constructed prisons, paroles had been exacted from military prisoners. In Missouri, the state militia taken at Camp Jackson were released on their oath not again to bear arms. In western Virginia, General McClellan followed the practice of releasing men on parole as soon as they were taken. An exception to this rule was, however, made in the case of officers who had resigned commissions in the service of the United States to accept commands under the rebel flag. These, by the order of Lieutenant General Scott, were sent to Fort Lafayette in New York harbor.[1]

The system of exacting paroles and releasing prisoners immediately after their capture might be as effective as it is humane in a conflict of minor proportions, but in warfare on a large scale, such a system presents difficulties. In the case of guerilla warfare, especially, the captor has no assurance that the prisoners so released will not again return to bushwhacking operations. If exchange is desirable, a system of indiscriminate paroling creates problems which are almost insuperable when the time comes for counting and evaluating the prisoners. Military conflict on a large scale and for a prolonged period necessarily presupposes that soldiers taken

[1] *Official Records,* series 2, III, 10.

in arms shall be retained as prisoners of war for the use and benefit of the capturing party.

When it was realized that Civil War was not to be a ninety-day holiday for the enthusiastic soldiers, preparations for the confinement of the inevitable prisoners became necessary. By law and army regulations the duty of preparing for the expected captives fell to the lot of the quartermaster-general of the army. General M. C. Meigs, in charge of this department, found time amid his other duties to take the necessary steps toward inaugurating a prison system.

By these army regulations an official bearing the title of commissary-general of prisoners was to assume charge of the prisoners. In the War of 1812, General John Mason of Virginia had held this position from 1812 to 1815 and the former British consul at New York, Thomas Barclay, had served in a similar capacity under the king of England. The duty of this officer was to keep an account of the prisoners, to manage the business of exchange in case a cartel for the exchange of prisoners was agreed upon, and to care for the captives taken by the armies of his government. It was his duty, also, to transmit to the prisoners held by the enemy such supplies and funds as were sent to them.

With these rules and precedents behind him, General Meigs, in the early days of July, 1861, addressed Secretary of War Cameron on the necessity of appointing a commissary-general of prisoners. Because of the powers and importance of the position Meigs suggested that only an accomplished gentleman should be appointed. The accomplishments of the gentleman must necessarily include a thorough knowledge of military law and custom.[2] It was not until October, after Meigs had several times repeated his suggestion for the creation of the office, that Lieutenant Colonel Hoffman, of the 8th Infantry, still on parole from General Twiggs' surrender of the Texas garrison, was selected for the duty of caring for prisoners held by the North.[3]

[2] *Ibid.*, 8.
[3] *Ibid.*, 32, 48-49.

The accumulation of prisoners in the available prison camps effected the final appointment of Hoffman to this post. Blockade runners and privateers taken by the blockading squadron increased the number, as paroles were not practicable for these prisoners. Former officers of the United States Army captured by McClellan in West Virginia were sent to Fort Lafayette; privateersmen were confined in Forts Warren, Lafayette, and McHenry, along the Atlantic coast. The number of these prisoners being small, no particular problems developed as a result of their detention. The situation, however, changed after the fall of the forts in Hatteras Inlet in North Carolina, during the latter part of August. The prisoners, 678 officers and men, were transported north and quartered on Governor's Island. The officers were placed in Fort Columbus and the men confined in the army quarters known as Castle William.[4] Colonel Loomis, in command of the post, allowed to the officers the liberty of the island on their paroles not to attempt to escape. From their homes the prisoners were allowed to receive supplies and money not exceeding twenty dollars at a time, but visiting was prohibited. Blankets were issued to the prisoners by the government.[5] Sutlers were permitted to sell specified articles to them.

The officers in Fort Columbus requested that servants be furnished or permitted to them to clean their quarters and cook their meals.[6] The men who were confined in Castle William had other worries. Accustomed to performing their own menial tasks they were desirous only of adequate arrangements by which they could do their cooking. The castle in which they were confined, in addition to being poorly equipped with the necessities of camp and garrison life, bore a reputation of being unhealthy, whenever large bodies of men were confined in it. Toilet facilities were inadequate, and the heating was poor. The men were clad in the sum-

---

[4] *Ibid.*, 34.
[5] *Ibid.*, 35, 39.
[6] *Ibid.*, 41.

mer garments of the southland. Moreover, it was difficult to enforce sanitary arrangements among the prisoners, and measles, typhoid, and pneumonia spread over the prison.[7] These unhealthful conditions caused Fort Warren in Boston Harbor to be equipped for the reception of the prisoners, the governor of Massachusetts furnishing a battalion of volunteers to guard the fort, and the prisoners were moved from Governor's Island and the unhealthy surroundings of Castle William.[8]

In the west, Camp Chase at Columbus, Ohio, originally designed as a camp of instruction for volunteers, became a depot for the confinement of political and military prisoners from Kentucky and western Virginia. In November, steps were taken for its improvement and complete devotion to the use of prisoners of war and state.[9] Still further to the west, citizens, guerillas, and Confederate soldiers from Missouri and surrounding states, were huddled indiscriminately in a confiscated medical college and in a deserted slave pen in St. Louis.[10] In December the McDowell College prison became so crowded that General H. W. Halleck found it necessary to move the prisoners. A new state penitentiary at Alton, Illinois, was acquired and the first of February prisoners were sent to the new prison. By the twelfth of the month, it was reported that this prison was also crowded.[11]

This scattered prison system which was developing was unsatisfactory from a military standpoint. At the same time that General Meigs recommended the appointment of a commissary-general of prisoners, he suggested to Cameron that a special camp for the confinement of prisoners of war be created. The prisons at Fort Warren, Fort Lafayette, and Governor's Island were unsatisfactory and insufficient. Meigs suggested that an island in Lake Erie, and particu-

[7] *Ibid.*, 47.
[8] *Ibid.*, 46-47, 50-51, 53, 122.
[9] *Ibid.*, 136.
[10] See *Ibid.*, series 2, II, for political prisoners and prisons. See also series 2, I, 151.
[11] *Ibid.*, series 2, I, 163, III, 257-59.

larly the islands in Put-in-Bay near Sandusky, Ohio, would
be an ideal location. This matter was not acted upon until
after the appointment of a commissary-general. Accordingly, the first instructions which Colonel Hoffman received
in his new capacity were orders to proceed on a tour of inspection of the islands of Lake Erie, with a view to the selection of a site for the quartering of prisoners.[12]

That a proper selection for the office of commissary-general of prisoners had been made was evidenced by the thorough report which Hoffman submitted on his return from
this trip of inspection. At an expense of time and patience
he minutely examined the available islands in Put-in-Bay
and with the military thoroughness of an officer of the regular army and a graduate of the United States Military
Academy, he reported his conclusions. Considerations of
safety (it was too near Canada) forced him to reject one
of the available islands. Exorbitant rent decided him against
another, while considerations of the possible demoralization
of the guard by a near-by brandy establishment placed
another of the islands in the discard. Finally, two and a
half miles from Sandusky and one mile from the mainland,
he found in Johnson's Island an ideal situation for a prison.
Three hundred acres, with entire control over the remainder
of the island, could be obtained at a rental of five hundred
dollars a year. Half of the available acreage was wooded
and the problem of fuel supply was therefore met. A forty-
acre clearing on the water front furnished a suitable location
for barracks for the guard and for the prisoners. The proximity of the city made an uprising against the guards impracticable, and the mile of water between the island and the
mainland cut off the possibility of escape as long as a warning cannon could arouse the loyal citizens of Sandusky.

The thoroughness of this report was characteristic of Hoffman, but a more characteristic phase of his nature was revealed in another feature. Although originally from New
York, the commissary-general exhibited a thriftiness which

[12] *Ibid.*, 8, 49.

is popularly supposed to be inbred among the natives of New England. For economy, the customary army barracks of one story were suggested for the prison quarters. A building, 125 feet long by 24 wide, with walls of 9 feet could be divided into 3 rooms to house 180 men. This building, with each of its rooms equipped with 2 stoves, could be built for $180. A smaller building of 12 rooms, divided by halls for purposes of discipline into groups of 4, would house officers and cost $1,100. This cost would be lessened if several of these buildings were connected, and would be still less if the buildings were of more than one story. The proximity of Sandusky obviated the necessity for storerooms, but a hospital and mess room were indispensable. Provisions for guarding the prison had also to be made and Hoffman suggested a plank fence on three sides, and a picket fence on the water front. Along the top of the fence, and outside, a platform for the sentinels to walk their posts was to be constructed. From a hundred to a hundred and fifty men would be needed for the duties of the guard, and a blockhouse with a howitzer, together with a guard boat, would complete the equipment of the prison. The total cost for these original outlays, the preparation being made for a thousand prisoners, was estimated at $26,266.[13]

General Meigs received this report and approved of Hoffman's suggestions and the proposed expenditure, but he urged upon the commissary-general the constant necessity for as great an economy as was consistent with the safe keeping and proper welfare of the prisoners. Hoffman was ordered to establish his headquarters in New York City, and to make inspection trips to the various camps to determine the needs and condition of the prisoners.[14]

A guard force was among the first needs of the prison at Johnson's Island. Since the prison was in Ohio, Secretary Cameron called upon Governor Dennison of that state to furnish Hoffman with a company of volunteer guards for

[13] *Ibid.*, 54-58.
[14] *Ibid.*, 122-23.

the prison, and requested the governor to consult with Colonel Hoffman in the selection of officers. These volunteers were furnished by the governor, and in December Hoffman called upon Governor Dennison for an additional company, recommending at the same time the appointment of William S. Pierson of Sandusky as major in charge of the prison. Though Major Pierson, who was ordered to assume command of the prison January 1, 1862, was not a military man, he had impressed Hoffman as combining the ability and qualities of a gentleman, with the willingness to fit himself for his duties as commander of the post. These duties at the beginning were to supervise the organization of the camp, especially the discipline and training of the volunteer guards, and to assist the quartermaster assigned from Hoffman's office in overseeing the construction of the camp.[15]

Within two weeks of his inspection trip, Hoffman had leased the island, let the contract for the construction of the buildings to a reliable company of Sandusky, and gained the promise that the prison would be ready for occupancy by the first of February. The entire enterprise cost $30,000. Among the preparations for the reception of prisoners was the employment of a physician and the gathering of sufficient medical supplies for six months. The location of the island, however, was supposedly healthful, and but little sickness was expected. By the first of February, the work on the island was completed, and a steam propeller for use as a guard boat was ordered. On February 24, the first detachment of five or six hundred prisoners was ready to be sent to the island.[16]

But before Johnson's Island was ready for the prisoners it became evident that the preparations made for their reception had been too modest. On February 16, 1862, Fort Donelson fell, giving fifteen thousand prisoners of war to the care of the North. Immediately the problem of disposing of the troops arose, and General Halleck looked about

[15] *Ibid.*, 123, 163, 171.
[16] *Ibid.*, 135-36, 196, 204, 284, 231, 257, 317.

for some place where they could be placed to relieve his army of the necessity of guarding them. Governor Morton had room for three thousand at Indianapolis,[17] while the Illinois executive offered to take three or four thousand at Springfield, and eight or nine thousand at Chicago.[18]

General McClellan sent orders to General Halleck to send all of the general and field officers taken at the fort to Fort Warren, and five hundred of the sick and wounded were sent to Cincinnati. Scattered groups went to Terre Haute, Fort Wayne, Lafayette, and Richmond, Indiana. Three thousand were sent to Springfield after it was decided that the Copperhead and dissatisfied elements there would not constitute more of a problem than would the concentration of the prisoners elsewhere. Three thousand more went to Indianapolis, and five thousand went to Chicago. With this disposition of the troops from Fort Donelson, there came into permanent existence camps Douglas at Chicago, Butler at Springfield, Morton at Indianapolis, and Chase at Columbus. In this latter camp were confined all of the officers other than those sent to Fort Warren.[19]

The establishment of these new prison camps increased the problems of administration. Guards had to be furnished, and regulations for the proper management of the various prisons had to be made. The prisoners within the camps had to be made amenable to the disciplinary measures necessary to their security and safe-keeping. The problem of feeding and clothing the prisoners, and caring for the sick among them, added to his functions as general supervisor of discipline, gave to the commissary-general of prisoners a variety of duties which would tax his ingenuity to the utmost. Already Hoffman had asked that his position be announced

[17] *Ibid.*, 270.

[18] *Ibid.*, 274.

[19] *Ibid.*, 269, 270-71, 276, 277, 281, 288. These figures do not total the fifteen thousand reported as having been taken at Donelson. At best the figures are approximations. The mayor of Chicago said seven thousand arrived in the city (see below). Prisoners, mostly sick, sent to the Indiana cities were later moved to the permanent camps.

to the army,[20] but this had not been done. Since Halleck had selected the new camps out of the necessities of the moment, he continued to give instructions to the officers in command of the prisons until Hoffman could take charge.

The first problem of the prisons was one of guards. When the seven thousand prisoners assigned to Chicago arrived, the mayor wired to Halleck that such a number of prisoners constituted a menace, as the city had no guards for its security. Halleck indignantly replied to this complaint: "I have taken these Confederates in arms behind their intrenchments, it is a great pity if Chicago cannot guard them unarmed for a few days." [21] After this rebuke the city found means to guard them and put the prisoners under the charge of the city police until after Colonel Mulligan had surrendered to General Price in Missouri. Mulligan's paroled forces were then ordered into service guarding the prisoners at Chicago.[22] Other camps were guarded by volunteer forces especially recruited under the authority of the governors for that duty.[23]

Among the first steps to be taken in caring for the prisoners was the promulgation of rules for the government and administration of the camps. As the essential features of such rules looked to the safe-keeping of the prisoners, they were required to give up all arms upon entrance to the prison;[24] their names were enrolled, and officers and men, if they were confined in the same camp, were divided into separate messes. To each mess, according to international law and the regulations of the army, was to be issued the same food in quality and quantity as was given to the enlisted soldiers in the forces of the United States. In addition, those for whom the prescribed ration did not furnish sufficient luxury or variety, were permitted to purchase from a licensed sutler other food and necessary supplies, except intoxicants.

[20] *Ibid.*, 156.

[21] *Ibid.*, 315-16.

[22] Tuttle, *History of Camp Douglas*, 10 ff.

[23] See, for example, the cases of Johnson's Island and Fort Warren above.

[24] By the terms of the surrender of Fort Donelson the officers were allowed to retain their side arms. These were taken at the camps but returned to them at exchange.

The prisoners were allowed to have money for these purchases, although large amounts sent or given to prisoners were administered by the commanding officer. Visitors, except close and loyal relatives of the sick, were not permitted. Finally, the prisoners were not permitted to leave the confines of the camp.[25]

Placing the prisoners in confinement, and establishing rules for the proper discipline of the camps were not the only necessities to which the United States had to attend. The laws of war oblige the captor to feed the prisoners, to clothe them, and to provide them with the necessary comforts of life. This was a minimum requirement, and might be modified by conventions with the enemy to supply specified kinds of food and clothing, or to allow other privileges to the captured. Since there was no arrangement with the forces of the seceding states, General Meigs early pointed out that the United States was only obliged to give the prisoners one ration a day. In case they needed clothing, they might be placed in a position to earn it by their own labor.[26] The regulation ration which the prisoners were to receive consisted of three-fourths of a pound of bacon or one and one-quarter pounds of beef, one and one-third pounds white or one and one-quarter pounds of corn-bread, one-tenth pound of coffee, one and one-half ounces of rice or hominy, one-sixth pound of sugar, a gill of vinegar, one candle, a tablespoonful of salt, and beans, potatoes, and molasses in small amounts.[27] Contracts were made at the various camps with local dealers for these rations, which were issued by a commissary at the camp to the prisoners; the average cost being from ten to fifteen cents per prisoner a day.[28] Except at

[25] *Official Records*, series 2, III, 337, 344-45, 357-58. This discussion is based ·on the rules established for the administration of Camp Chase, and while the details varied from camp to camp in accordance with local conditions the essential features of the rules were the same for all prisons. Later changes were made as experience showed their necessity.

[26] *Ibid.*, 32.

[27] *Ibid.*, series 2, IV, 157.

[28] *Ibid.*, series 2, III, 604-5.

Johnson's Island, the prisoners were required to do their own cooking.[29]

Since these rations, which consisted mainly of meat, bread, and rice or hominy, were considered too much for men leading a sedentary life, portions of the issues were ordered withheld. The sale of this non-issued portion went into a prison fund which was expended for the benefit of the prisoners. Stoves and cooking utensils were bought from this fund. At Camp Morton an oven, itself an economy-producing device, was built out of the savings. At all of the prisons, the fund was applied to the purchase of tobacco, stamps, and stationery for the prisoners. A tax placed on the authorized sutlers and others trading with the prisoners; the saving in fuel, made by contracting by most of the camps for the baking, added to the mounting fund. Hoffman, whose constant suggestions in the direction of greater economy occasioned the adoption of these features, was also responsible for the addition of another saving: "Farmer's Boilers" were substituted for the customary camp equipment of kettles, which by enabling the prisoners to cook in messes rather than in individual portions increased the saving in rations. By June, Camp Morton reported that there was $2,400 in the prison fund after all of these minor articles had been provided for the prisoners; and in addition to the bake house and ovens, a hospital had been built.[30] At Camp Butler, Hoffman's instructions regarding the creation of a fund were not carried out and there was no saving there until Hoffman's assistant, Captain Freedley, arrived in July on a tour of inspection. He reported that the prisoners were accustomed to selling their surplus rations back to the contractors.[31] In July the fund at Camp Douglas amounted to $4,000, although Colonel Mulligan had appropriated $1,500 of it to some unaccounted for use.[32] Newspapers were even furnished the prisoners from the excess fund at Camp Morton; but

[29] Barbiere, *Scraps from the Prison Table*, 131.
[30] *Official Records*, series 2, III, 338, 432, 518-19, 549-50, 562, 647.
[31] *Ibid.*, series 2, IV, 130-31, 156-57.
[32] *Ibid.*, 180.

Hoffman, fearing perhaps that the benefits of economy were leading to extravagance, ordered such procedure stopped.[33]

In general the food issued to the prisoners was of good quality, although the prisoners, as the inevitable discomforts of their status made natural, found occasion to complain that the bacon was all fat and the beef all bone; the bread was generally sour to the prisoner's palate.[34] Inspectors, of course, found the food of proper quality. At Camp Chase, however, Captain Lazelle, another of Hoffman's assistants and a former subordinate of the commissary-general in Texas, found that the poorest food, shanks and necks of beef, low-grade flour, few vegetables, and the most inferior Rio coffee were served to the prisoners by the contractors. Most of this was due to an inefficient commissary, who was dismissed from the service on Lazelle's representations.[35]

In addition to feeding the prisoners, it was necessary for the United States Government to guard them against exposure due to their insufficient clothing. Prisoners were allowed to receive gifts from friends but it was obvious that this method would not suffice to keep any large proportion of them well clad. Citizens of New York made gifts of clothing to the prisoners who were confined on Governor's Island,[36] and after the Hatteras captives were removed to the more healthful Fort Warren, money and clothing were sent to them by citizens of Boston.[37] Since such a system of clothing the prisoners might be expected to be spasmodic and inefficient, Meigs instructed Hoffman to furnish them with "such clothing and bedding as may be absolutely necessary for their health and comfort."[38] In the latter part of January, 1862, Hoffman was informed that defective clothing which had been rejected as unfit for army use, was

[33] *Ibid.*, 306, 325-26.

[34] Barbiere, *op. cit.*, 105-6.

[35] *Official Records*, series 2, IV, 677-86. The commissary was later restored to the army as a result of Schuyler Colfax's interference and his appeal to Lincoln. See *Ibid.*, series 2, V, 3-5.

[36] New York *Times*, October 8, 1861.

[37] *Official Records*, series 2, III, 762-63.

to be issued to the prisoners of war. He was also authorized to issue army blankets as they were needed. Hoffman decided that blankets and clothing would both be needed, as he believed that it would be necessary to discard the filthy clothing worn by prisoners when they arrived at a camp.[39]

When the prisoners from Fort Donelson arrived, Hoffman found his expectations justified. Reports from Camp Butler declared that they were the "hardest looking set of men ever brought together." Their uniforms were rags of all colors, and they were equipped with strips of carpets for blankets.[40] Such of their clothing as was fit for use was adapted to a warmer climate than that of the northern camps.[41] Clothing was issued to the prisoners from the condemned stock, and from supplies of materials not of the regulation color or cut. Friends were allowed to send clothing to the destitute and some of the prison commanders had a tendency to neglect issuing clothing in order to force the prisoners' friends to take action in their behalf. New clothing was issued even to the eve of exchange, being stopped just before exchange was completed, since such issues would be gifts to the Southern armies.[42]

The problems of administration of the prison system were complicated by the fall, in April, of Island Number 10. The problem of disposing of the new captives was similar to those which had confronted the commanders after Fort Donelson. Although Hoffman had repeatedly requested that his position be announced to the army,[43] the announcement had not been made, and the new capture found Halleck making the decisions in regard to the distribution of the prisoners. A wire to Governor Yates brought the information that an increase of guards at Springfield and Chicago would afford accommodations for twenty-five hundred. Governor Morton was ordered to prepare for one thousand, and plans were

[39] Ibid., 221, 238, 241.
[40] New York Times, February 24, 1862.
[41] Harper's Weekly, April 5, 223.
[42] Official Records, series 2, IV, 123, 155-57, 187, 195-208, 406, 457.
[43] Ibid., series 2, III, 389.

made to send two or three thousand of the remainder to Camp Randall at Madison, Wisconsin. The officers were sent to Camp Chase, and the general and field officers to Fort Warren, as in the Donelson capture.[44]

The congestion of prisoners resulting from this capture made it necessary to shift the officers from Camp Chase to Johnson's Island. Governor Tod suggested that, for purposes of discipline, some two hundred of the more dangerous officers should be sent to the island prison.[45] General Meigs advised that all of the officers at Camp Chase, numbering over a thousand, should be moved, and it was finally decided to make Johnson's Island a prison for officers only. The removal of the officers was completed by the first of May.[46] In the east, the island upon which Fort Delaware was situated was fitted with shed barracks for the reception of two thousand prisoners. Political and naval prisoners were already confined on the island.[47] This became a principal depot for prisoners in the east.

Maladministration and disorder marked the camp at Madison[48] but such conditions were avoided in most of the prison camps by effective means of discipline. The first step toward internal discipline was made by separating officers and men immediately after capture. The separation of general and field officers from the line officers furthered the plan.[49] Within the camps, the prisoners were divided into squads and messes, and the roll of these divisions was called after reveille and at retreat each day, thus making other features of discipline easy. Each of the squads was responsible for the police of its quarters. After retreat, the men were confined to the quarters of their squad, and visiting was forbidden.[50] Prisoners who ventured too close—usually

[44] Ibid., 433.
[45] Ibid., 433.
[46] Ibid., 439, 448, 465.
[47] Ibid., 470-71.
[48] Ibid., 509, 526-27, 542, 578-86, 598, 632, series 2, IV, 52.
[49] Ibid., series 2, I, 169; III, 236-38.
[50] Barbiere, op. cit., 131-32. Official Records, series 2, III, 590; IV, 102, 152. Violations of these rules were to be punished by the withholding of either one-third or one-half rations of a squad in case the individual violator could not be ascertained; individuals were confined in cells.

a distance of twenty feet—to the confines of the prison, were shot after being warned by the sentinel. "Crossing the dead-line" resulted in numerous deaths at the hands of watchful guards.[51]

Despite the rules laid down for the camps, discipline in some of them was lax. This was particularly true of Camp Chase during the period that the officers were confined there. Some of the Donelson officers ordered to Camp Chase were sent by way of St. Louis, where they were allowed to stop at hotels, and were entertained by Southern sympathizers in their homes. Halleck corrected this practice, after popular opposition was aroused in the city.[52] The officers were sent under guard from St. Louis to Camp Chase. But when they arrived in Columbus, Ohio, they found that the restrictions which had been placed upon them en route were removed. Reports of a lax discipline reached the ears of the officials in Washington, and Stanton ordered Governor Tod to stop the practice of allowing disloyal persons to visit the prison. An inspector was sent to investigate a report that the officers wore their sidearms and swords, and were allowed to come and go at will. The governor denied that there was a laxity in discipline, insisting that Colonel Granville Moody, the commandant of the prison, was a strong antislavery Republican, and performed his duty faithfully and discreetly. Tod admitted that permission had been given sick officers to leave the prison to be cared for by friends in Columbus, and the inspector left satisfied that there were no disciplinary problems at the camp.[53] Citizens of Ohio, however, reported to Lincoln that rebel officers in uniform continued to wander the streets of Columbus and to register at the best hotels as belonging to the "C. S. Army."[54] A committee of the state senate investigating the reports found that they were true, and that rebel officers in full uniform had been invited to occupy "honorable" seats within the bar during the sessions of the senate. Moreover, the officers at Camp Chase were

[54] Ibid., 498-500.
[51] Barbiere, op. cit., 82, 120 ff.
[52] Official Records, series 2, III, 379.
[53] Ibid., 410, 412, 420, 427.

permitted to retain their negro servants who had been with them at Donelson. To the Republican committeemen such a condition was unpardonable, and they demanded the immediate release of the negroes with certificates of freedom. Despite their feeling that conditions at the camp were deplorable, the committee was, nevertheless, able to whitewash both the governor and the commanding officer.[55] Captain Lazelle, who was sent from Hoffman's office to check the reports which were coming in, was, unfortunately, unable to be so easily convinced of the governor's efficiency. He found that Tod had permitted visitors to the prison, and that the camp was becoming a center of public interest as a curiosity. A regular line of omnibuses ran from the capitol to the camp and anyone who wanted to spend twenty cents could go even to the officers' quarters. These omnibuses and numerous private vehicles disturbed the discipline of the camp. The officers and men of the guard, and even the commanding officer [in July], Colonel Allison, were infused with a desire to show their authority. The commanding officer was vain of his position and both he and the governor were opposed to prohibiting the visitors; "the object seems to be to make Camp Chase popular." Despite the vanity which the officers showed, Lazelle declared that they all, both civil and military, possessed "the most astonishing ignorance of the most ordinary practical military functions." The Ohio executive told Lazelle that the commanding officer of Camp Chase should be a good lawyer rather than a good soldier. To a regular army man, such a statement must have appeared absurd, but it seems that the idea was literally acted upon. "Colonel Allison is no soldier," Lazelle wrote Hoffman, adding that he was "utterly ignorant of his duties and he is surrounded by the same class of people. But he is a good lawyer and the son-in-law of the Lieutenant Governor."[56]

[55] Ohio *Senate Journal*, 1862, Appendix 155-56.

[56] *Official Records*, series 2, IV, 195-208. It was on this same inspection trip that Lazelle discovered the fraudulent contracts and the inefficient commissary mentioned above.

Hoffman, as a disciplinarian, could appreciate the horror of his subordinate at the conditions of the camp. He ordered Tod to recall the paroles which the officers had given, and to limit visiting to the agents of Governor Johnson of Tennessee who were sent to induce the prisoners from that state to return to their allegiance.[57] Since the exchange of prisoners began a few days after Lazelle's report was made, it was decided that Camp Chase should be abandoned as a prison camp—"or things there will be better arranged than they are now."[58]

Aside from the daily roll calls and the police of their quarters the duties of the prisoners were few. For the most part they enjoyed all of the liberties consistent with their position. Their confinement was a necessity, and visiting was prohibited on the grounds of public policy. Disloyal visitors sometimes lent aid to prisoners who planned to escape, and the restriction of visiting was found to be conducive to better discipline.[59] Mail from the prisoners and letters coming into the prison camp were subjected to a censorship, and the prisoners were limited to one page of personal matter in their letters.[60] Money was allowed to the prisoners, although large amounts possessed by them at the time of capture, or sent to them, were controlled by the prison commandant. The money might be expended for supplies from the sutlers who were authorized to sell to the prisoners. In addition to the regular sutlers, authorized vendors of milk, vegetables, papers, and sweets were admitted with their wares to the prison. Spirituous liquors sometimes found their way into the prison camps, although forbidden by the rules.[61]

Many prisoners who did not have friends and relatives to supply them with money undertook the manufacture of rings, breast pins, and other trinkets. These were usually made of bone, or from the buttons of their uniforms, and were sold to visitors, or, when visitors did not have as free access to the prison as at Camp Chase, to the sutlers.[62]

[57] *Ibid.*, 242.
[58] *Ibid.*, 371.
[59] *Ibid.*, *series* 2, III, 421, 411.
[60] *Ibid.*, series 2, IV, 152-53.
[61] Barbiere, *op. cit.*, 123, 126.
[62] The Camp Chase Letters.

Aside from such voluntary work, the prisoners did little. By international law they were expected to earn their own clothing by engaging in some occupation, but clothing was furnished them and they devoted their labor to obtaining luxuries for themselves.[63] Prison labor was used to make improvements in their camps. Generally, the prisoners did not object to this work. Hoffman marveled that they did not even complain of having to do things of such "doubtful propriety" as putting up the fences which enabled their captors to hold them more securely.[64]

Prisoners who worked were enabled to overcome, to some extent, the mental depression attendant upon their condition. The deprivation of liberty rested heavily on men who were accustomed to a life without restrictions.[65] The nerves of the prisoners were constantly on edge, and they passed from periods of excitement to ones of depression as the ever current rumors of exchange varied from hopeful to hopeless.[66] To overcome the effects of confinement on the nervous system and to pass away the time in prison, the prisoners played games, gambled, and, in their nervous condition, even fought. Two prisoners were reported killed by their fellows at Camp Douglas.[67] To relieve the depression religious services were held in the prisons.[68] Chaplains among the prisoners held services in the officers' prisons at Camp Chase and Johnson's Island and received a full attendance while poker games were stopped.[69] However, the ministers who were furnished to the prison from the local talent were not always accorded such a cordial reception. To their intense disgust, the Fort Donelson captives were compelled to listen to a patriotic sermon delivered by their fellow-Tennesseean, Parson Brownlow, over the walls of Camp Chase. The prisoners also seemed to resent the Christian ministrations of Colonel Granville Moody, the "Antislavery Republican" in charge of them. One prisoner speaks of him as "another

[63] *Official Records*, series 2, III, 122-23.
[64] *Ibid.*, series 2, IV, 324.
[65] The Camp Chase Letters.
[66] Barbiere, *op. cit.*, 257-58.
[67] New York *Times*, April 19, 1862.
[68] *Official Records*, series 2, III, 152-53.
[69] Barbiere, *op. cit.*, 117.

light and 'specimen brick' of the church militant."[70] A Catholic priest of Sandusky was permitted to perform the offices of his church among its communicants at Johnson's Island.[71]

Although such spiritual consolation as they received may have ameliorated, it did not overcome the mental depression of the prisoners. Many of them were sick or wounded when they were taken captive, and others fell victims to the colder climate and the inevitable exposure.[72]

Aside from the consequences of exposure and mental depression, much sickness resulted from the physical conditions of the several camps. Camp Chase, built on low flat ground, was muddy, and uncovered sinks, ten by five feet, were above the cisterns which supplied the drinking water for a thousand prisoners.[73] At Camp Douglas, President Bellows of the United States Sanitary Commission found deplorable conditions. Declaring that only some special providence, or some peculiar efficacy of the lake winds, could prevent the camp from becoming a source of pestilence, he called upon Hoffman to abandon the location before "the amount of standing water, of unpoliced grounds, of foul sinks, of general disorder, of soil reeking with miasmatic accretions, of rotten bones and the emptying of camp kettles," resulted in disaster. Such conditions were "enough to drive a sanitarian mad," and he did not believe that drainage would "purge that soil loaded with accumulated filth, or those barracks fetid with two stories of vermin and animal exhalations." The services of the architects of the Sanitary Commission were offered to aid Hoffman in drawing up a plan for a new camp. The post surgeon indorsed this report with the declaration that the hospital was overcrowded[74] and Hoffman recommended to Meigs a system of drainage for the

[70] *Ibid.*, 221 ff.

[71] *Official Records*, series 2, IV, 423, 498.

[72] New York *Times*, February 27, reported that the prisoners were exposed before their arrival at the camps. Sickness resulted from allowing the prisoners to stand in the rain and cold during delays en route. See also *Harper's Weekly*, April 5, 223.

[73] Barbiere, *op. cit.*, 221, 224.

[74] *Official Records*, series 2, IV, 106-7.

camp.[75] The cost of the drainage system would be about $15,000 and Meigs refused to approve of the expenditure, declaring that "the United States has other uses for its money than to build works to save them [the prisoners] the labor necessary to their health."[76] Hoffman then ordered Tucker, successor to Colonel Mulligan as commandant of the prison, to begin a system of police which should clean the camp, although he explained to Meigs that the use of prison labor would considerably reduce the estimated expense.[77] Meigs, however, would authorize only minor improvements for the camp, justifying his action by an appeal to humanity, which required that the prisoners be given the treatment of enlisted men in the United States Army, and by the further argument that, whatever the prisoners received, it would be better than the rebels accorded to their prisoners.[78]

The sick and wounded whose condition was caused or complicated by mental depression and bad environment were usually under the care of their own surgeons.[79] The sick among the prisoners received the same treatment as sick soldiers in the United States Army. Women at Lafayette, Indiana, where some of the sick from Donelson were sent, equipped a hospital for the prisoners. The government issued sheets to the sick in addition to the blankets which were given to all prisoners.[80] A hospital fund was created by the method of withholding and reselling the excess portions of the regular rations, and luxuries for the sick, not comprehended in the army rations, were obtained from this fund.[81] The fund at Camp Butler built an addition to the city hospital in Indianapolis.[82]

[75] Ibid., 110.　　　　　　　　　　　[77] Ibid., 162, 166.
[76] Ibid., 129.　　　　　　　　　　　[78] Ibid., 238.
[79] Ibid., series 2, III, 185, 196, 204, 284, 312, 356, 359, 386. At Johnson's Island, a contract physician was employed, although at first rebel surgeons were distributed among the prison camps. This system of contract physicians was generally accepted, after it was agreed between the belligerents that surgeons should be treated as non-combatants.
[80] Ibid., 281, also series 2, I, 169, series 2, III, 221-22, 211, 336, 370.
[81] Ibid., 152-53.　　　　　　　　　[82] Ibid., 386-87, 400.

Most of the diseases among the prisoners were due to these factors of mental depression and bad physical surroundings; epidemics were not general. There was smallpox at the Alton penitentiary which resulted in a quarantine of the prison and the withholding of new prisoners for a time.[83] Smallpox was also found at Camp Chase, where a contract was made with the directors of the Franklin County, Ohio, Infirmary to care for the patients.[84] In general, however, proper police of the prisons kept disease and death at a minimum.[85]

Prisoners who died were given a decent burial and marked graves. Property belonging to deceased prisoners was given to relatives, if any appeared as claimants, or, in the absence of such claimants, it was sold, and the proceeds added to the hospital funds.[86] Before the cartel, preference was given to sick prisoners in being selected for special exchange. With the formation of the cartel, those among the sick who were able to travel were first sent through the lines.

The formation of the cartel and the beginning of exchange relieved the United States government of the necessity of caring for the prisoners, and prison camps were abandoned. The political prisoners held by the government were concentrated at Johnson's Island and McDowell's College. Some of the camps, however, were soon called into service to house the prisoners from the South, who returned to the North on parole.

[83] *Ibid.*, 551-52, 562.

[84] *Ibid.*, series 2, IV, 658-59.

[85] *Ibid.*, 130-31. Freedley reported to Hoffman a 70 per cent decrease in mortality at Camp Butler after new police measures were established. Cf. also *Ibid.*, 253-56, 195 for results of police.

[86] *Ibid.*, 248, 319.

CHAPTER IV

SOUTHERN PRISONS 1861—1862

Although the opening guns of the Civil War found the newly organized Confederate States already in possession of prisoners of war—the forces surrendered by General Twiggs in Texas—the care of these prisoners was not the result of orders from the Confederate authorities. The control over these remnants of Twiggs' forces was exercised by the military authorities of the department. The secretary of war, at Richmond, had too many other duties in connection with prisoners nearer headquarters to concern himself especially over the disposition and fate of the quondam frontier garrison of the southwest, for at the very beginning of the war the Richmond authorities faced the problem of enemy forces taken in arms against the South. The Confederate army regulations, adaptations of those of the United States Army, provided that prisoners should be disarmed and sent to the rear of the lines upon capture, their private property was to be respected, and they were to receive one ration a day, regardless of rank. Other rations were to depend upon conventions with the enemy.[1] On May 21, 1861, the Confederate Congress enacted rules to further cover the subject of the treatment of prisoners of war. These rules directed that captives be transferred to the secretary of war, who should instruct the quartermaster-general to provide for their sustenance while they were retained in custody. The rations furnished should be those of regularly enlisted men in the Confederate service.[2]

On June 8, before any considerable number of prisoners had been taken, Secretary of War Walker addressed Governor Henry T. Clark of North Carolina in reference to securing a prison for the expected military prisoners. Clark

[1] *Official Records*, series 2, III, 691.
[2] *Statutes at Large, Provisional Congress of the Confederate States*, 154.

was asked to investigate the available sites, and to enlist a guard for a prison, the Confederate government assuming the cost.[3]

Upon receipt of this communication, Governor Clark sent an agent to investigate the available locations. At Salisbury the agent found that an abandoned cotton factory, with surrounding buildings, could be obtained for $15,000. The buildings would hold fifteen hundred or two thousand prisoners, and Governor Clark privately informed Walker that the property would easily sell after the war for from thirty to fifty thousand dollars.[4] Bars for the windows and other repairs were estimated at two thousand dollars, but there was five hundred dollars worth of machinery included in the buildings. The owner was willing to take the bonds of the Confederacy in payment. The location was reported as good, the prison was shaded by a grove of oaks, and the water was plentiful. The secretary of war approved the report and asked the North Carolina governor to make the necessary repairs.[5] Clark expressed his willingness to furnish guards for the prisoners, but when he turned to the task he found that the citizens of North Carolina refused to volunteer for the specific service of guarding prisoners because they considered that such service was degrading.[6]

While Secretary Walker was looking for a place to house the prisoners, the Battle of Bull Run was fought, and approximately a thousand prisoners were unexpectedly thrown upon the hands of the Confederacy. There were no preparations made for their reception, and they were entrusted to the care of Brigadier General John H. Winder, who had been appointed inspector-general of the camps near Richmond.[7]

[3] *Official Records,* series 2, III, 681-82.

[4] *Ibid.,* 682.

[5] *Ibid.,* 696. History and Tabular Statement of the Prison at Salisbury, N. C. (War Department Archives).

[6] *Ibid.,* 693.

[7] *Official Records,* series 2, III, 683. Jones, *A Rebel War Clerk's Diary,* I, 59-60. General Winder, who continued in charge of the prisoners in the South until his death

When the unexpected prisoners were brought to Richmond, they were conducted to an unused tobacco factory in the district of the city known as Rockett's. The officers were confined in a warehouse formerly belonging to the firm of Liggon and Sons, and the men were placed in near-by buildings.[8] General Winder apologized to the prisoners for the poor accommodations, and stated to them that he was having some neighboring buildings fitted for their use.[9] Accordingly, some of them were removed to an adjoining building on July 24. The officers were quartered on the ground floor, above them were the prison guards, and on the upper stories were placed the enlisted men who were effectively cut off from their officers by the quarters of the guard. The rooms of the buildings were about seventy-five by thirty feet; a row of tobacco presses divided the quarters of the officers and occupied about one-half of the room on their floor.[10]

The buildings in which the prisoners were confined were strongly guarded on all sides. Among the officers of the guard was a Lieutenant Todd, Mrs. Abraham Lincoln's half brother, whom the officers united in proclaiming a tyrant.[11] Within a week, two companies from Louisiana were assigned to the duty of guarding the prisoners.[12] The guards seem to have taken their duties seriously, for a short time after the prisoners arrived, a guard shot at one for putting his head out of the window. Colonel Corcoran, among the prisoners taken at Bull Run, protested to General Winder, and received the assurance that such proceedings were unauthorized and would not be repeated.[13]

in 1865, was a son of the General Winder whose ill-fated Maryland militia had failed to hold the British forces in their advance on Washington in 1814. A major in the United States Army at the outbreak of the war, General Winder resigned the commission which he had held since his graduation from West Point, in 1820, and applied for a commission in the Confederate service. Too old for active service, he proposed to act as an inspector of camps and as commander of the prisons in the Confederacy.

[8] Jeffrey, *Richmond Prisons 1861-1862*, 7-8.
[9] Corcoran, *Captivity of General Corcoran*, 27.
[10] Jeffrey, *op. cit.*, 10.
[11] *Ibid.*, 13 ff. *Official Records*, series 2, III, 687.
[12] *Ibid.*, 700. Henry Wirz belonged to one of these companies.
[13] Corcoran, *op. cit.*, 27. Ely, *Journal of Alfred Ely*, 23 ff.

General Winder made a favorable impression on the prisoners, most of whom were sufficiently young in the service to admire a man of habitual military bearing. Congressman Ely, who had been unable to find his carriage when the retreat from Manassas began and had thus been taken a prisoner of war, described Winder as one possessing courtesy and kindliness, and although a strict disciplinarian, a man of humane feelings without a disposition "to exercise his power beyond its proper limits." "He is withal a handsome officer." For his kindness to him, Ely declared that it would be his "dutiful pleasure to speak of him on some future public occasion, in a manner which his merits deserve."[14]

Colonel Corcoran, perhaps a better judge of military merits, concurred in praising Winder for doing all in his power to make the prisoners comfortable,[15] although he did not deign to honor a rebel in such a conspicuous manner as his fellow prisoner promised to do. A third prisoner was unable to appreciate the general's qualities, and declared that Winder was a martinet of forty years' standing, abrupt, profane, and coarse in speech, and noted that his visits to the prison inevitably resulted in the roughening of the prisoners' comforts.[16] This uncomplimentary opinion was shared by the people of Richmond, who condemned Winder and his Maryland associates for their rule in Richmond, particularly in connection with the issuance of passports to the North, a matter which also came under Winder's duties. He was accused of collusion with the prison undertaker, and of speculation in the burial of the dead.[17]

From the fact that the prisoners were not subjected to undue hardships, it would seem that the opinions of Corcoran and Ely on the character of the general were correct. However, a breakfast of the usual rations of dry bread, coffee, and boiled beef, served to the prisoners on the morning after their arrival in Richmond, convinced them that

[14] *Ibid.*, 96.
[15] Corcoran, *op. cit.*, 29.
[16] Harris, *Prison Life in the Tobacco Warehouse at Richmond*, 126-27.
[17] Jones, *op. cit.*, I, 91, 93. Harris, *op. cit.*, 127.

luxuries were not included on the prison menu.[18] These rations were reduced after the fall of Hatteras Inlet which had cut off the possibility of importations, and the prisoners were informed that sugar and coffee could no longer be issued by the Confederate authorities.[19] The officers then began to send out for vegetables and other foods to supply the deficiencies of the issued diet.[20] Servants from among the enlisted men were permitted to cook for and wait upon the officers.[21] The food issued to the enlisted men was the same as that received by the officers, but the natural scarcity of ready money among this class of prisoners forced them to restrict their diet to the issued rations. Smoking tobacco was furnished the prisoners liberally, and occasionally a favored officer was invited to dine in the city with one of the young officers of the guard.[22]

By law, the Confederate authorities were required to furnish clothing to the prisoners, and friends were allowed to send gifts of clothing to them.[23] Straw and comforts were issued to the prisoners,[24] but the scarcity of clothing, even for the army, prevented any issue to the men, and the prisoners eventually became destitute.[25]

The prospect of a long confinement stimulated the prisoners, soon after their arrival, to devise some means for passing away their time. Despite the statements of Northern newspapers, the captives were not forced to work and only those who volunteered for service in the kitchens were confronted with any other task than that of amusing themselves.[26] The

[18] Jeffrey, op. cit., 9.

[19] Ely, op. cit., 117. Jeffrey, op. cit., 19.

[20] Ibid., 86, 115. Ely, op. cit., 101.

[21] Ibid., 100. Cf. Merrell, Five Months a Prisoner, passim.

[22] Jeffrey, op. cit., 98-99.

[23] Official Records, series 2, III, 694.

[24] Harris, op. cit., 31. Harris denies that the officers were allowed servants and declares that for months they slept on the floor without covers and with wooden blocks for pillows. There is no supporting evidence for such statements and all of the other accounts of prison experiences unite in stating that servants were allowed to the officers. Cf. Official Records, series 2, III, 725.

[25] Ibid., 724. New York Times, October 9, 1861.

[26] Ely, op. cit., 104.

officers formed the "Richmond Prison Association" to supervise their life, to make rules for cleanliness, and to furnish
entertainment.[27]

The association on its serious side served as a clearing house
for prison opinion. One of the most inharmonious of its
sessions was devoted to debating the advisability of prevent-
ing escapes from the prison. The privileges allowed to the
prisoners rendered escape from the prison comparatively
easy, and some few took advantage of the opportunity to
return to the North. The escape of a surgeon while acting
in his humane capacity led to the imposition of restrictions
on the remaining prisoners. They were not allowed to go
to the city and newspapers were for a time forbidden them.[28]
These restrictions resulted in the association considering the
propriety of permitting no more of their members to escape.
It was decided that a prisoner had the right to escape, but it
was evident that many prisoners were opposed to such a step.
Several of the prisoners complained that their attempts had
been frustrated because of information given to the authorities by their companions.[29]

Visitors were permitted, and many came to see the Yankee
prisoners. Congressman Ely was especially annoyed by these
visitors, and complained to General Winder. Passes to the
prison were then discontinued.[30]

Not all of the experiences of the prisoners were attended
by such a small amount of inconvenience as the matter of
visiting. Despite the fact that a correspondent of the London *Morning Herald* reported that the prisoners wept at the
"uniformly kind" treatment which they received, their treatment was not uniformly kind.[31] The quarters of the prisoners

[27] Corcoran, *op. cit.*, 28-29. The seal of the association was engraved with a circle
of *pediculi* and bore the motto "Bite and Be Damned."

[28] Ely, *op. cit.*, 56.

[29] *Ibid.*, 226-27. These attempts at escape, several of them successful, led General
Winder to demand that the saloons near the prisons be closed and that all saloons
in Richmond be ordered to refuse intoxicants to the prison guards. *Official Records*,
series 2, III, 719. This action would not increase his popularity in Richmond.

[30] Ely, *op. cit.*, 67.

[31] Quoted by W. E. Daniel to Secretary Walker. *Official Records*, series 2, III, 709.

were infested with lice,[32] and the early promise of Winder to permit no more shooting of prisoners was soon forgotten by the guard. The latter part of September, a sentinel killed a prisoner for cursing and abusing the guard from an upper window.[33]

The greatest inconvenience of prison life was the crowded condition of the prisons. The assembling of the prisoners in Richmond was unexpected, and they were crowded into two buildings; 52 officers and 261 men in the one, and 551 men in the other. The police of the buildings was bad, and the surgeon-general of the Confederacy reported to the secretary of war that pestilence was imminent if the conditions remained unchanged. He recommended another building and a better system of police.[34] General Winder shifted the blame for these conditions to the surgeon-general, who had taken one of the buildings designed for the prisoners and converted it into a hospital. Although Winder acquired another building for the prisoners,[35] this step did not relieve conditions permanently. Constant arrivals soon crowded the new building. Generals in the field were asked to retain their captives until better arrangements for them could be made in Richmond.[36]

To relieve the situation in Richmond, prisoners were sent to North Carolina immediately after the Bull Run captives had arrived. Governor Clark, who was urging the selection of Salisbury as a site for a prison, was, nevertheless, unprepared for any prisoners at the time, because the citizens of his state refused the "degrading" service of guarding the Yankees. Since the presence of the prisoners was so "odious" to the people, the governor suggested that some state farther to the south be selected for the duty of caring for them. At the same time, however, the adjutant general of North Car-

[32] Cincinnati *Daily Commercial*, September 18, 1861. Jeffrey, *op. cit.*, *passim*.

[33] *Ibid.*, 21-22. Ely, *op. cit.*, 130-33. Jeffrey says that three prisoners were shot at the prison. Harris (*op. cit.*, 33), who reveals a tendency to exaggerate the horrors of prison life makes the number seven.

[34] *Official Records*, series 2, III, 698.

[35] *Ibid.*, 700. Jeffrey, *op. cit.*, 112.

[36] Adjutant General Cooper to Huger, *Official Records*, series 2, III, 726.

olina urged the secretary to prepare Salisbury as a prison. The country about Salisbury was represented as being rich in produce; fruits and garden vegetables were abundant, and the thousand recruits who had answered the call to arms had brought about a proportionate increase in the already surplus production of the country.   There was no reason to doubt, the adjutant general assured Walker, that the commissary-general of North Carolina could make a contract to feed the captives at less than the cost of army rations.   These arguments convinced the secretary, who ordered Governor Clark to rush the repairs on the Salisbury property, and to notify the Richmond officials as soon as it was possible for the prisoners to be cared for there.[37]

The crowded conditions in Richmond occasioned the removal of 156 prisoners to Castle Pinkney in Charleston Harbor, September 10.   Among the forty officers moved to the new prison was Colonel Corcoran, whose presence in a Southern prison was to prove of great benefit to the Confederacy in forcing the United States to agree to an exchange of prisoners.   The prisoners selected were those who had evinced the most insubordinate disposition.[38]   Ten days later 253 prisoners were sent from Richmond to New Orleans.[39]

At Castle Pinkney the prisoners found their Richmond experiences duplicated.   Gifts of food came from the friends of the prisoners in the city; the "Castle Pinkney Brotherhood" was created on the model of the Richmond Prison Association.   Coffee and sugar remained on the rations here until October 16 when the effect of the blockade was brought home to the prisoners in the same fashion as it had been in Richmond.   The last of October the prisoners were removed from the castle and taken to the Charleston jail.   A few

[37] *Ibid.*, 695-96, 966, 702.

[38] Jeffrey, *op. cit.*, 17-18.   Ely, *op. cit.*, 108.   Corcoran, *op. cit.*, 39.

[39] Ely, *op. cit.*, 110. Jeffrey, *op. cit.*, 23, says that September 25, 250 privates were sent farther south. These, of whom there is neither official nor confirming record, if sent at all—and it is possible that Jeffrey is confusing them with the 253 sent to New Orleans—were sent to Mobile, Alabama.   For these prisoners see the New York *Times,* October 9, 1861.

weeks later some of them were moved again—this time to the jail at Columbia.[40]

These accommodations were still insufficient, and when Judah P. Benjamin succeeded Walker as secretary of war, he set about to find a new prison. After considerable correspondence with the governors of Alabama, Georgia, and North and South Carolina,[41] Benjamin decided to equip an abandoned paper mill at Tuscaloosa, Alabama, for the regular prisoners. An agent sent to begin the preparations[42] made a contract for the buildings, but the quartermaster-general of the Confederate army advised its repudiation on the grounds that the mill was eminently unsuitable for the purpose. The first story lacked a floor; one room was without sills. The grounds were low and damp, the walls full of holes, and chimneys or any cooking arrangements were lacking.[43] But before these conditions were known, a quartermaster had been appointed for the prison and preparations had begun.[44] Prisoners were sent from Richmond in November under the charge of Sergeant Henry Wirz.[45]

Sergeant Wirz, who was placed in charge of the prisoners at Tuscaloosa, had appeared in Richmond as a private with the Madison Infantry of Louisiana volunteers. Assigned to special duty with General Winder in August,[46] he soon made himself invaluable at the Richmond prisons where his rank was raised to that of a sergeant. Known to the captives as the "Dutch Sergeant," he was described as the "essence of authority."

Officers and men in the warehouse, and negro cooks in the yard, ignored the existence of all authority in the Confederacy save what centered in our Dutch Sergeant. He was a good fellow at times and a very bad one at others . . . He was an infallible dog—thought himself omnipresent and omniscient.

[40] Corcoran, op. cit., 60-72, 90 ff.
[41] Official Records, series 2, III, 730-33.
[42] Ibid., 734.
[43] Ibid., 751.
[44] Ibid., 745.
[45] Ely, op. cit., 230, Jeffrey, op. cit., 42-44.
[46] Official Records, series 2, III, 711.

Reports soon came to the prisoners at Richmond that Wirz was very popular among the prisoners at Tuscaloosa because of his obliging nature; he was still noted for his infallibility as well as for his usefulness.[47]

The citizens of Tuscaloosa aided the guard in the work of securing the prisoners, but their safe-keeping was endangered by Unionist sentiment in the surrounding country. Although the prisoners were sufficiently remote from their lines to prohibit their attempting a return to their own country, danger existed in the possibility of the Union men in the country joining with the prisoners in an uprising against the guards. In January, 1862 a hunting encampment near the prison aroused excitement among the officers of the prison, but it eventually moved away, or was broken up, without any untoward development.[48]

The prisoners reported that they were better off in Tuscaloosa than they had been in Richmond, although the unaccustomed heat caused more sickness in their numbers.[49] Their destitute condition[50] in regard to clothing had been relieved by gifts from the United States.[51] Blankets of bagging were issued to the prisoners at Tuscaloosa and Selma, Alabama, by the Confederate and state authorities.[52]

When Governor Clark reported to Benjamin the cessation of the former negotiations for the purchase of the prison at Salisbury, the secretary immediately ordered the buildings

[47] Harris, *op. cit.*, 135-36. Merrell, *Five Months in Rebeldom* (1862), declared all the officers were kind except Todd and "Wurtz" who were cruel. "Wurtz" thought that if "dem tam Yankees" got him they would kill him. *Official Records*, series 2, III, 751. When the report of the unsatisfactory condition of the paper mill at Tuscaloosa was received, an attempt was made to secure the lunatic asylum as an additional prison. *Ibid.*, 757. Governor J. G. Shorter protested against this action on the pleas that the asylum was crowded and that an attempt to seize the building, which he had heard was contemplated, would disorganize the institution while it aroused the indignation of "a loyal and Christian people." *Ibid.*, 758, Benjamin denied any intention of seizing the building which the trustees refused to vacate, and promised to send no more prisoners to Tuscaloosa.

[48] *Ibid.*, 795.

[49] New York *Times*, March 3, 1862.

[50] Jeffrey, *op. cit.*, 42-43.

[51] Prisoner to the Cincinnati *Daily Commercial*, February 11, 1862.

[52] *Official Records*, series 2, III, 853.

and grounds to be purchased and put in proper shape for the prisoners who were removed from Richmond and sent to Salisbury at the same time that Tuscaloosa was occupied.[53]

The guard force, raised by the North Carolina executive, was mustered into the service of the Confederate States,[54] and in January Major G. C. Gibbs was assigned to the command of the prison. The actual enlistment of the guards, and the arrival of the prisoners, produced a change in local sentiment. Governor Clark wrote to Benjamin that while he did "not know how many prisoners we may be blessed with," if it was decided to send any more prisoners from Richmond, he could recommend the purchase of a college building about thirty-five miles from Salisbury. In May, 1862, the contemplated removal of Colonel Gibbs brought the governor back to his former sentiments, until he was assured that Gibbs and an adequate guard would be retained.

The prisoners at Salisbury found that the food issued to them was more abundant, but of poorer quality, than that received in Richmond. Soup from cowpeas was issued and they received beef, which the prisoners declared to be of doubtful origin—either horse or mule—although this issue was varied by one of pork which the impoverished commissary department obtained by forceful confiscation of the stock of citizens of Union sentiments in the locality.[55] The prison itself consisted of the factory and several buildings which had formerly been used as boarding houses; a board fence surrounded all.[56] Clothing was not furnished by the Confederacy and gifts from the North do not seem to have been delivered at this prison.[57]

Despite the fact that the laws of the Confederacy required that the prisoners be furnished with clothing, no provision for making any issues was ever devised by the authorities.[58]

[53] Ely, op. cit., 225-26.
[54] Official Records, series 2, III, 758, 760, 770, 767, 861.
[55] Jeffrey, op. cit., 150.
[56] Ibid., 149.
[57] Official Records, series 2, III, 533-34.
[58] Ibid., 704.

Blankets and coverlids were issued to them, but they received no clothing. Northern newspapers carried stories of the prisoners clad only in blankets, and the prisoners themselves complained that "the rags the Government gave us won't last forever."[59] Letters from the prisoners to Congressmen carried the information that their poor clothing would not even withstand the rigors of a southern climate.[60] On November 4, Secretary Seward wired to General McClellan to secure permission from the President to send an officer, under a flag of truce, across the lines to make arrangements for supplying prisoners with blankets and clothing. General Wool communicated the desires of his chiefs to General Huger, and asked whether the requisite permission to send the supplies would be allowed by the Confederate authorities. On November 11, he reported that an arrangement had been made with General Huger, the position of the government not having been compromised by any approach to recognition of the Confederacy. Huger agreed to receive articles which might be sent south by way of the Southern Express Company, and also agreed to receive moneys sent for the payment of freight charges. General Meigs, quartermaster-general of the United States Army, ordered two thousand suits of infantry clothing, shoes, overcoats, blankets, and caps, to be sent to General Wool for transfer to Confederate hands. Permission was given by the Confederate authorities to send coffee, sugar, and tea to the captives; although the seeming implication that the prisoners were underfed was vigorously denied by the Confederates. Money was sent north under the reciprocal features of the agreement.[61]

When the prisoners were moved from Richmond to the other prisons, Wool demanded that he be allowed to send gifts to them at the new prisons, and asked that he be informed where they were sent, in order that he might forward packages to their proper destination. Massachusetts and Indiana sent outfits for their soldiers in Southern prisons,

[59] New York *Times*, December 11, 1861.
[60] *Official Records*, series 2, III, 152-53.
[61] *Ibid.*, 125, 129, 130, 142, 749, 149.

although the Federal government delayed sending the supplies which had been ordered for the use of the prisoners. The Sanitary Commission was informed by the war department that General Wool would transmit any supplies which they might desire to send forward.[62] Prisoners received the gifts of their countrymen with but little delay.[63]

In January, 1862, the military committee of the House reported a bill authorizing the secretary of war to furnish to the prisoners in the South the necessities of life, and to employ such agents as might be necessary.[64] Acting on this resolution, Secretary Stanton, as the first act of his official career, commissioned Ames and Fish to proceed to Richmond for the purpose of relieving the wants of the prisoners. The Commissioners were refused admission by the Confederate authorities who turned the question to the exchange of prisoners.

After the Ames and Fish mission had been diverted from its original purpose, Huger, on the suggestion of the war department, suggested to Wool that each side should appoint a commissary to look after the interests of its soldiers in the other's prisons; and to receive and ship the supplies and gifts which passed through the lines at Fort Monroe. Wool promptly declined to join in this proposed action, as he thought such collaboration would be an implication of the belligerent status of the Confederacy.[65]

While negotiations for an exchange of prisoners were pending, the concurrence of military events served to hasten the formation of a cartel. The battle of Shiloh in the early part of April brought a number of prisoners to the South. Most of these were released on parole but some were retained. In Virginia, the Peninsular campaign brought an increased number of prisoners to the tobacco warehouse at Richmond.

[62] *Ibid.*, 150, 155, 158, 169.

[63] Harris, *op. cit.*, 38. Philadelphia *Inquirer*, March 1, 1862. A letter published in the New York *Times*, January 30, 1862, declared that none of the supplies had ever been received. This is evidently propaganda as the official reports cited show that there was no idea that such supplies were not received by the prisoners.

[64] See Supra, page 20, also Moore, *Rebellion Records*, IV, 12.

[65] *Official Records*, series 2, III, 839. See Supra, page 28.

When Jackson, in the Shenandoah valley, made a large capture, it was decided to retain his prisoners in Lynchburg, Virginia, since the prisons at Salisbury and Richmond were too crowded to receive them.[66] The quartermaster at Lynchburg reported that it was almost impossible to obtain sufficient food for the prisoners, and the quartermaster-general informed the new secretary of war, Randolph, that the growing deficiency in the resources of the Confederacy made an exchange of prisoners imperative.[67] The prisoners at Lynchburg were given poor quarters (stables on a fairground), and there was an insufficient supply of blankets. Added to this, a quarrel over the exercise of authority between the commander of the post and the quartermaster assigned for duty at the prison resulted in the prisoners being deprived of their already scanty rations for twenty-four hours. Orders were given to the quartermaster to stop shipments from Lynchburg to Richmond and to impress whatever food was necessary for the sustenance of the prisoners and their guards.[68]

A similar deficiency in foodstuffs developed in Richmond a few weeks later. Difficulties were experienced in getting bread for the prisoners, and General Winder was instructed to use all of his available forces to prevent an uprising of the captives. General Lee considered that there was no reason for a lack of bread, declaring that in Richmond there was plenty of flour, which, with proper arrangements, could be made available.[69] These difficulties in supplying the prisoners with food, at a time when a battle was being fought a few miles away, were relieved by the ratification of the cartel for the exchange of prisoners on July 22, within a week after the bread shortage in Richmond. Exchange began immediately, and the suffering of prisoners in the South because of the inadequate resources of the Confederacy was relieved until after the cessation of exchanges under the cartel.

[66] Richmond *Examiner*, June 16. New York *Times*, June 21.
[67] *Official Records*, series 2, IV, 777.
[68] *Ibid.*, 779, 788-89.
[69] *Ibid.*, 822.

CHAPTER V

EXCHANGE UNDER THE
CARTEL

With the formation of the cartel by Generals Dix and Hill, the hope of exchange, so long delayed, bore promise of being realized. Public opinion had so long demanded exchange that questions of recognition were relegated to a temporary oblivion, and the joyful news of the cartel was announced to the prisoners in the tobacco warehouses and the prison camps. Hope rose North and South with the tidings, and the country joined in the wish that this news, unlike similar reports in the past, would prove to be true. The people were tired of the delays and postponements hitherto attendant on the question, and demanded an immediate preparation for the execution of the cartel provisions.[1]

The Confederacy lost no time in appointing an agent of exchange, selecting for the task the Honorable Robert Ould, even before the cartel was completed. Ould, formerly district attorney of the District of Columbia and a lawyer of distinction, was acting at the time as the judge-advocate of the armies of the Confederacy.[2] In selecting him the war department chose a man destined to become a most vigorous defender of the rights of the South. Secretary Stanton delayed the appointment of an agent but sent Dix up the James River to Aiken's Landing to promise that prisoners would soon be forthcoming from the prison camps of the North.[3] Lorenzo Thomas was then ordered to assume the functions of agent of exchange in addition to his other duties as adjutant general of the army,[4] and on August 3 he arrived at Aiken's Landing with the first detachment of prisoners from

[1] New York *Times,* July 24.
[2] Jones, *Diary of a Rebel War Clerk,* I, 143.
[3] *Official Records,* serieis 2, IV, 283-84.
[4] *Ibid.,* 291-92.

Forts Delaware and Warren. For these three thousand, he returned North with three thousand and twenty-one from Ould. He also arranged an exchange for a number of officers on parole; Hoffman's exchange was arranged for; and the valuable Corcoran, soon to style himself "The Hero of Bull Run" after his reception by the Irish population of the cities of the North, was delivered up to the Federal agent.[5] His presence had been of great service to the Confederacy. After these exchanges were completed, Thomas remained near Aiken's until he was able to announce that all but the sick and wounded in the east had been exchanged.[6]

Exchanges in the west were to be made at Vicksburg. Here the Confederates appointed a Major Watts, who was to act under the instructions of Ould. The system of having two officers carrying on the work of exchanges independently, as seemed to be contemplated by the cartel, gave way to having the arrangements for exchanges made by the agents closest to the respective capitals, and Vicksburg became merely a place for the delivery of the prisoners. The agent there performed only the functions of receiving and receipting for the prisoners. The rolls were sent east to the principal agents.[7] The United States appointed no agent of exchange for the west; Hoffman sent Freedley and Lazelle to deliver the prisoners at Vicksburg,[8] and Thomas went west to supervise the arrangements.[9] By the middle of September most of the prisoners in the west had been delivered.[10]

[5] *Official Records*, series 2, IV, 349-50. Corcoran conferred this laudatory title upon himself when he published an account of his captivity. See title page of his *Captivity of General Corcoran*. For his reception in the North see New York *Times*, August 18, and *Harper's Weekly*, September 6, 562. Corcoran was made a brigadier general and formed an Irish brigade from New York. His book was undoubtedly written to promote recruiting.

[6] *Official Records*, series 2, IV, 406.

[7] *Ibid.*, 394, 841.

[8] *Ibid.*, 365-66, 414, 419, 420.

[9] *Ibid.*, 413.

[10] Barbiere, *op. cit.*, 268-78. Throughout the exchange opportunities were given in the Northern camps for the prisoners to take the oath of allegiance and remain in the North. When exchange first became a possibility many prisoners requested to be allowed to take the oath. Andrew Johnson was especially anxious that this opportunity

The delivery of the prisoners was not unattended with difficulties, and the early troubles were singularly indicative of those which were to come in the future. On the day before the signing of the cartel, Secretary Stanton issued an order directing that the military commanders in the Southern states might seize for their use any necessary personal or real property belonging to disloyal citizens within their commands. On the day of the cartel General Pope, in Virginia, ordered the removal of disloyal male citizens from their lands in the rear of his lines with the penalty of death as spies hanging over them in case they returned. A few days later, John Letcher, governor of Virginia, filed with the war department a demand that the officers of the enemy be surrendered to him for trial in the courts of the state on charges of treason and inciting slave insurrection. The treason consisted in aiding the "usurped" government of Pierpont. Letcher also called attention to the seizure of peaceful citizens and their removal from their lands as threatened by Pope's orders. He asked that a provision be inserted in the cartel which would prevent this practice.[11]

Under this stimulus,[12] Davis instructed Lee to inform General McClellan that these orders would be considered by the South as the inauguration of a system of uncivilized warfare. To this he added a condemnation of a subordinate of Pope's, Brigadier General Steinwehr, who had issued orders

to return to their old allegiance be given to the prisoners from Tennessee and he was given permission to send an agent into the prisons where soldiers from his state were confined to persuade the men to renounce the South. President Davis reported that 309 took the oath in the east, and 918 were reported as having taken the oath at Camp Douglas. Cf. in this connection, *Official Records*, series 2, IV, 223, 289, 307, 312, 328, 333-35, 364-65, 551-52.

[11] *Official Records*, series 2, IV, 836, 828-29.

[12] The assumption that Letcher's letter influenced the action of the Confederate president is based on the comparative dates of the communications involved. Letcher wrote Randolph July 28, Davis' letter to Lee is dated July 31, and on that date Randolph replied to Letcher. *Ibid.*, 849. Unfortunately, Randolph's reply is not found. There is no reason to suppose that Davis might not have taken this action without the "stimulus" offered by Letcher's concurrence. The Richmond *Dispatch*, August 1, 1862, opposed the cartel because it deprived the South of the means of protecting her citizens by a resort to retaliation. The next day the paper approved Letcher's course.

directing that citizens should be held as hostages for the
safety of his men from the assaults of bushwhackers.
McClellan was to be informed that Pope, Steinwehr, and
their commissioned officers would be considered "to be in
the position which they have chosen for themselves—that of
robbers and murderers and not that of public enemies entitled if captured to be considered as prisoners of war." The
enlisted men, being regarded as unwilling instruments in the
execution of these orders, were to be accorded the treatment
of prisoners of war. It was only the much vaunted Southern
sense of honor, it seems, that prevented Davis from refusing
to execute the "generous cartel" which had just been ratified. Davis was sure that the orders of the generals and
those of the Northern government furnished a complete
justification for such a course.[13]

This was not the first protest that Lee had sent to McClellan concerning the actions of the Federal government. On
July 6, under directions from the Secretary of War, Lee had
demanded that information be given and explanation offered
regarding the hanging of a citizen of New Orleans, William
B. Mumford, by General Butler, who had him executed for
hauling down the United States flag from the government
mint in that city. The Confederates alleged that Mumford's
patriotic gesture had been made before the occupation of the
city by the Federal troops. At the same time McClellan had
been asked for an official explanation of the execution, as the
Confederate reports alleged, without trial, of a Colonel
Owen, of the Missouri State Guard, on a charge of bridge
burning.[14] McClellan had professed his ignorance of these
matters and had forwarded Lee's letters to Stanton,[15] from
whom no reply was received.

Now, August 1, since the practice had already begun of
informing the Federal officials that there were limits to the

[13] *Ibid.*, 830-31. The Richmond *Dispatch*, August 9, 1862, wanted to know "why
should the mongrel crew who march under the banners of Lincoln be exempted from
punishment?"

[14] *Official Records*, series 2, IV, 134-35.

[15] *Ibid.*, 170.

Confederate patience, Lee was ordered by President Davis to demand some reply from the United States to his letters about Mumford and Owen, and to add to that an inquiry whether the actions of Generals Hunter and Phelps and Colonel Fitch were sanctioned by the Northern authorities. These generals were accused of having armed slaves "for the murder of their masters" in South Carolina and New Orleans. Colonel Fitch was accused of the murder of two citizens in retaliation for the murder of one of his soldiers. The South would deem no reply to these letters an admission that they were true; and retaliation would result.[16]

The North interpreted this action by the South as an attempt to affect the draft.[17] That there may have been such an idea in the Southern mind is believable when it is remembered that exchange was considered a necessary stimulus to the rapid recruiting of the Northern armies. General Lee recommended that the enlisted men who were captured from Pope's army should be immediately sent home, believing their statements that they were tired of fighting and inclined to surrender; "those who sell themselves, especially since a draft is ordered by the authorities of the United States, will find it easy to make their money."[18]

On August 9, General Halleck returned Lee's letters with the statement that they were insulting to the United States government, and he must therefore decline to receive them. The only observable result in the North was the cessation of preparations for exchanges at Vicksburg until after the return of General Thomas from Aiken's Landing.[19] There is no evidence that the question was discussed by the commissioners, possibly because the ten-day period for the delivery of the prisoners had not expired and no issue was definitely presented in the course of their business.

[16] *Ibid.*, 835, 329-30.

[17] New York *Times*, August 11. The *Times* also suggested that enough Southern prisoners be held to enable the U. S. Government to retaliate for any ill treatment accorded the officers in the South.

[18] *Official Records*, series 2, IV, 843.

[19] *Ibid.*, 362, 376, 391.

When Halleck refused to receive Lee's letters, Governor
Letcher returned to his former demand. Since the soldiers
from Pierpont's government had been sent north in exchange,
he assumed that his request to subject them to the justice of
the commonwealth was not acceded to; but there remained
Pope's officers. He hoped that these at least would be surrendered to him for trial. The President, however, was
hoping for national action on the question and insisted that
Letcher present charges and specifications before making a
demand for the officers.[20] Turning to his newly assembled
congress, two of whose members had already presented bills
for the rendition of negroes taken in arms to the state authorities while their officers were to be shot,[21] the Confederate
executive demanded support for a policy of retaliation.[22]
Orders were issued to the army to execute the officers of
Colonel Fitch's command, while Generals Hunter and
Phelps and their officers were to be denied the rights of
prisoners of war and considered as outlaws.[23]

The execution of the cartel was attended with other difficulties than those growing out of the retention of these
officers. The Confederate practice of paroling men immediately after a battle, as after Shiloh and during the Peninsular campaign, forced the Northern government to begin a
system of handling these paroled troops. It had been customary to discharge bodies of men from the army when they
had been returned to their own lines on parole. But as this
custom resulted in the men's being lost to the service, the war
department of the United States, anticipating a number of
troops on parole, established, June 28, camps of instruction
at Annapolis, at Camp Chase, and at Benton Barracks, Missouri. All men on parole were ordered to report to the camp
designated for their section of the country. All furloughs

[20] *Ibid.*, 849-50.

[21] New York *Times*, August 27.

[22] *Official Records*, series 2, IV, 854-55.

[23] *Ibid.*, 857. The question in regard to Pope was passed by his removal and the
assurance that his orders were no longer in force. The latter part of September Ould
delivered to Thomas those of Pope's officers who had been held in the South. *Ibid.*,
552, 913. The question of the negroes remained to complicate the future.

were recalled and no more were to be issued.[24] The Shiloh prisoners were the first to come under this order and were sent to Benton Barracks where there developed a problem which was increasingly to embarrass the administration for the coming year.

The prisoners quartered at the Benton Barracks had returned to their lines with the expectation that they would receive eight months' back pay and a furlough to their homes until they were exchanged. The majority of the prisoners were from Iowa and objected to being sent to a camp outside their own state. Moreover, slight preparations had been made to receive them, and they found themselves without camp equipment, cooking utensils, and other necessary conveniences of the soldier. There were no officers to look after their welfare. To cap the misfortunes of the soldiers, they were ordered under arms to relieve a regiment which had been on guard duty.

Such duty was considered by the men a direct contradiction to their paroles 'not to bear arms or to aid the United States directly or indirectly until they were exchanged.' They appealed to General Halleck, the administration's authority on international law, who had a remarkable ability to adapt the rules of his subject to fit the exigencies of the moment and to marshal opinions to support the policy of the government. Halleck replied that the prisoners were obliged to perform guard and fatigue duties and to maintain order within their own camp. Those who refused such duties were mutinous.[25] But the adjutant general of Iowa interfered with the good effects which this dictum might have had and petitioned Stanton for the return of the Iowa troops to their own state where they would not be subjected to the danger of violating their pledged word—and thus avoid disastrous consequences in case they again had the misfortune to fall into rebel hands. Halleck's opinion was therefore reversed and Adjutant General Thomas ordered that all duties inconsistent with the paroles which the men had given should be

[24] *Ibid.*, 94.   [25] *Ibid.*, 242.

stopped. Later decisions added that paroled officers might drill paroled men for purposes of discipline but could not request them to serve as guards, or perform any functions which might release others for service in the field.[26]

With the ratification of the cartel, a more serious problem developed in the Northern armies. Generals in the field found that the system of paroles established by that instrument acted as an inducement for soldiers to fall into the hands of the enemy in order to be paroled and sent home. A premium was thus placed upon straggling in the vicinity of the enemy in order to obtain, according to one soldier, a "little rest from soldiering."[27] General Buell, in headquarters at Huntsville, Alabama, was the first to take official notice of this dilatory tendency of his men. On August 8, therefore, he issued an order admitting that the system of paroles as practiced in his army had "run into intolerable abuse" and ordered that henceforth any officer captured by the enemy must obtain the consent of his general before he could give his parole; any parole not receiving such assent would be considered void. The system was also to apply to Confederates who were placed under the necessity of obtaining the consent of their commander before they would be released.[28] General Sam Jones, opposing Buell, called the latter's attention to the cartel provisions which made obligatory the release of men within ten days of their capture,[29] so the order was rescinded.[30]

[26] *Ibid.*, 242, 246, 250, 288, 295-300, 336.

[27] McElroy, *Andersonville*, 98.

[28] *Official Records*, series 2, IV, 360.

[29] *Ibid.*, 414-15.

[30] *Ibid.*, 452. During the period when the exchanges were in progress the South maintained a balance of prisoners which resulted in most of their men going into the ranks as soon as they could be reorganized after coming from prison. Money, despite its constantly decreasing purchasing power, was available to pay the prisoners. Those in the east were ordered upon their return to report to their regiments in the field or to Winder, in Richmond, and the senior officer of each regiment was authorizd to act as paymaster for the returned men. *Ibid.*, 841. The prisoners who were delivered at Vicksburg were greater in number and presented more of a problem in that it was not always easy to return them to their regiments. Bragg ordered General Tilghman, himself a returned prisoner, to establish a camp near Vicksburg and reorganize the prisoners as they returned, sending them to their regiments where

Two defeats in Kentucky brought the defects of the system of paroles more emphatically to the attention of the Federal government. On August 30, the Confederates captured four thousand prisoners at Richmond,[31] and followed this by administering defeat and exacting a surrender from the Union forces at Mumfordsville, September 17.[32] Governor Tod indignantly informed Stanton that "the freedom in giving paroles by our troops in Kentucky is very prejudicial to the service and should be stopped. Had our forces at Richmond, Kentucky, refused to give their parole it would have taken all of Kirby Smith's army to guard them." Stanton heartily agreed that this was one of the most dangerous evils which had appeared in the army and confessed that he saw no remedy. "There is reason to fear," he admitted, "that many voluntarily surrender for the sake of getting home." In order to check the nuisance, Stanton sent fifteen hundred to Camp Chase with orders that they should be closely confined to quarters, drilled diligently every day and allowed no leaves of absence. Tod, however, had another remedy. The Indians in Minnesota had gone on the warpath and were causing the government considerable trouble. What could be better than to send the homesick soldiers against this new foe? Besides, "it is with great difficulty that we can preserve order among them at Camp Chase." A few days later Tod reported there were four thousand prisoners at Chase utterly demoralized through lack of organization,[33] and Stanton sent General Lew Wallace to organize the prisoners for the Indian expedition.[34]

September 15, the garrison of Harpers Ferry, Virginia, surrendered and the troops there were released on parole; ten thousand of the prisoners released were sent to Annapolis,

possible. Furloughs were not granted to the men but they were paid off and comfortable clothes issued to them. *Ibid.*, 852-54. Because of this care and the early return to duty, disciplinary problems did not develop in the South as early as they did in the North.

[31] *Ibid.*, series 1, XVI, part 1, 906-52, part ii, 458 ff.

[32] *Ibid.*, series 1, XVI, part i, 959-90, part ii, 518 ff.

[33] *Ibid.*, series 2, IV, 499, 519.

[34] *Ibid.*, 522.

and Adjutant General Thomas went there to decide what
disposition was to be made of them. Orders had already
been given that police duty was not contrary to the obliga-
tions of their paroles, and the men had been paid off and forbidden to leave the camp.[35] After disbanding an Ohio regiment the twelve thousand available for service against the
Indians were sent to Chicago for reorganization.[36] But it
happened that the Harpers Ferry prisoners had been told by
the Confederates that their paroles meant that they were to
be sent home, and the prospect of a campaign in Minnesota
was a severe disappointment. They began to declare that
such service would be a violation of their paroles, and the men
of the 32d Ohio made public announcement of their intention
to pay a visit to their homes while en route through their
state. Thomas warned Stanton to expect many desertions
and much straggling on the way.[37]

The arrival of Wallace at Camp Chase did not quiet the
camp. He and Tod united in presenting to Stanton the need
of the soldiers for their back pay, which some of the prisoners,
they said, had not received for a year. With the troops paid,
the work of organization might get under way. Despite the
protest of the paymaster's department that funds were low
and more valuable troops in the field were owed greater
amounts, a paymaster was sent to Columbus and supplies for
the prisoners were forwarded.[38]

To the already existing complications was now added another. Governor Morton, seeing the confusion at Camp
Chase, requested that the Indiana prisoners there, five thousand from Mumfordsville and two thousand from Richmond, Kentucky, be sent to their home state, representing
that inasmuch as he had available facilities equal to those at
Chase, a transfer of prisoners to Indiana would remove dis-
satisfaction. "Indiana feels very sore," he informed Stanton,
at the imbecility which had caused the Kentucky surrenders,
and Morton felt that it would be something of a salve to

[35] Ibid., 529, 540.   [37] Ibid., 546-47, 550-51.
[36] Ibid., 540-42.   [38] Ibid., 545-46.

have the paroled prisoners now at Chase near their homes. Since this was exactly what Stanton wished to avoid, he replied to Morton that while he was not surprised at the soreness, the suggested salve would be but an added "inducement for shameful surrender."[39]

Wallace, meantime, would have been glad to rid himself of the presence of some of his incorrigible charges and demanded that no more be sent him. The men refused to be armed or to perform any duty whatsoever;[40] numbers deserted, and all were opposed to the Indian service. The promise to pay them had resulted in recruiting one regiment but most of these men had taken their pay and absconded. Confusion was confounded by the exchange of some of the troops while others remained on parole. Those exchanged were sent to their old commands in the field.[41]

The erstwhile defenders of Harpers Ferry arrived in Chicago from Annapolis about the first of October. Their trip across the country had not been attended by conditions conducive to reconciling them to the service planned. Crowded by railroad companies into freight cars, they were provided with neither water nor toilet facilities. The men got off at stops and were left behind by conductors who refused to wait for them. General Tyler, in charge of the troops, boasted thirty years of railroad management and admitted investments in transportation facilities, but he pronounced the service, at a charge of $623 for a regular $168 cattle car, "outrageous."[42] The condition of the soldiers on arrival was

[39] *Ibid.*, 562. The governors of Kentucky and Pennsylvania added their pleas to those of Governor Morton; the one to have the Kentucky troops remain in the state and the other to have the Pennsylvania prisoners returned to the state from which they had been recruited. The Pennsylvania executive represented that the prisoners would rather have remained in Richmond than to undergo the hardships which had befallen them at Annapolis. *Ibid.*, 588-89, 594, 620. Stanton would doubtless have preferred the prisoners in the Confederate capital but he failed to comply with either request. However, some Indiana prisoners were given a furlough on the excuse that they had been promised it before they were suddenly ordered into the field in Kentucky. *Ibid.*, 585-86.

[40] *Ibid.*, 563.

[41] *Ibid.*, 569-71.

[42] *Ibid.*, 595-96.

one of complete destitution,[43] and immediately upon their arrival Stanton ordered the officers with them to return to Washington. Tyler protested against such a course as he feared that mutiny would result. "You have taken the heads of every regiment we have," he told Stanton, adding that two New York regiments refused every duty. Only parts of five other regiments were available for use and they were not reliable; the 9th Vermont was the only loyal regiment in the camp. And added to that Pope had sent for a regiment! Tyler gave the men one day to suppress their insubordination,[44] and two days later one of the New York regiments fell in. But hardly had this point been reached when the Chicago *Tribune* published the cartel by which the men learned that they were forbidden to do field, police, guard, or constabulary duties. "The publication is unfortunate," complained Tyler, concluding that if the cartel were complied with, the United States could only hold and feed the paroled prisoners.[45] It was not until October 23, that Tyler was able to report that the crisis had been passed. But before the recalcitrant troops finally allowed their reluctant spirits to yield to proper military subordination they fired three buildings of Camp Douglas and, to prevent the camp from being burned to the ground, fourteen others had to be torn down.

When the news of the proposed Indian expedition came to the South, the reaction was similar to that of the paroled prisoners in the North. Protests appeared in the Richmond *Dispatch* which were subjected to vituperative countercharges in the New York *Times*.[46] In Virginia General J. E. B. Stuart cautiously exacted paroles specifically excluding service against the Indians.[47] Lincoln appealed to the ingenious Halleck who, after reversing his opinion twice, finally decided that the cartel did not forbid service against the Indians. However Ould protested to Thomas when he learned of the contemplated misuse of the prisoners, and Thomas informed

[43] *Ibid.*, 566.   [45] *Ibid.*, 600.
[44] *Ibid.*, 596.   [46] New York *Times*, October 3, 1862.
[47] *Official Records*, series 2, IV, 593, 598.

Stanton that the project was illegal.[48] But General Pope, who had been removed from Virginia, had been successful in his campaign against the Indians, and there was no longer any necessity for sending the prisoners to serve with him on the frontier.[49]

With conflicting interpretations of the permissibility of military service being passed back and forth at Washington, it fell to Hoffman to give the final interpretation which satisfied all angles of the question. If the cartel was to be interpreted as it read, the paroled soldiers could perform no service whatever. But, declared the commissary-general of prisoners, the war department had the right to determine whether military duties could be exacted from the returned men. It was the government and not the soldier who gave the parole, and the responsibility for its observance fell upon the government and not upon the men. Hoffman admitted that this assumption of responsibility by the government might not please the officers who had given their word of honor to abide by the cartel's provisions. In case the officers refused to submit their sense of honor to the first duty of the soldier, Hoffman feared that the court martial which would have to be assembled might agree with the officer in interpreting the cartel as it read and thus frustrate the plan of the government.[50] Seemingly, this was not a satisfactory solution, but it was the only conclusion which gave the department ground upon which to stand. And that kaleidoscopic jurist, Halleck, adopted this interpretation as his own![51]

Even with the passing of the Indian danger, the excess prisoners in the parole camps did not return to obedience. Governor Morton continued to demand that the Indiana soldiers be returned to the state, offering the hope that Camp Morton would be better disciplined than Camp Chase, and Stanton finally promised to send the prisoners home if the arrangements could be made.[52] The hopes of getting some order in the parole camps led Stanton to ask Hoffman to

[48] Ibid., 600-603, 621.
[49] Ibid., 607.
[50] Ibid., 652, 697.
[51] Ibid., 697.
[52] Ibid., 638, 641, 652-54.

suggest a plan for the payment of the troops, while Tod
recommended that the men at Chase and Douglas be given
a dishonorable discharge.[53]

In the east, disorders were as great as in the west, and
here they were complicated by inadequate care and provisions.
The governor of Wisconsin protested at the suffering caused
to his troops by the lack of food and clothing at Alexandria,
Virginia, where a temporary camp had been established. The
governor of Iowa demanded that his troops be removed from
Annapolis to their home state.[54] Hoffman, inspecting in
November, found that the prisoners were housed in tents
furnished with stoves and sufficient clothing had been issued,
but the officers were as insubordinate as the men. The sick,
however, had been poorly cared for. There were other
troubles as well; a private demanded of the commander of
the post that something should be done to stop the gambling,
robbery, and even murder which prevailed in the camp. "A
person is not safe to step out to meeting or anywhere else
after dark," he complained, adding that liquor was smuggled
into the camp contrary to the rules. Wisconsin troops protested against the disorders, and Hoffman ordered the commander to make a report on the conditions.[55] The commander
made a report, which admitted everything but murder, and
for relieving the situation outlined a program, the chief point
of which was to furnish adequate guards for the camp.[56] By
the middle of December he had inaugurated a new system
which promised to bring success.

Despite these conditions in the parole camps, which were
probably now known in the army,[57] the tendency to take a

[53] *Ibid.*, 673, 688. Tod, however, expressed his regret that the 60th Ohio had
been so discharged at Camp Douglas.

[54] *Ibid.*, series 2, IV, 689, 696.   [56] *Ibid.*, series 2, V, 38-42, 58-69.

[55] *Ibid.*, 692-93, 727, 749, 771.

[57] The administration papers, which were the ones of general circulation in the
army, were singularly free from any hint of conditions in the parole camps. Even
such papers as the Columbus, Ohio, *Crisis*, almost within sight of Camp Chase, has
but the slightest reference to conditions there. The New York *Times*, *Tribune*,
Herald and *News*, *Harper's Weekly*, Philadelphia *Inquirer* and Cincinnati *Daily Commercial* have been examined and all seem to have been totally unaware that the administration was facing a disciplinary problem of considerable proportions.

vacation by falling into the clutches of the enemy continued. Rosecrans, commanding the department of the Cumberland, announced, November 14, that he was "pained" to learn of these conditions. Such conduct was "even more base and cowardly than desertion." He ordered that all paroles in the future would subject the one who gave the parole to arrest.[58] The South was taking advantage of this situation; a spy reported to Davis that while he had been a prisoner a number of privates had asked him what disposition would be made of them if they should be captured and seemed delighted when they were informed that they would be sent home.[59]

While the administration had been dealing with the problems growing out of the excess of prisoners on parole, the agents of exchange in the east had been meeting the routine problems of their offices. The first problem of any importance which the agents faced was the necessity of deciding what men and classes of troops were to be considered as coming within the scope of the cartel. Hardly had that instrument been signed, than General M. Jeff. Thompson suggested to Secretary Randolph that there were confined in Chicago, St. Louis, and Alton, as prisoners of war, former members of his brigade of the Missouri State Guard who had been arrested at their homes after the expiration of their terms in order to prevent their re-enlistment. He also called attention to the case of men who were captured while engaged in raising commands, but who had not yet been mustered into the Confed-

[58] *Official Records*, series 2, IV, 713.

[59] *Ibid.*, 949-50. Despite the fact that the excess of prisoners held by the South enabled the Confederacy to return their prisoners to the ranks soon after their return, the Southern soldier revealed the same tendencies in parole camps as his Northern adversary. General M. L. Smith, writing to General French in regard to deliveries at City Point, said "the camp of paroled prisoners at this point has given more annoyance and trouble than any other of the many charges upon the command in Richmond, and you will be fortunate and deserve unusually if you succeed where we have well-nigh failed in managing it satisfactorily. The men arrive full of the idea of deserving unusual privileges because of their capture and will at once besiege your officers for furloughs, pleading the unusual merit of their position, and upon being refused, as they must be in every instance except when furnishing a certificate of disability, they become exceedingly unruly, mutinous and difficult of management." French was instructed to employ a large guard and forbid troops to leave camp except in small numbers and for one day. *Ibid.*, 940-41.

erate service.[60] In the North, Stanton urged upon Thomas the necessity of securing the release of the Texas prisoners, a number of telegraph operators and surgeons, and directed that persons who had offered to take the oath of allegiance to the United States should not be offered in exchange unless they were necessary to release prisoners actually held in the South.[61] To this Gideon Welles added the demand that blockade runners should not be given in exchange, as it was through their efficiency that his blockade was constantly in danger of becoming ineffective.[62] Men accused of being bush-whackers and guerillas were retained at Johnson's Island after the other prisoners were sent for exchange.[63]

By the first of October a sufficient number of cases had arisen to justify Ould in writing to Lieutenant Colonel W. H. Ludlow, an aide to General Dix who had been carrying on the business of exchange until he had come to be regarded as the agent, a protest against a number of practices. He protested against the arrest of Missouri citizens; the confine-ment of a number of officers and men of the Missouri State Guard at Johnson's Island and other prisons; the retention of a blockade runner; the refusal to deliver Partizan Rangers who were declared to be a part of the regularly commissioned forces of the Confederacy but who were held by the North as guerillas; the holding of citizens as prisoners after Pope's orders had been rescinded and his officers released; the keep-ing of prisoners in New Orleans by General Butler after they had been exchanged; the use of the paroled prisoners against the Indians; and, finally, the arrest of citizens by the North-ern forces and generals. Ould requested that either Thomas or Ludlow meet with him to adjust these and other diffi-culties.[64] General Thomas suggested to Stanton that he should reply to Ould that the arrest of the citizens of Mis-souri was legitimate as the state was still within the Union; the Missouri State Guard and Partizan Rangers were to be placed on the same footing as other prisoners of war; Gen-

[60] *Ibid.*, 827-28.
[61] *Ibid.*, 306-7.
[62] *Ibid.*, 346.
[63] Barbiere, *op. cit.*, 130.
[64] *Official Records*, series 2, IV, 600-603.

eral Butler would be instructed to release the prisoners at
New Orleans; the use of paroled troops against the Indians
was illegal; and so long as the Confederacy arrested citizens
for their Union sentiments, the United States had the right
to arrest citizens for disloyal sentiments.[65] This answer was
not sent, but the concessions to the Southern contentions were
communicated to the Confederate commissioner. Other matters remained to cause trouble. The middle of November,
Major General Ethan Allen Hitchcock, of Stanton's staff,
was appointed "Commissioner" for exchange, with Ludlow,
who had declined the first place, his assistant.[66]

The continued failure of Federal authorities to answer the
questions presented by Ould led the South to adopt what had
hitherto been an effective means of forcing the Northern hand
—the threat of retaliation. The confinement of the hostages,
Corcoran especially, for the privateersmen had forced the
cartel from the reluctant government of Lincoln. The proclamation against Pope had been followed by the removal of
that general to other fields and the announcement that his
orders were no longer in force. May 9, a proclamation by
Lincoln had reversed Hunter's orders in regard to the
negroes of South Carolina and Florida.[67] This consistent
yielding to the Southern demands, despite the fact that in
two of the cases the reasons had had but little to do with the
threats of the rebel executive, inevitably had the effect of
inducing in the minds of the Confederate officials an abnormal
confidence in the potency of such threats. November 10,
Benjamin, then secretary of state, advised Randolph to demand that the Partizan Rangers and other prisoners who
were held by Butler in New Orleans be released. If an answer were not received in fifteen days the South should retain
as hostages all commissioned officers taken prisoners. He
also suggested that a demand be made for a reply in the case
of Mumford.[68] Accordingly, two weeks later, Ould wrote

[65] *Ibid.*, 621-22.
[66] New York *Times*, November 18.
[67] Richardson, *Messages and Papers of the Presidents*, VI, 91.
[68] *Official Records*, series 2, IV, 937.

to Ludlow that he had not received replies to his inquiries in regard to Missouri citizens, the citizens arrested under Pope's orders in Virginia, the prisoners retained in New Orleans, or the citizens of the Confederacy arrested. He added a demand for a reply in the case of Mumford and informed Ludlow that if a reply was not forthcoming within fifteen days the South would consider that an answer was refused and would proceed to retain the officers.[69] Ludlow replied that he had asked for instructions and that the release of prisoners from Forts Warren and Lafayette indicated the course of his government on those points.[70] December 24, President Davis issued a proclamation setting forth the attempts which had been made to settle the questions. He then pronounced General Butler a felon and outlaw for the murder of Mumford. "And I do further order that no commissioned officer of the United States taken captive shall be released on parole before exchange until the said Butler shall have met with due punishment for his crime." This "due punishment" was to be hanging, and the commanding officer of any detachment which should be so fortunate as to capture the "Beast" was instructed to hang him immediately. Butler's officers were not to be treated as prisoners of war, and all negroes taken in arms should be delivered to the civil authorities of the states wherein they were captured.[71]

The sections in this proclamation referring to the negro troops and their officers were inserted as the result of a problem which had been agitating the Southern mind for some time. It has already been pointed out that the congress which met in September had come prepared to discuss the question. September 19, they called upon Randolph to learn what disposition was made of negroes taken in arms, but Randolph told them that no such troops had been captured.[72] September 21, came Lincoln's preliminary emancipation proclamation

[69] *Ibid.*, 770-71.

[70] *Ibid.*, series 2, V, 19, 20.

[71] *Ibid.*, 795-97. The Richmond *Dispatch*, December 24, 1862, approved the president's proclamation and hoped it would be carried out to the letter. "The black flag is the only answer to the unheard of crimes of these enemies of the human race."

[72] *Official Records*, series 2, IV, 892.

and the Confederate authorities reached the point of desperation. In November a negro was taken in South Carolina and
Seddon, succeeding Randolph as secretary of war, advised
the president that the negro be executed as an example.[73] In
the North reports were current that the negroes who were
captured in the South were sold into slavery,[74] although
Stanton told Congress that he did not possess information of
any such cases.[75] The problem of the proper treatment of the
negro soldiers was one which touched the Southerner closely
and the imminence of the final proclamation of emancipation
doubtless led to their inclusion in Davis' proclamation against
Butler.[76]

Davis had selected a moment of victory for his proclamation as Lincoln had done for his preliminary emancipation
proclamation, but the effect in the two cases was different.[77]
The North had yielded to Confederate threats of retaliation
in the case of the privateersmen only under the pressure of
public opinion. But by this time, the experiences with the
paroled prisoners had not been such as to create a love for the
cartel in the Northern mind. Stanton instructed Ludlow to
deliver no more commissioned officers to the Confederates
and the same instructions were given to commanders in the
field.[78] It was reported that the first intention of the government was to cease exchanges under the cartel altogether.[79]

If the intention had been to intimidate Lincoln, the attempt of the Confederate president was unsuccessful. The
emancipation proclamation appeared on time. When the
newspapers carrying the text of the proclamation appeared in
the South, Davis turned to the newly assembled congress with
indignation, "tempered," he said, "with a profound contempt
for the 'impotent rage' disclosed." It was impossible for him,
as it was for any slaveholder, to perceive anything in the
proclamation other than a call for the negroes to rise in the
most horrible of all warfare—a servile insurrection. Despite

---

[73] *Ibid.*, 945-46, 954.   [75] *Ibid.*, 42.
[74] *Ibid.*, series 2, V, 9.   [76] New York *Times*, December 28.
[77] The battles of Fredericksburg were fought December 12-15, 1862.
[78] *Official Records*, series 2, V, 127-30.   [79] New York *Times*, December 31.

his contempt for the impotent rage of the Northern President, Davis again resolved to try the effects of retaliation; January 12, he addressed his congress on the subject and declared that, unless it refused to support him, he would turn the commissioned officers of the North over to the state authorities to be punished under the laws of the several states for exciting slaves to rise against their masters.[80]

Despite the fact that these two utterances of the Confederate president prohibited the officers from being released on parole in accordance with the terms of the cartel, the exchanges of noncommissioned officers and enlisted men went on without interruption. Ludlow believed that it was the intention of the South to carry out the threats, although he wrote to Ould to ask him to a conference in regard to whether the Confederacy actually intended to deal with the officers as Davis had suggested.[81] However, his real reason for demanding the interview was to obtain the release from their paroles of ten thousand troops who had been delivered before. After the first proclamation of Davis, Ludlow had rushed to City Point, now the exchange point in the east, and had made arrangements for some general exchanges of irregular paroles. These had been largely in favor of the United States, and Ludlow reported that out of twenty thousand declared exchanged he had been the gainer by seven thousand; "if an open rupture should now occur in the execution of the cartel we are well prepared for it." He hoped now to obtain the release of all of the officers in the South who had been taken before Davis' message.[82] This was possible since the President's proclamation did not affect exchanges but only prohibited the release of officers on parole before exchange. Ould agreed to make an exchange of all officers taken before January 12.[83]

Hope came to Ludlow when he learned the reception which the message of Davis had been given in the Confederate congress. Richmond papers informed him that a strong

[80] *Official Records,* series 2, V, 807-8.   [82] Ludlow to Hitchcock. *Ibid.,* 181.
[81] *Ibid.,* 178.   [83] *Ibid.,* 186-87.

opposition, led by W. L. Yancey, had developed.[84] The
Virginia legislature overruled Governor Letcher who had
attempted to have prisoners tried under state laws, and turned
over the entire control of the prisoners to the Confederate
government.[85] An embarrassing obstacle to rigorous action by
the South was that the Northern government held a majority
of prisoners.[86] Ludlow hoped the cartel would be resumed,[87]
the wish being based upon the reports of the suffering of the
officers in the South due to the lack of provisions.[88]

Another problem complicating the arrangements for the
exchange of prisoners was the failure of the Federal authorities to deliver the captives taken in the west, particularly at
Arkansas Post, through Vicksburg. Grant declared that it
would be criminal to send the prisoners to reinforce the garrison there at the very time he was attempting to reduce the
forts.[89] Accordingly the prisoners were lodged in the Alton,
Illinois, penitentiary[90] from whence it was planned to send
them east to be delivered at City Point.[91] This delivery was
postponed for various reasons, chiefly those growing out of
the cost of transportation. Ould became insistent that some
reasonable explanation be given him for the delay.[92] On
March 16 after three months' dickering orders were finally
given to send all of the enlisted men from the west to the
eastern exchange point.[93]

The suffering of the prisoners in Richmond led Ludlow to
so press their cause upon the authorities[94] that a decision
finally came from the secretary of war authorizing him to exchange the officers, man for man, without reference to the
cartel.[95] By April 1, arrangements were complete for the
exchange of all of the officers.[96] Ludlow announced to Ould
that all such exchanges must be special until Davis' offensive
proclamation and message were revoked.[97] The implication

[84] *Ibid.*, 119.
[85] *Ibid.*, 358.
[86] *Ibid.*, 244.
[87] *Ibid.*, 286.
[88] *Ibid.*, 396.
[89] *Ibid.*, 176.
[90] *Ibid.*, 179-80.

[91] *Ibid.*, 238-39, 248-49.
[92] *Ibid.*, 223-4.
[93] *Ibid.*, 357.
[94] *Ibid.*, 389, 394.
[95] *Ibid.*, 397.
[96] New York *Times*, April 1.
[97] *Official Records,* series 2, V, 431.

that the Confederacy had broken the cartel was resented by
Ould who cited the retention of officers and men in Northern
prisons as the first breach which had forced the President of
the Confederate States to issue his order refusing paroles to
Union men in Southern prisons until the Confederates should
have been released. "If captivity, privation and misery are
to be the fate of officers on both sides hereafter, let God judge
between us. I have struggled in this matter as if it had been
a matter of life and death to me. I am heartsick at the termi-
nation but I have no self-reproaches," declared the Confederate commissioner,[98] as he inaugurated a correspondence
which eventually developed such bitterness that exchanges
became entirely impossible, and which served at last to bury
the real points at issue under a maze of ill-tempered vitupera-
tion. Ludlow failed to be deluded by the appeal to humanity
and divine judgment, and callously demanded whether the
South intended to resume the retention of the United States
officers as soon as the South held the greater number of
prisoners.[99]

While the agents of exchange troubled themselves over
the responsibility for the violation of the cartel and sought
to exchange officers in spite of obstacles, the officials in Washington continued to face the problem of the paroled prisoners
and the tendency of the men to take a "little rest from soldiering" by falling into the hands of the enemy. In the
parole camps conditions continued bad, and the governors of
Illinois and Indiana demanded that their troops be sent to
camps in their home states.[100] Increasing difficulties and
complaints led to the establishment of better facilities for the
care of the returned prisoners[101] but Lazelle reported after
an inspection of Annapolis that an increased guard force was
necessary before the discipline of the camp could be greatly
improved.[102] Since this need was not met, disorders continued to prevail.[103] By the last of March Hoffman was
finally convinced of the necessity of having the parole camps

[98] Ibid., 469.
[99] Ibid., 478-79.
[100] Ibid., 292, 289.

[101] Ibid., 232, 255.
[102] Ibid., 326-37.
[103] Ibid., 248-49.

in the several states; but he still refused to designate particular camps for the troops of any state, fearing that if the information became general throughout the army, desertion would be increased.[104] However, the need for parole camps was soon to pass.

In September, 1862, a citizen of Columbus, Ohio, seeing the conditions in Camp Chase, wrote to Stanton:

I have seen enough of the paroled prisoners and heard enough of them talk to know that unless the paroling system is abandoned we will be beaten by the number of paroled prisoners we shall have. It is an inducement not only for cowards, but for men discontented with their officers, or even homesick to surrender. . . . The paroled prisoners also become outlaws and refuse to serve again in any capacity. An order ending all paroling will force upon the South the necessity of feeding or releasing our soldiers, and if our men understood positively that they are to be prisoners in the South if taken they would strike with more energy and desperation.[105]

The denial of paroles to the officers did not affect the non-commissioned officers and enlisted men. If the citizen above quoted was correct, the retention of the officers might even have resulted in the increase of voluntary surrender by men who wished to rid themselves of unpopular chieftains. Certain it is that the tendency to fall into the hands of the enemy did not cease. It was not even necessary for the men to be captured since a number adopted the practice of forging parole certificates and wandering off to parole camps.[106] The commandant at Annapolis reported that not five hundred men in his camp knew to what army corps they belonged, and half of those who knew were wrong. "If the men of my camp were a sample of our army," he told Hoffman, "we would have nothing but a mob of stragglers and cowards." In this classification he placed three-fourths of the paroled men.[107]

The army under Rosecrans seems to have been particularly infested with this type of men, and the general sought for some means by which the evil might be checked. He found it in the cartel. By the terms of that instrument all prison-

[104] *Ibid.*, 373-74.
[105] *Ibid.*, series 2, IV, 576.
[106] *Ibid.*, series 2, V. 169.
[107] *Ibid.*, 194.

ers were to be delivered at Vicksburg, or City Point, within
ten days of their capture. Rosecrans thereupon issued an
order declaring that no paroles would be recognized unless
delivery were made at one or the other of these places.[108]
Farther to the west Grant made the same discovery in the
cartel and issued, January 20, a similar order, with the added
provision that all officers and soldiers who were captured
while straggling would be court-martialed.[109] Generals
Dodge at Corinth, Mississippi, and Sherman added orders on
the subject within a week while Rosecrans called to Stanton's
attention the Confederate practice of paroling troops wher-
ever they were taken.[110] Stanton informed Rosecrans that a
general order would be issued on the subject, giving due
notice to the enemy that in the future paroles must be given
and deliveries made in accordance with the terms of the
cartel.[111] Accordingly, February 29, General Orders No. 49
was issued from the war department. By this order it was
declared that paroling must take place by the signing in
duplicate of parole certificates, none but commissioned officers could give paroles for themselves and their commands,
and "no inferior officer if his superior is within reach"; no
paroling on the battlefield or just after a battle, nor should
bodies of troops be sent to their own lines simply with the
declaration that they were paroled; "any officer who gives a
parole for himself and his command on the battlefield is a
deserter"; no noncommissioned officer or private could give
his parole except through a commissioned officer; if the engagement made by an individual soldier was not recognized
by his government "he is bound to return and surrender
himself as a prisoner of war"; paroles were only binding
against a specific belligerent.[112] This order was considered of
particular force against the giving of paroles to guerilla commanders, and it was hoped that Ould would accept it and
cancel all such irregular paroles.[113]

[108] *Ibid.*, 198.
[109] *Ibid.*, 216.
[110] *Ibid.*, 231, 237-38. February 1 and 5.
[111] *Ibid.*, 301-2.
[112] *Ibid.*, 306-7.
[113] *Ibid.*, 359.

Ould, however, was more critical of the order and reported to Secretary Seddon that some parts of it were unacceptable while others were contradictory, and the provision that a parole applied only to a specific belligerent was entirely contrary to the provisions of the cartel.[114] However, Ould's opinion of the order was not submitted to the Northern government because he had not received the order through the formal channels.

After the Virginia legislature surrendered the entire control of prisoners of war to the Confederate government, the congress returned to the attempt to define the Southern attitude toward the negro soldier and his officers in the army of the enemy. May 1, a joint resolution was passed by the congress purporting to be an answer to the message of the president which had caused the cessation of exchanges for officers. The resolution declared that the officers of the United States ought not to be turned over to the authorities of the several states as the president had suggested but that they should be tried for violations of Confederate law by the national courts. The emancipation proclamation, according to the resolution, was designed to incite servile insurrection, and this attempt on the part of the United States should be met by retaliation. Davis was therefore authorized to retaliate for every violation of the laws of war. It was also provided that all white officers of negro troops, or of troops serving with negroes, were to be put to death. The negro soldiers themselves were to be turned over to the several states.[115] Although Ludlow believed that this act had been passed against the will of the more intelligent of the congress under the necessity of yielding to what was thought to be public opinion, and that it was not what Davis had asked for in his message, it was still sufficiently broad to cause a number of new and serious complications.[116]

Two cases to test the principle of retaliation arose almost immediately. The first of these grew out of the execution of

[114] *Ibid.*, 860-61.   [116] *Ibid.*, 286.

[115] *Ibid.*, 940-41

two Confederate officers on a charge of recruiting behind the Union lines in Kentucky. General Burnside, commanding the Department of the Ohio, arrested Captains McGraw and Corbin and tried them by court-martial.[117] Newspapers carried to the South the news of the execution and Lincoln's approval, and Ould informed Ludlow that two Federal officers would be shot in retaliation.[118] Ludlow in turn immediately recommended to Hoffman that all Confederate officers, even those who had been exchanged and were awaiting delivery, should be held to await developments; and he wrote to Ould that every execution by the South would be met with retaliation on the part of the United States.[119]

The other case, developing at the same time, which arose to test the efficacy of retaliation came as the result of the capture near Rome, Georgia, of the command of Colonel A. D. Streight, consisting of Indiana troops. But Governor Shorter of Alabama had information that two companies of Colonel Streight's command were composed of natives of Alabama and that the entire command was guilty of enticing slaves to rebel. The governor demanded that the officers, as well as the Alabama citizens, be punished either by the Confederate States or surrendered to the justice of the courts of Alabama.[120] Seddon ordered that the officers be held,[121] and the Confederate President ordered that the officers and men who remained in the South—some having been sent in exchange before the arrival of Shorter's letter—should be tried by the Confederate courts.[122] General Forrest, who made the capture of Streight, reported that there were neither negroes nor Alabamians with the Indiana troops,[123] but the officers were, nevertheless, held in Libby, largely for the reason that Ludlow did not have the officers to offer in exchange for them.[124]

Meantime the Union authorities were continuing to take action to check the lax system of paroles which had developed. April 24, there was issued from the war department

[117] *Ibid.*, 556-57.
[118] *Ibid.*, 691.
[119] *Ibid.*, 701-4.
[120] *Ibid.*, 946-47.
[121] *Ibid.*, 952.
[122] *Ibid.*, 955-56.
[123] *Ibid.*, 960-69.
[124] *Ibid.*, 701-4.

a General Order No. 100 and entitled "Instructions for the Government of Armies in the Field." The order purported to be a summary of the laws and usages of war and was written by Professor Francis Lieber, Professor of International Law at Columbia University.[125] Section 7 of the order related to prisoners of war and embodied the rules in regard to paroles which had been promulgated in General Order No. 49.[126] This order, as well as No. 49, was sent to Ludlow to be transmitted to Ould with the announcement that all paroles given after the date of the earlier order would be considered void. That this was hardly fair is seen by the fact that it was not until May 20 that these orders were delivered to Ludlow, and several days elapsed before they were sent by him to Ould.[127]

In regard to General Order No. 100 Ould addressed Ludlow to inquire whether the order went into effect when it was issued or when it was delivered to him, citing as his reasons for making the inquiry the outrages alleged to have been committed by Federal troops in Virginia—such outrages being forbidden by the laws of war as set forth in the order.[128] Ludlow referred the question to Hoffman[129] who replied that General Order No. 100 went into effect for the United States on the date of its issue and that it went into effect against the enemy on the date of its delivery to Ould. Further, it was intended to work both for and against the government which issued it. General Order No. 49, however, was operative from the date of its publication, even though it was embodied in the later order. It might not be binding, however, under special circumstances; to be left to

[125] *Ibid.*, series 2, VI, 863-64.   [126] *Ibid.*, series 2, V, 671-82.

[127] *Ibid.*, 670, 689. During the controversy between Ould and Meredith the date of the delivery of the orders became an additional subject for the ill-temper of the agents' correspondence. Ould insisted that he received 49 before 100. Meredith proved by Ludlow's letter book that the two orders were delivered at the same time. This seems to be the correct interpretation, Ould's contention that he received the earlier order before 100 being due to the fact that he received unofficial information of the order from the papers or through some general in the field. The subject was of comparative unimportance except that Ould at the time was insisting that paroles should be governed by the orders according to their dates of issue.

[128] *Ibid.*, 744.   [129] *Ibid.*, 755.

the discretion of the major general commanding in a department.[130]

After May 25, the exchange of officers ceased entirely, although the exchange of noncommissioned officers and men continued as usual. The Northern government had hopes of forcing the Southern hand. Ludlow reported that the retention of officers by the North had resulted in a strong opposition in the South and there were indications that the entire subject of retaliation was becoming unpopular among the Confederates. He lost no opportunity to insist that the South return to the cartel.[131] An additional piece of good fortune came to the United States in the person of Brigadier General W. H. Fitzhugh Lee (son of the great commander) who fell wounded into the Federal hands. "His retention settles all questions about hanging our officers," decided Ludlow. Moreover, Ludlow believed that the operation of General Orders 49 and 100 had added a great advantage to the North; for the Confederates were forced by them to reduce every capture to possession, unless the commanders of opposing armies made other agreements under the provisions of Article 7 of the cartel.[132]

In this situation with officers retained, prominent Confederates available in case hostages were needed, the problems of the paroled prisoners and the tendency to desert under way of being settled, the Northern government was content. For the first time since the beginning of hostilities they were in a position to resist Confederate demands and the pressure of public opinion. Threats of retaliation, hitherto successful, had at last been met with counter-retaliation. The next move must come from the South, and under these circumstances President Davis sought to obtain a settlement of the difficulties by direct negotiations with President Lincoln. Accepting the "patriotic" offer of Vice-President Stephens to bear a message, the Confederate executive commissioned him a

[130] *Ibid.*, 767-68.
[131] *Ibid.*, series 2, VI, 32-33.
[132] *Ibid.*, 69.

special agent to visit Washington with a letter addressed to Lincoln calling attention to the numerous disputes which had arisen in the execution of the cartel which Davis declared he was prepared at all times to execute in good faith. It also bore the Confederate complaint against hostilities being waged against noncombatants. To these points there was added a protest against the shooting of the recruiting officers in Kentucky with the declaration that retaliation had not been resorted to.[133] Stephens was commissioned to adjust the difficulties and to make arrangements which would prevent such troubles from arising in the future.[134]

Accompanied by Ould as secretary, July 4, 1863, Stephens arrived in Hampton Roads with a flag of truce and requested permission from Admiral S. P. Lee and General Dix to pro-

[133] While Stephens lay at Hampton Roads waiting to deliver a message to Abraham Lincoln that no such retaliation had been made, prison officials in Richmond selected Captains Henry Washington Sawyer and John M. Flinn, of New Jersey and Indiana respectively, to be executed in retaliation for Captains McGraw and Corbin. *Official Records,* series 2, VI, 82, 87. The unfortunate victims of a drawing of lots, fearing that their government might delay in coming to their aid, with a commendable zeal for self-preservation besought General Winder to spare their lives on the plea that they were in no way connected with the Department of the Ohio. Hardly commendable was their further suggestion that two of their fellow prisoners, whom they specified by name, would, because of their connection with Burnside's army and for other reasons, make suitable sacrificial material. *Ibid.,* 107. However, the plight of the officers soon became known in Washington (Ludlow to Halleck and Halleck to Lincoln, *Ibid.,* 108-9), where President Lincoln ordered that General Fitzhugh Lee and another officer be placed in close confinement to await execution in case any officer of the United States was put to death by the Confederates contrary to the laws of war. *Ibid.,* 118. The other officer selected was Captain R. H. Tyler, of Virginia, and Ould was informed of the president's order. As Ludlow had remarked when he learned of the capture of General Lee, his retention settled all questions of retaliation.

Ibid., 122. By some unknown means, possibly because of a similarity in sound, the impression became general, and was shared even by Ludlow and Hoffman, that a Captain Winder, presumably a son of the Confederate prison commander, had been selected as the co-hostage with General Lee. See *Ibid.,* 219; also Domschcke, *Zwanzig Monate in Kriegs-Gefangenschaft,* 50.

Official Records, series 2, VI, 127. In reporting that hostages had been chosen the colleague of Lee was not named, Ludlow stating that Lee's name would be enough. There is no evidence that the Confederate Commissioner ever learned that a Captain Winder or Tyler had been selected. Cf. Godfrey, *Sketch of Major Henry Washington Sawyer.*

[134] *Ibid.,* 74-76.

ceed to Washington with his communication. The Federal commanders in their dilemma detained him until they could receive instructions from their respective chiefs. After a day's delay Welles and Stanton informed their subordinates that Stephens' request was inadmissible and that the customary agents and channels were adequate for all needful communications between the belligerents. Since Stephens' mission was due to the failure of these customary channels and agents, this communication was manifestly unsatisfactory.[135] Essentially, the Southerner's request was refused because Lincoln and his cabinet feared that any dealings with an accredited emissary of the Confederacy would give the South the recognition which they had been careful to deny.[136]

The decision to reject the mission of Stephens had not been reached without due consideration of other events. At the time when the Confederate vice-president was presenting his request to be allowed to go to Washington, General Lee was being defeated at Gettysburg and the Southern Cross was being replaced by the Stars and Stripes over the long beseiged Vicksburg. The news of the victories of Meade and Grant placed the North more securely in a position to resist any demands which might be made by the South.[137] When Stephens left Richmond neither of these events was known, although the fall of Vicksburg was felt to be imminent. Lee, however, had been victorious on the preceding day. "Whatever may have been the object of his mission," remarked the New York *Times*, "there is no doubt that he expected to effect it rather easily at that juncture."[138]

After the first day's fighting at Gettysburg General Lee offered to exchange prisoners with General Meade. Meade immediately refused the proposition, stating that he did not have the power to enter into the suggested arrangement.[139] A number of Lee's prisoners were released on parole, mostly wounded whom it was impossible to take with the army on its

---

[135] *Ibid.*, 84, 94-95.   [136] New York *Times*, July 16.
[137] For these battles and the resulting correspondence in relation to the prisoners see Official Records, series 2, XXVII, part ii, 529 ff; parts i, ii, iii (Index).
[138] New York *Times*, July 10.   [139] *Official Records*, series 1, XXVII, iii, 514.

retreat, while some were taken south. Lee exchanged some
prisoners with General Couch of the Pennsylvania Militia,
but the action was disavowed by General Meade.[140]

At Vicksburg General Grant released on parole some
thirty thousand troops; the Gettysburg prisoners amounted
to twelve thousand, and on the same day as the great battles,
Helena, Arkansas, fell and twelve hundred prisoners were
added to swell the total. On July 9 Port Hudson in Louisiana was surrendered, and seven thousand more prisoners
came into the possession of the United States. The enlisted
men among these latter prisoners were released on parole
while the officers were confined.[141]

On July 3, just before the great battles, the subject of
paroles had been given a finishing touch by a new General
Order No. 207. This order called the attention of commanders in the field to the cartel, particularly Article 7. "All
captures must be reduced to actual possession and all prisoners of war must be delivered at the places designated. . . .
The only exception allowed is the case of commanders of two
opposing armies who are authorized to exchange prisoners or
to release them on parole at other points mutually agreed
upon. . . ."[142] Halleck in transmitting this order to Ludlow
told him to inform Ould that releases not in conformity with
the cartel would not be accepted as valid by the United States,
nor would they expect the Confederacy to so regard them.
All releases since May 22, the date when Ould received General Order No. 100, would be considered illegal if not made
at the designated places.[143] Ludlow informed Halleck that
it had been distinctly understood he and Ould had agreed to
consider all paroles, except those issued by special agreement
of commanders, illegal if not in conformity with the cartel.[144]

Hardly had the ink become dry on these orders and correspondence before news came to the department of Grant's
paroling the prisoners he had taken at Vicksburg. Halleck

[140] *Ibid.*, series 2, VI, 101-3.   [143] *Ibid.*, 85.
[141] New York *Times*, July 9, 17.   [144] *Ibid.*, 90.
[142] *Official Records*, series 2, VI, 78.

immediately wired him to stop this procedure, fearing, he declared, that paroling the Vicksburg garrison without delivery to a proper agent might be construed by the Confederates as an absolute release and the men be immediately returned to service: "Such has been the case elsewhere."[145] A closer study of the orders and the cartel enabled the versatile jurist to wire Grant that a "full examination" of the question had convinced him that Grant had the right to agree with the commander of the Vicksburg garrison for the delivery of the prisoners on parole.[146] When Port Hudson fell, Halleck wired Banks that he feared the enemy would not recognize the paroles which that general had allowed the captured garrison. "They gave notice in May last that prisoners must be delivered and paroled as provided in the seventh article of the cartel, and that any parole given in violation of these provisions would be considered null and void." Halleck added that in view of this the United States would not be justified in protesting if the Confederacy returned these prisoners to the ranks.[147] Banks replied that he had made arrangements with General Gardner of the Confederate forces before paroling and declared that this had been necessary because he did not have sufficient men to guard the prisoners. This arrangement was made immediately after the surrender.[148]

On July 13 orders were given by Stanton, acting on the fear that the rebels would be able to use them in the campaigns about Richmond, to deliver no more prisoners at City Point until further instructions.[149] Evidently the excess of prisoners in the hands of the North made it possible now to

---

[145] *Ibid.*, 92-93.   [147] *Ibid.*, 147-48.

[146] *Ibid.*, 97.

[148] *Ibid.*, series 1, XXVI, part i, 55-56. These paroles were not considered binding by either side, and they eventually were not counted. However, as soon as the Confederate agent decided that they were not valid, their legality was asserted by the United States. The validity of these paroles became one of the minor issues in the dispute between Ould and Meredith. It will be noticed that Halleck put into the mouth of the Confederates his own former statements when the situation was reversed. See below, page 107.

[149] *Ibid.*, series 2, VI, 112.

enforce the desires of the administration on all subjects. Ludlow declared that he had no reason to believe that prisoners were ever used by the South before they had been exchanged and stated that he could expect no more deliveries unless he continued to send prisoners.[150] But he was informed that it had been decided to make no more deliveries until there was a better understanding of the cartel; the only exchange which could be permitted was one for ten thousand of the Vicksburg prisoners to balance that number held on parole in the North.[151] Most of these were men who had been released after the battle of Chancellorsville.

As if to prove that the South did not have to await the formal delivery of more prisoners, Ould, on the same day that Stanton's order was issued, addressed to Ludlow a statement that he had declared exchanged Lieutenant General Pemberton, Major Generals Forney, M. L. Smith, and Bowles, eight brigadier generals, and three colonels, taken and paroled at Vicksburg. Ludlow was informed that he could select the equivalents for these prisoners out of the paroled men released after Chancellorsville.[152] Ludlow declared himself astounded at Ould's proceeding and informed the Confederate that he declined to unite in such a declaration, averring that since Ould held Colonel Streight and his officers prisoners and had refused to exchange them, no special exchange could be agreed to until they were released. He also stated that in making exchanges he would first exchange those of equal ranks before beginning to assimilate the grades of the officers and invited Ould to return to the cartel.[153] To this Ould replied that he had done only what Ludlow had frequently done and charged that the Federal agent had even gone so far as to declare exchanges for troops who were needed when he had no equivalents to offer. The fifth article of the cartel, which he cited, authorized one party to discharge its prisoners from parole upon delivering an equal number of the enemy and Ludlow's consent was not need-

[150] *Ibid.*, 126.
[151] Hitchcock to Ludlow, *Ibid.*, 129.
[152] *Ibid.*, 113.
[153] *Ibid.*, 116.

ed.[154] But Ludlow declared that the cartel provided for the exchange of equivalents only after those of equal ranks had been discharged from parole, and since the North held the excess of prisoners, the South could not make a declaration for the exchange of their generals. But, even so, the cartel had been so long ignored that the Confederacy could not consistently appeal to its provisions.[155] In reply Ould took a parting shot at Ludlow, who was removed from the business of exchange, with the statement that the North had violated the cartel by retaining prisoners contrary to its provisions, and pointed out that Ludlow, whose letter was dated from New York, evidently did not have a copy of the cartel before him or he would have perceived that there was no such provision in it for prior exchange of those of equal rank. It had been customary to reduce all officers to their equivalent in privates and to make exchanges for numbers of privates. Ould also added that frequent boats were sent to City Point without prisoners and declared that this was a covert attempt on the part of the United States to take prisoners without giving any in exchange.[156]

On July 25, Ludlow was removed from the position of agent of exchange and Brigadier General Sam A. Meredith was appointed in his place. Colonel John Mulford, who had served under Ludlow in charge of the truce boats, was made Meredith's assistant.[157] Whether or not Ludlow's removal was caused by his desire to be fair and humane, as was charged by Ould in his letter cited above, the effect certainly justified this opinion. The relations between the commissioners became more and more strained until all hopes of adjustment through them were finally given up.

To start off the work of Meredith, Ould began by making a formal denial that he had ever agreed with Ludlow that

[154] *Ibid.*, 125. Since the battle of Chancellorsville was fought before the fall of Vicksburg it would seem that a correct interpretation of the cartel would have permitted Ludlow to make this exchange and that Ould's declaration was a perversion of the terms of the article which he cited.

[155] *Ibid.*, 136.   [157] *Ibid.*, 141.
[156] *Ibid.*, 151-52.

all captures must be reduced to possession before their paroles would be considered valid. He admitted that Ludlow had informed him that this would be the practice, but he denied that he had ever consented to adopt or acquiesce in such a ruling.[158] Ould was quite willing, however, to adopt any rule which worked to his advantage and so demanded that, under the terms of General Order No. 207, the officers who had been paroled by Lee at Gettysburg and whose paroles had not been recognized by the United States, should be delivered to him to be confined in the South. The United States, he declared, must by the terms of this order either recognize the paroles or deliver the officers.[159] To this extraordinary demand the Confederate Commissioner added protests against the failure to deliver noncommissioned officers and enlisted men,[160] and against the frequent sending of flag-of-truce boats to City Point under the pretense that they were carrying mail to and from the prisoners. Every boat arriving without prisoners was a violation of the cartel.[161]

To settle these and other complicated questions Ould sought an interview with his new opponent. Meredith was not familiar with the duties of his office or with all of the questions involved but, with the approval of Stanton, he went into the conference prepared to insist upon the immediate delivery of Streight and his officers and that negroes and their officers should be treated as prisoners of war.[162] At the same time Halleck armed Meredith with an opinion on the return of the Gettysburg officers. Since Meade had refused to ac-

---

[158] *Official Records*, series 2, VI, 167-68.   [160] *Ibid.*, 180-82.
[159] *Ibid.*, 179-80.   [161] *Ibid.*, 182-83.

[162] *Ibid.*, 185. Another question which was constantly before the commissioners grew out of the retention and trial in the Virginia courts, on charges ranging from murder to horse-stealing, of a Doctor Rucker, from the western part of the state. It was not clear whether the doctor was a member of a guerilla band or whether he was a citizen who was forced to guide a party on a bridge-burning and thieving expedition. He was a Union man in his sympathies. Claimed by the North, his delivery was refused by the Confederates, largely because his release could not be obtained from the Virginia courts. A surgeon was held as a hostage for him after an earlier attempt had been made to secure his release by withholding all surgeons from exchange. The escape of the doctor finally settled the questions in his case. For details of the case see Index of the *Official Records*, series 2, IV, V, and VI.

cept an offer of exchange, Lee's paroles were illegal, and Ould's "extraordinary" demand could not be complied with. In order to avoid any difficulties over paroles, however, Meredith was authorized to agree that all paroles from May 22 to July 3 on either side were to be considered illegal.[163] Since the majority of the paroles between these dates were in favor of the South, this offer was justifiably regarded with suspicion by the Confederate agent.

When these questions were considered by the commissioners, Ould made counter propositions to the effect that all paroles should be counted in accordance with the rules set forth in the United States General Orders 49, 100, and 207 according to their respective dates. If this were unacceptable, he proposed that all paroles should be counted as they had been in the past. Streight and his officers held as prisoners of war would be exchanged as soon as the regular exchange of officers was resumed.[164] But Ould would not consider any proposition in regard to negro prisoners, declaring that the South "would die in the last ditch" before it would give up the right to return the recaptured slaves to their masters. An exception might be made in the case of free negroes, but here Meredith appreciated the difficulties in the way of proof as to the prior status of the individual negro. Ould offered to exchange officers grade for grade with the exception of those commanding negro troops. This Meredith promptly declined. The Confederates were eager to continue the exchange of the noncommissioned officers and privates.[165]

[163] *Official Records*, series 2, VI, 199.

[164] Meredith also learned that General Neal Dow, of Maine Law fame, had been turned over to the Alabama courts for trial. The charges seemed to have arisen out of accusations against the general of stealing furniture while he had been associated with Butler at New Orleans and in other parts of the South. Stanton ordered that General Morgan, already a hostage for Streight, be chosen as a hostage for General Dow (*Ibid.*, series 2, VI, 229), but the Confederates were not be informed of this. *Ibid.*, 235-37. Dow was released by the courts of Alabama on the grounds that although he was guilty, the crimes which he had committed had been prior to the date of the joint resolution and the courts, therefore, had no jurisdiction. *Ibid.*, 669-73.

[165] *Ibid.*, 225-26.

Meredith submitted Ould's counter proposition in regard to paroles to Hitchcock and Halleck. On September 7 Ould informed Meredith that since he had, as he expected, received no reply to his proposition, although one was promised, the Confederacy would pursue any course which it deemed proper. As it was desirable to get some commitment in regard to the Vicksburg prisoners, Meredith offered to exchange one of the generals. Ould immediately informed the Federal commissioner that the general in question had been exchanged and that the equivalent had been given.[166] Further proof that the Confederates were not intending to reverse their position in this matter was given four days later in an announcement from Ould that he would, on the next day, declare exchanged a number of the prisoners taken at Vicksburg. He had, he declared, enough valid paroles in his possession to cover them, and in addition he had delivered some ten or twelve thousand prisoners at City Point since the last declaration of exchange. It had been the practice, he informed Meredith, when one party made an exchange for the other to select the equivalents, but he added that if Meredith did not do so he would select the equivalents from among the Union prisoners on parole. Accordingly the next day, September 12, he declared exchanged the officers and men of several divisions of the Vicksburg prisoners and all those who had been delivered at City Point.[167]

After the surrender of Vicksburg General Pemberton had made a virtue of a necessity and given furloughs for thirty days to his men who had already gone home without his permission.[168] These were ordered to reassemble at a camp at Demopolis, Alabama, where the South began to experience all of the difficulties which had hitherto been the peculiar misfortune of the North. The prisoners assembled under protest and held that no service could be required of them until they were exchanged. They were encouraged in this

[166] Ibid., 230, 265-66.
[167] Ibid., 279-80, 295-96.
[168] Jones, op. cit., II, 3.

attitude by prominent citizens, and Pemberton recommended to Seddon that the troops be assembled at camps in their own states unless there was a prospect of immediate exchange. The men refused to stay in the camp established for them at Demopolis. Some of the prisoners were mustered out of the service and others were distributed to other parole camps.[169]

The desire to rid the government of the troublesome problems connected with these troops induced Ould to make his declaration of exchange. The experience of the North in attempting to solve the same problems had led to orders in regard to paroles which had produced confusion, contradictions and disputes; the experience of the South was to lead to similiar difficulties. The question at issue between the commissioners from this date was whether Ould's declaration was justified.[170] Halleck immediately pronounced Ould's declaration illegal, citing the fourth article of the cartel which declared that prisoners should be released before their equivalents were declared exchanged, and demanding that Ould release prisoners to balance those declared exchanged. In order for the exchange to be complete, it would be necessary for Meredith to declare an exchange for an equal number. Meredith was therefore instructed that he should demand that prisoners in the South should be released in order to make the exchange complete. However, it was definitely settled that none of the prisoners in the North would be given up. Meredith was ordered to frame an exchange which would release the Southern prisoners but not touch those held by the United States.[171] Halleck sent Ould's "spurious" declaration to General Grant, who had been puzzled by the appearance of General S. D. Lee before him without an exchange.[172] Halleck in telling him that there was no justifica-

---

[169] *Official Records*, series 2, VI, 224, 273, 229, 232-33.

[170] Ould's declaration of exchange released 1,027 officers and 14,915 privates of the Vicksburg prisoners. Seventy-two officers and 8,014 men were released at City Point, making a total of 24,208 covered by this declaration. *Ibid.*, 470, Note.

[171] *Ibid.*, 300.

[172] *Ibid.*, 303.

tion for Lee's appearance there[173] had admitted that under the cartel the South could release all their prisoners of war and the United States could not protest but merely make another agreement, but he had not thought that Davis would commit such a breach of faith.[174] Nothing in this former admission, however, prevented him from pronouncing Ould's declaration illegal.

According to the computation of the commissary-general of prisoners, Ould's declaration released 1,028 officers and 22,879 men, making a total, reduced to privates, of 29,433. There were in the United States 76 officers and 19,083 privates on parole, leaving a balance due from Ould of 10,024. Hoffman recommended that Meredith be instructed to declare all the paroled men exchanged and to call upon Ould to deliver 10,000 from prisons in the South.   Hoffman, although seeming to accept Ould's declaration in this recommendation, stated that he thought Ould's action was illegal but that while the question was being discussed the paroled troops would be in arms against the United States.[175]

In a meeting with Ould, which Meredith hastily sought when this unexpected exchange was declared, Ould admitted that his actions were not justified by the words of the cartel but that he was justified by the practice of the agents while Ludlow had been representing the United States.   Meredith accepted his explanation, but when they came to a discussion of the balance of the prisoners Ould insisted upon having credit for 4,800 paroled at Gettysburg.   This demand caused the meeting to break up without an agreement, and Meredith continued to press for the 10,024 prisoners, insisting that the declaration was not authorized by the cartel and complaining that the required list of the prisoners exchanged had not been sent to him.   He even continued to assert that Ould had agreed with Ludlow that all paroles after May 22, not given at an exchange point, would be null and void.[176]

[173] *Ibid.*, 273, see also *Ibid.*, series 1, XXX, part iii, 694, 224.
[174] *Ibid.*, series 2, VI, 296-97.
[175] *Ibid.*, 306-7.
[176] *Ibid.*, 314-16.

These developments led Ould to send a Major I. Szymanski across the Mississippi to gather up paroles[177] while he
sparred for time with Meredith. Though Ould admitted
that he did not know how many prisoners he had discharged
from their paroles, he was still able to find fault with the
figures from City Point. By his calculation, instead of owing
Meredith 10,024, the Federal agent owed him 7,500 prisoners. He also repeated his denial of the alleged agreement
with Ludlow.[178]

To add to the complications with regard to figures Ould
declared that the Port Hudson paroles were invalid and returned the troops to duty.[179] These paroles had not been
counted by Hoffman or by Meredith in presenting their accounts to Ould, and he felt justified in assuming that the
paroles were illegal. Northern official opinion was reversed,
however, as soon as Ould took advantage of the situation;
and the Federal agent was able to add this to the charges
against Ould.

As the dispute over the validity of paroles continued,
Hoffman coached Meredith to tell Ould that as the cartel
was older than the orders, and was more fundamental, the
orders could not set aside its terms; therefore, Ould's proposition to count paroles according to General Orders 49, 100,
and 207 could not be permitted and the North would abide
by the terms of the cartel. He added that Ludlow had never
made such a declaration as Ould claimed, either ignoring
Ould's citations of dates or else interpreting the various exchanges to fit his own thesis.[180]

When Meredith made his declaration to balance Ould's,
the Confederate agent immediately declared him in excess
and issued another declaration to balance the alleged fault.
As he did so, he announced that he had adopted the rules of
the United States' orders in counting his paroles, of which he

[177] *Ibid.*, 320-21.
[178] *Ibid.*, 333-34. Some very involved computations are given in Ould to Meredith, *Ibid.*, 339-40.
[179] *Ibid.*, 367, see note 148 above.
[180] *Ibid.*, 369-70.

claimed enough to cover all his declarations; but offered to adopt any just, fair, and reciprocal standard of computation.[181] When this was known, Hitchcock determined to put a stop to all declarations of exchanges until some adjustment was made. In order to make this adjustment he wisely decided that it would be well to draw from Ould a statement of the paroles which he claimed as a basis for his declarations.[182]

Meantime Meredith had found a new charge to bring against his opponent. He discovered that Ould had informed him that the Confederacy would declare exchanges whenever it felt that it had the right to do so "for the purpose of putting men into the field." Meredith, with his customary sarcasm, informed Ould that he had no objection to the Confederate's acting according to his conscience so long as that conscience was guided by the laws of war, but there was no reason to believe that Ould had a responsible conscience. With such a statement to back him, Meredith rejected Ould's offer to release men on parole until an adjustment was made, declaring to Ould that the men would be immediately returned to the ranks by the Confederacy. According to Meredith the Vicksburg prisoners had been used in the battle of Chickamauga a few days after Ould had made his illegal declaration.[183] With equal ill-temper, Ould replied that while he had relied partly on his own sense of right he had also relied to some extent on Meredith's. He denied that the prisoners from Vicksburg had been used in Tennessee: "Why not come out and say that our soldiers are more valuable than yours?"[184] With two men so unwilling to meet on

[181] Ould to Meredith, *Ibid.*, 387.

[182] *Ibid.*, 400.

[183] *Ibid.*, 441-42. Meredith later acknowledged that Ould's alleged statement was made to him in conversation. Since Ould denied having made such a statement the point is as impossible of settlement as any other in this vituperative correspondence. Since Meredith cited similar statements, which did not go to the length of "putting men into the field," but which Meredith claimed represented the Confederate's attitude, it seems reasonable to suppose that Ould never made the statement but that Meredith put into Ould's mouth his own suspicions.

[184] *Ibid.*, 452-55.

reasonable grounds to adjust their differences but so very willing to engage in verbal mud-slinging, it is not surprising that exchanges were not resumed.

The sufferers in this situation were not the officials who carried on the correspondence or their prompting associates, but were the prisoners who were condemned to long captivity by the continuation of these bickerings. Ludlow in June had been anxious to alleviate the sufferings of the prisoners in the South. Winter was now approaching, and it was doubtful whether the dictates of humanity would be in sympathy with the technical questions involved in the squabble over the validity of paroles. Doubtless with a realization of this, November 2, Meredith suggested to Hitchcock that he should be allowed to exchange man for man until all the prisoners in the South were released. If this were not acceptable, he suggested that he offer to Ould that each side should provide for its soldiers in the enemy's prisons. Hitchcock did not believe that Ould would accept the first proposition, especially as the North could not yield on the negro question, and he considered the second impracticable.[185] However, he thought that Ould should be informed that the sufferings of the prisoners in the South resulted in increasing the ill feeling of the people of the North against the Confederacy.[186]

Just before this, October 27, Ould presented the list of paroles upon which he had based his declarations of exchange. This listed by dates of capture and officers giving the paroles, 18,867 paroles in forty-four places, mostly in Kentucky and Tennessee.[187] When Hitchcock saw this list, he immediately set about to discover flaws in it. He found that the parole list did not distinguish between officers and men or specify points of delivery, which meant that they had been paroled without having been reduced to possession;[188] and he asserted

[185] *Ibid.*, 457-58.   [186] Hitchcock to Meredith, *Ibid.*, 468.   [187] *Ibid.*, 430.

[188] In this connection Hitchcock stated that the cartel was in complete accord with General Order 100. At the same time Hoffman was writing to Meredith that the general orders were contrary to the terms of the cartel and were therefore set aside by the more fundamental document. *Ibid.*, 466-68.

that the paroles probably included many given by citizens which would be invalid.[189] Meredith dutifully transmitted the findings of his chief to Ould, adding to them his usual pointed remarks on the character of the Confederate's actions.[190] To all of these statements Ould made a complete denial, explaining that the list of paroles was only a summary of the several paroles which he held and which he would submit to a decision of the Federal agent with full facts in regard to places of capture and with such complete evidence of their validity that they would have to be accepted. There were no paroles of citizens in the list submitted. More than thirty of the forty-four captures on the list had been made before May 22, regarding which there had never been controversy, and any after that date would be counted in accordance with the general orders of the United States.[191] Hitchcock expressed his regret that he had obtained a false impression of Ould's parole list and declared that he would talk the matter over. But even if these paroles were acceptable, he pointed out that the retaliatory resolutions of the Confederate congress still stood.[192] On the same day that he saw these paroles and made his apology for assuming that they were irregular, with the approval of the secretary of war, Hitchcock wrote to the New York *Times* a letter purporting to explain the entire situation. In this letter he repeated the statement that the paroles were those given to citizens of Kentucky and Tennessee. The main burden of the letter, however, was designed to prove that the South refused to deal justly with the negro troops.[193]

It was necessary for such a letter as this to be sent to the public at this time. The New York *Times* had declared that twelve thousand prisoners were being starved because Meredith would not give way in the matter of paroles. The *Times* advised that no more exchanges be made because the rebels could not be trusted, but they admitted that such a course

[189] *Ibid.*, 471-73.   [191] *Ibid.*, 549-50.
[190] *Ibid.*, 504-7.   [192] *Ibid.*, 590-91.
[193] *Ibid.*, 594-600. Cf. also *The National Intelligencer*, December 3, 7.

would have a bad effect on recruiting.[194] In November the reports of starving prisoners in Richmond led to the sending of supplies from the United States Government and Meredith was instructed to ask for the release of the prisoners, pledging the government to respect their paroles.[195] Halleck in his annual report informed Stanton that the prisoners in Richmond received treatment equal to that given in Tunis, the British prison hulks, and the Black Hole of Calcutta.[196]

As a sign of the approaching public disapproval of the exchange and parole controversy came an offer from General Butler, now in command at Fort Monroe, that he be allowed to try his hand at arranging exchanges. He informed Secretary Stanton that he believed that he could induce the rebels to exchange man for man. Stanton replied that he knew that the rebels would make such an exchange but as they would not exchange negroes and their officers—"and on this point the whole matter hinges"—Butler was told that he should not interfere with Meredith.[197] Butler assured Stanton that his record was above reproach on the negro question but that the negro had been lost from sight in the commissioners' quarrel over the counting of paroles. Further, Butler pointed out that the North could exchange the prisoners in the South and still hold enough prisoners to insure that the negroes and their officers received just treatment. The North held twenty-six thousand prisoners while the South had only thirteen thousand, so that thirteen thousand would remain in the North as hostages for the security of the negro troops. Besides, relations between Ould and Meredith necessitated a change of commissioners before negotiations could continue.[198]

Butler's assertion that the negro had been lost from sight seems to have been true. That he had never occupied an

---

[194] New York *Times*, November 10.   [196] *Ibid.*, 523-24.
[195] *Official Records*, series 2, VI, 515.   [197] *Ibid.*, 527-28.
[198] *Ibid.*, 532-34. Cf. the *National Intelligencer*, December 2, 1863 which stated that the prevalent belief was that the rebels had not brought up the negro question but the war department was looking for some excuse to stop exchanges. It was generally believed, according to this paper, that if Meredith and Ould could be superseded and new commissioners allowed to proceed without interference the prisoners could be exchanged in two weeks.

important place in the controversies of the commissioners is evident. It was not until the country showed signs of restlessness that the negro was brought forward as a reason for the non-exchange of prisoners. The solicitor of the war department explained the government's position on the negro soldier to a citizen of Ohio,[199] but the Copperhead press of that state, represented by the Columbus *Crisis*, was unable to see anything but an abolitionist attempt to force the negro down the Northern throat, while it declared a cessation of exchange for the sake of the negro soldiers was a needless cruelty.[200] This attitude of the democrats was paralleled by that of many people, who, having read the correspondence of the commissioners in the newspapers, had come to the conclusion that the negro was not of much importance in the controversy.[201] To correct this impression, Hitchcock added a postscript to his public letter to prove that the negro was the cause of all the administration's problems with the South.[202]

December came with no change in the status of the exchange question. On the third Hitchcock offered his resignation as commissioner but it was not accepted.[203] On the seventh General Halleck offered to General Lee to exchange the prisoners in Richmond, leaving the questions in regard to the other prisoners and the whole matter of paroles to be settled by the commissioners.[204] Lee refused, declaring that the cartel had been formed to regulate exchanges and he would not interfere with it.[205] When this effort failed, Hitchcock was ordered to Fort Monroe to take advantage of Butler's offer of his services. December 17, Butler was appointed a special agent of exchange with Meredith acting under his instructions. He was authorized to exchange man for man, officers for officers of equal rank, with negro troops and their officers on the same plane as the white. The questions regarding the parole were to be waived for a time.[206]

---

[199] Columbus, Ohio, *Crisis*, December 2.   [200] *Ibid.*, November 18.

[201] Senator Davis of Kentucky characterized the employment of negro troops "Stanton's cruelty." *Congressional Globe*, December 16.

[202] *Official Records*, series 2, VI, 615-17.

[203] *Ibid.*, 638-39.   [205] *Ibid.*, 691.

[204] *Ibid.*, 659.   [206] *Ibid.*, 711-12.

CHAPTER VI

LIBBY AND BELLE ISLE

The beginning of exchange under the cartel brought relief to the Confederate States by taking away an accumulation of prisoners who were rapidly leading to the bankruptcy which Commissary-General Northrop foresaw in the depleted granaries of his department. The commissary-general urged the necessity for an exchange of prisoners, pointing out to the secretary of war the danger to the city of Richmond which a large number of hungry prisoners with insufficient guards caused.[1]

But the relief to the Confederacy which was brought by exchanges was least noticeable at the capital. The prisoners at Tuscaloosa and Mobile, at Atlanta and Macon, at Lynchburg and Salisbury were released; but at Richmond the prisoners en route for delivery across the lines at City Point or Aiken's Landing were concentrated. The sick from the prisons and the wounded from the battlefields were brought to the city to crowd the hospitals while awaiting that convalescence which would make possible their removal to their own lines.[2]

This continuation of the city of Richmond as a prison center necessitated the retention of the prison system which had developed before the cartel. Part of the prisoners were placed in the tobacco warehouses, and others on Belle Isle, a small island in the James river, which had been used for the prisoners before the cartel.[3] General Winder continued to exercise his functions of supervision of the prisons, assisted by Wirz, now a captain and relieved from the duties in charge of prisoners at Tuscaloosa. Captain Montgomery was placed in direct command of the prisons in Richmond,

[1] See pages 61 and 68.
[2] *Official Records*, series 2, IV, 433.
[3] Sanitary Commission, *Narrative of Sufferings in Rebel Prisons*, 45 ff.

114

confining his attention, however, to Belle Isle, until in October, 1862, Captain Thomas P. Turner assumed command.[4]

Not only was Richmond used as a depot for holding prisoners for exchange during the usual ten-day period provided for in the cartel, but these cases of the detention of officers and men growing out of the attempt on the part of the Southern president to force the North by threats of retaliation, were also held in the capital. With the number of such prisoners increasing as the execution of the cartel became more difficult, the effect of the policy of holding the prisoners in Richmond began to be apparent. The arrival of prisoners in large numbers inevitably caused the market prices of necessities to increase. In January, 1863, it was reported that beef rose from forty to sixty cents a pound and butter went from one to two and a half dollars in one day due to the sudden arrival of several thousand prisoners from the army in the field.[5] When the exchange under the cartel came to an end in the summer of 1863, the prison officials faced, in an intensified form, the problem of providing rations for the prisoners.

The rations furnished the prisoners in Libby and on Belle Isle decreased in quality and quantity as the year 1863 passed from summer to autumn. In May it was reported that the rations consisted of good flour, bread, and salt pork, while the officers continued to exercise the privilege of sending out for purchases of apples, sugar, eggs, molasses, and corn.[6] The officers cooked for themselves, but they regarded this as an indignity. "Imagine a staff officer detailed to clean pots and pans," enjoined one horrified prisoner, or "a national colonel with his hands in the dough." The prisoners did not doubt that this was a punishment inflicted on them by the fiendish cruelty of the rebels.[7]

In August the commissary-general suggested to Secretary Walker that rations of meat should be no longer issued to the

[4] *Official Records*, series 2, IV, 865-66, 928.
[5] Jones, *A Rebel War Clerk's Diary*, I, 240.
[6] Richardson, *The Secret Service, The Field, The Dungeon and The Escape*, 336.
[7] *Official Records*, series 2, V, 385-87.

prisoners and oat and cornmeal gruel, pea soup, soft hominy, and bread be substituted. This was not allowed by the secretary, although Northrop justified the action by citing the harsh treatment which the North gave to its prisoners and the destruction of Southern crops by the invading armies. Walker declared that the law permitted the prisoners the same rations as received by the Confederate soldier.[8]

At this time the prisoners were receiving about a half pound of beef and a pound of bread with rice, peas, or soup.[9] To Colonel A. D. Streight, confined in Libby after his surrender to General Forrest, in Georgia, these rations seemed insufficient. Declaring that the officers received but a fourth of a pound of poor fresh beef, half a pound of bread, and a half a gill of rice or beans a day—an amount he believed insufficient to sustain life—he wrote to Secretary Seddon that the officers in the prison spent a thousand dollars a day for vegetables to eke out their scanty fare.[10] General Winder answered this communication by pointing out to the colonel the cruel treatment accorded to the Confederate prisoners at Point Lookout and Fort Delaware. He promised to investigate Colonel Streight's rations to determine if any were being withheld.[11]

According to this promise an investigation was made of the rations and Captain Warner, the assistant quartermaster at the prison, succeeded in eliciting from several of the mess sergeants a report of the rations received. The mess sergeant of Streight's floor, himself a lieutenant of Streight's command, reported that he had 254 prisoners on the floor for whom he received from the "urbane and attentive" commis-

---

[8] Jones, *op. cit.*, II, 11.

[9] It is almost impossible to determine the exact ration issued to the prisoners at any one time. Official reports of rations are lacking and the accounts of prisoners are open to suspicion of exaggeration. It is difficult to imagine that a prisoner writing from three to twenty years after his release from captivity is able to remember the rations issued in any given month. Prisoners' narratives place the amount of meat anywhere from one ounce to one-half pound. Bread is usually not mentioned by weight but some accounts state that the prisoners received a half pound of cornbread.

[10] *Official Records*, series 2, VI, 241-42.

[11] *Ibid.*, 267.

sary 127 pounds of beef and 235½ pounds of bread. By a subtle arithmetic computation the prisoner arrived at the conclusion that this was one-half pound of beef and one and one-eighth pounds of bread per man. The prisoner in charge of another floor made the same error in regard to bread, stating that he received 236 pounds which made one and one-eighth pounds for each of his 299 men.[12] This report was endorsed by two other prisoners, a Colonel Tilden of Maine and Lieutenant Colonel James M. Sanderson, commissary of subsistence in the United States Army.[13] This action on the part of four of their number aroused the indignation of the other prisoners. A meeting of some of the officers passed resolutions condemning the action of the two colonels and approving Streight's letter to Seddon.[14]

[12] *Ibid.*, 278. More amusing still is the fact that Roach, a lieutenant under Streight, writing to defend his commander cites these documents and condemns the authors without perceiving the error in arithmetic. Cf. *The Prisoner of War*, 53-56.

[13] *Official Records*, series 2, VI, 279.

[14] *Ibid.*, 301-3. Roach, *Prisoner of War*, 56-58. There was an underlying reason for this disagreement between the officers. Colonel Sanderson had been a hotel proprietor before the war and had gained a reputation as a cook because he wrote a book on camp cooking which had been published by the government for distribution to the army. Sanderson, *My Record in Rebeldom*, Appendix, iii-iv. On his arrival at the Libby prison he was called upon by his fellow prisoners to superintend their cooking arrangements. "A very short experience convinced me," Sanderson declared, "that but little dependence was to be placed on the forbearance or courtesy of my fellow prisoners." Accordingly, he posted a set of regulations for the use of the stoves and utensils so that confusion about the limited supply of stoves might be overcome. These regulations had been approved by the Confederate officers who had given Sanderson disciplinary power to enforce their execution. The ex-hotel keeper, older than most of the prisoners, possessed a stern demeanor; his insistence upon military obedience in the execution of his cooking regulations brought him many enemies among the prisoners, among whom was Colonel Streight who became offended when Sanderson refused to support him in a political argument. When Sanderson approved of the statements of the mess sergeants, Streight took the occasion to arouse the prisoners against his enemy. (*Ibid.*, 25-30. See, however, Domschcke, *Zwanzig Monate in Kriegs-Gefangenschaft*, 50 ff.)

Not all of the prisoners had the privilege of cooking for themselves and hence fared worse than the prisoners in Libby. Cooking for the prisoners, both privates and officers, was done in the lower rooms of the Libby building. Davidson, *Fourteen Months*, 540 ff. Jones, *op. cit.*, II, 73. Privates, however, received the same rations as their officers. Jones contends that the prisoners received one-half pound of beef and "plenty of good bread and water." *Harper's Weekly*, October 17, 667; declared they received eighteen ounces of bread and one-quarter pound of meat with some salt, rice, and vinegar.

The latter part of October saw a crisis develop in the matter of meat rations for the prisoners. The prison commanders reported to Winder that no meat had been issued to them; Winder informed Secretary Seddon that this was the fourth time that the prisoners had been so deprived. "No force under my command can prove adequate to the control of 13,000 hungry prisoners," announced the general. Quartermaster-General Lawton asked Seddon to intervene between the commissary-general and General Winder.[15] Under Seddon's guidance a dispute between the commissary-general and the quartermaster-general was settled by the former's agreeing to furnish rations to the prisoners. It was decided that when the rations given to soldiers in the field differed from the rations given to soldiers at posts, the prisoners were to receive the same rations as the latter. If it should become impossible to feed both the prisoners and the soldiers, it was agreed that the soldiers should have the preference. In the temporary shortage General Winder was instructed to purchase for his charges beef which was being shipped through en route to the Richmond market,[16] but this was stopped when the arrangement was made for the commissary-general to supply the prisoners.[17]

Ten days after this arrangement was made, the prison officials reported to General Winder that there was not an ounce of meat for the prisoners and the commissary-general could promise but 2,500 pounds of beef for the 14,000 prisoners in the city. This would make it impossible to hold the prisoners. Secretary Seddon informed the commissary-general that the law and his agreement demanded that the prisoners should receive the same food as was issued to soldiers.[18] Colonel Northrop ignored the call for rations, and the fear that the prisoners would mutiny led the officers to

[15] *Official Records*, series 2, VI, 439-40. Cf. also Richmond *Examiner*, October 29, 30; *Whig*, October 30; *Enquirer*, October 31. These papers declared that the prisoners were comfortable while the people of the city were starving. Cf. also *National Intelligencer*, November 11.

[16] *Official Records*, series 2, VI, 821.

[17] *Ibid.*, 456.   [18] *Ibid.*, 497-98.

consider sending their families from the city.[19] On November 11 and 12 there was still no meat for the prisoners, but on the twelfth help started from the United States where Hitchcock, learning of the conditions in Richmond, instructed Meredith to send the needed rations through the lines.[20]

Sending supplies to the prisoners in the South had been practiced before the cartel and was continued after the formation of that instrument. Political prisoners in the prison known as "Castle Thunder," and sick soldiers in the hospitals were the beneficiaries of boxes of medicine and hospital supplies sent to the Southern prison officials.[21] September 28, 1863, Ould notified Meredith that supplies of blankets and clothing sent for the prisoners in Richmond would be issued in accordance with the instructions accompanying them.[22] Prisoners in Libby wrote Meredith that they were suffering and dying from exposure as a result of insufficient clothing. Hats, shoes, socks, blankets, overcoats, and shirts were lacking, and the officers slept on bare floors without sufficient covers. The Confederates were reported unable to furnish these articles but willing to allow a board of prisoners to issue any supplies which their government chose to send them.[23] As a result of this plea five hundred blankets were sent to the senior officer among the prisoners, General Neal Dow, of Maine, as an experiment. If this proved successful, the United States promised to forward clothing.[24] Money was also sent through General Meredith for the prisoners.[25]

The blankets were received and distributed by General Dow, and Meredith immediately sent a thousand suits and fifteen hundred blankets for the famous prohibitionist to

---

[19] Jones, op. cit., II, 94. The Richmond Dispatch, November 13, declared that the people could not buy meat because it was needed for the prisoners. The presence of thirteen thousand prisoners in a city that was already crowded inevitably caused distress. Seventy bullocks were killed daily for the prisoners. This paper declared that the recent overcrowding had forced the authorities to put prisoners on Belle Isle. December 22, the Dispatch stated that any shortage in food in the prisons had been merely temporary. The tendency to blame Northrop was criticized by the editor.

[20] Official Records, series 2, VI, 497-98. [23] Ibid., 354.
[21] Ibid., series 2, V, 830-34. [24] Ibid., 384.
[22] Ibid., series 2, VI, 324. [25] Ibid., 431-32.

distribute.[26] General Dow gave his parole to the officers in Richmond and distributed the clothing and blankets to the prisoners on Belle Isle. A single visit to the island was sufficient to acquaint him with conditions, and he sent, through a member of the sanitary commission who had been released from imprisonment, a full report of affairs on the island. The island was low and unhealthy, reported the general, and the 5,400 prisoners confined there were dying at the rate of ten a day. Not more than half of the prisoners had tents, while the remainder slept on the ground without clothing or blankets. Many had no pants, shirts, or shoes, and were on half rations without fuel or soap. The result was an inexpressible filthiness, and Dow foresaw that by January, 1864 the men would die at the rate of one hundred a day. Hussey, the sanitarian who carried this report to the North, added his experiences in Scott's factory in Richmond where a hundred and sixty privates, wounded at Chickamauga, were confined without stoves, fuel, soap, candles, straw, bunks, or clothes. To relieve these depressing conditions General Dow proposed that the government smuggle Confederate money to the prisoners. He asked that $100,000 be sent him, via the Sanitary Commission, sealed in tin cans and packed in other cans of jelly, butter, molasses, and milk. The officers were to receive credit for this issue of money at the current rate of exchange.[27]

To the suggestion of General Dow neither Meredith nor Hitchcock, both of whom must have realized the consequences of such action, made a response, but when, November 12, Meredith forwarded twenty-four thousand rations to the prisoners, he entrusted them to a captain of his acquaintance among the prisoners rather than to the Maine general.[28] This supply of rations was accompanied by an offer to Ould

[26] *Ibid.*, 458-59.
[27] *Ibid.*, 482-83.
[28] *Ibid.*, 503, 526. Sanderson, *op. cit.*, 37-38. Sanderson, who, as a hotel-keeper, had an intense dislike for temperance by legislative enactment, states that the author of the "Maine Law" was removed from the duty of distributing the supplies because of an abusive letter to General Winder in which he complained of the rations.

to take the prisoners off the hands of the Confederates and
keep them on parole,[29] and the offer was backed up by the
statement that the prisoners in Northern prisons were given
meat three times a day, coffee, tea, molasses, chicken, soup,
and mush. They were confined in comfortable quarters, and
slept on beds. They had plenty of clothing. Meredith asked
Ould to submit a similar report on the prisons in Richmond.
The surgeon-general of the Confederate armies recommended that a report be made in reply to that of Meredith.[30]

In reply to Meredith's request for information on the
Richmond prisons Ould sent a report from the provost marshal of Richmond, all of whose statements were endorsed as
accurate by the commissioner. There were in Richmond
11,650 prisoners, including 1,044 officers. Sixty-three hundred of these were confined on Belle Isle and the others in
tobacco warehouses known as Libby, Crews', Pemberton's,
Smith's, and Scott's. In hospitals were 728. The Libby
prison for officers contained eight rooms, 103 by 42 feet.
There was a water-closet on each floor, and the rooms were
thoroughly policed each day. This was also the practice in
the other prisons where the privates were confined. Belle
Isle was described as being equipped with tents placed on a
dry knob from the surface of which water was easily drained.
The police was aided by the river, and eight wells supplied
water to the prisoners. The report which was enclosed for
Meredith showed that between July 1 and September 30,
453,845 rations had been issued. These included beef,
bacon, flour, beans, rice, vinegar, candles, soap, and salt. The
amounts showed an issue of less than the army ration, but it
was explained that this was made up by the extra rations
issued to the hospitals. The rations after September 30 had
been the same, Meredith was assured, except in the case of
meat which had been temporarily deficient. The ration at
the time of this report, November 18, was stated as consisting
of one pound of bread, one-half pound of meat, and a half

[29] *Official Records,* series 2, VI, 515.
[30] Jones, *op. cit.,* II, 98.

pound of potatoes with rice, beans, salt, vinegar, and soap. Soup was served daily. Ould admitted that there was a possibility of individual cases of hardships, due to a prisoner's neglect of himself or the cruelty of his fellow prisoners. A case was cited of a prisoner whose mess sergeant had refused to issue food to him. Many were filthy because they refused to keep themselves clean.[31]

At the same time a counter report was made to General Meredith by a group of surgeons who were released from captivity in the Southern capital. These men reported that the Libby prison had unplastered walls which subjected the officers to exposure to the cold; each officer had only 276 cubic feet of air. The officers did their own cooking with an inadequate supply of fuel. The water-closet on each floor, of which Ould had boasted in his report, became in the surgeons' report a privy which rendered foul one end of the room and polluted the entire building. On Belle Isle there was an insufficient supply of tents and no blankets or bedding. The good hospitals of the Ould report here became inadequate, while the rations of a pound of bread and a half pound of beef were reduced by surgical calculations to a maximum of three-fourths pound of bread and a half pound of beef. Two ounces of beans were also issued. Then after a time the bread had become cornbread of unsifted meal, rice was substituted for beans, and then, taking the place of both rice and meat, one small sweet potato was received. For the last two weeks of their captivity the surgeons declared that three-fourths pound of cornbread had been the entire ration. The cleanliness of the prison lost its sanitary significance in the eyes of these men who had been subjected to it. They were unable to see anything but an added indignity. Twice in the past two weeks the floors had been washed at sunset and once the scrubbing squad had arrived a full half hour before the officers were ready to rise in the morning. "Thus in various

---

[31] *Official Records*, series 2, VI, 544-48. Two days after Ould made his report on conditions in Richmond, another shortage of meat began in the city. However, 100 tons of rations arrived from the North to relieve the situation. Jones, *op. cit.*, II, 103.

ways do the authorities seek to make our condition not only uncomfortable, but dangerous."[32]

The report of the surgeons stated that but two hundred blankets had been issued to the officers in Libby, and failed to mention the rations received from the North. Two of the surgeons volunteered the information that they had been informed by a cook and a carpenter at the prison that the rations had been divided, one-half of the supplies from the United States going to Lee's army. On the strength of this information, Meredith decided to withhold any further supplies until he was sure that the rebels were not misappropriating them.[33] The prisoners in Richmond were sure that the rebels were stealing their rations,[34] but Meredith was able to assure Hitchcock that he did not doubt that the prisoners received the rations although he had learned that some of the officers about the prison had been cashiered for withholding some of them.[35] Supplies from the Sanitary Commission continued to be forwarded from Fort Monroe and it was publicly announced that "there is no doubt of the supplies sent to Richmond being received by our men."[36]

The issue of supplies by a committee of officers in prison continued, although the prisoners claimed that the guards received more of the clothing than they did.[37] On December 3, the officers reported that their work was nearing completion, and agreed that the Confederate officers had given them every assistance in the distribution of clothing,[38] but in the North rumors that the supplies had not been issued continued to circulate. On December 12, Ould informed Meredith that the matter had been the occasion of so much abuse and misrepresentation that he could receive no more provisions. The materials on hand would be issued to the prisoners and "when that supply is exhausted they will receive the same rations as our soldiers in the field."[39] This action was

[32] *Official Records*, series 2, VI, 572-75. Moore, *Rebellion Records*, VIII, 15.
[33] *Official Records*, series 2, VI, 569. [37] Ransom, *Andersonville Diary*, 14.
[34] Byers, *What I Saw in Dixie*, 14. [38] *Official Records*, series 2, VI, 642-43.
[35] *Official Records*, series 2, VI, 625. [39] *Ibid.*, 686.
[36] New York *Times*, December 8, 1863.

interpreted in the North as being partly due to the lack of transportation facilities but mostly as the result of a spirit of petty hatred and revenge.[40]

After the decision by the Confederates to receive no more supplies from the United States Government, the former conditions again prevailed. The arrival of Christmas saw the prisoners without rations for the day;[41] prices quoted in the city of forty dollars for a bushel of potatoes, one dollar for a six-ounce loaf of bread, and fifty dollars a bushel for onions made it impossible for the privates to make purchases, while the former thousand dollars a day spent by the officers, even if it had been continued, would not have made an appreciable increase in the prison fare.[42] In January the prisoners on Belle Isle captured the pet poodle of Lieutenant Bossieux, the commandant, and ate it.[43] Food was scarce in Richmond, where bread riots were reported.[44]

The middle of January saw a repetition of the meat shortage. On January 14, the prison quartermaster received three thousand pounds of salt beef for fourteen thousand prisoners. This was repeated on the fifteenth, while on the three succeeding days neither beef nor a substitute for it was issued to the prisoners.[45] On the twenty-first the quartermaster-general ordered Captain Warner to purchase meat in the city markets without regard to the commissary-general. Secretary Seddon, however, January 26, ordered Warner to stop the purchases, as he was informed that the soldiers in the city were also without meat. The situation was deemed especially dangerous as the prisoners were likely to make a break, and there was a possibility that the inhabitants of the city would join with them. The city battalion could not be depended upon for service against the populace.[46]

The cutting off of supplies from the North resulted in

[40] Philadelphia *Inquirer*, December 17, 18.
[41] Page, *The True Story of Andersonville*, 51-52.
[42] Glazier, *The Capture, the Prison Pen, and the Escape*, 77.
[43] McElroy, *Andersonville*, 114-15, Ransom, *op. cit.*, 25. Byers, *op. cit.*, 23.
[44] Ransom, *op. cit.*, 23.
[45] *Official Records*, series 2, VI, 851-52.   [46] Jones, *op. cit.*, II, 131-35.

increasing the hardships of the prisoners. The high prices prevailing in Richmond prevented large purchases even when the prisoners had money; the greater part were destitute. Prisoners were not allowed money in large amounts and even small amounts were taken from them at times. It was customary to search the prisoners for contraband and excessive amounts of money when they arrived in Richmond. Such money as was found on the prisoners was held for their use and the remainder returned at the time of their exchange.[47] Money was received for the prisoners, although some never reached them.[48] Prisoners were searched at the Libby Prison before being distributed to the various tobacco warehouses. In general, small amounts of money were left in the possession of the prisoners.[49] The largest amount of money taken from an individual prisoner at Richmond was taken from Colonel Streight. By an agreement with General Forrest at the time of his capture in Georgia, Colonel Streight purchased from his surgeons about a thousand dollars in Confederate currency. When the case came before the secretary of war on the plea of the Indiana colonel, Ould advised Seddon that the United States took only large amounts from prisoners and disavowed any tendency to deprive them of their per-

[47] See Captain T. P. Turner to Colonel Mulford, enclosing money which the prisoners had at the time of their capture, *Official Records*, series 2, V, 806.

[48] Richardson, *op. cit.*, 369-70. Richardson claimed that Captain Turner was given fifty dollars in greenbacks to hand to Richardson but that Turner gave him fifty dollars in Confederate script.

[49] The memoirs of prisoners are almost unanimous in stating that all of the money which they possessed at the time of their capture was taken from them by the officials of the Libby Prison. This is usually accompanied by a venomous condemnation of Major Turner and a "Dick" Turner—sometimes confused by the prisoners (See for example, Darby *Incidents and Adventures in Rebeldom*, 104; Day. *Fifteen Months*, 12; Drake, *Narrative*, 5; Dufur, *Over the Dead Line*, 52.)—for the brutality and thoroughness with which they were searched. The contemporary evidence on this point, except in newspapers where it served a propaganda purpose, is almost entirely lacking, and creates a serious doubt as to the accuracy of the prisoners' accounts. Page, *op. cit.*, 37-40 denies that he was searched or that anything was ever taken from the prisoners. The prevalence of money, abundantly proved by the evidence, tends to disprove the statements that small amounts were confiscated. See Richardson, Abbott, Hyde, McElroy, and the *Libby Chronicle* for statements of the robbery of prisoners. Cf. Johnston, *Four Months in Libby*, 52 ff.

sonal property.[50] Since General Forrest vouched for the accuracy of Streight's statements[51] it was decided to retain the money but to allow the colonel to have a hundred dollars a month to meet his expenses while in prison.[52] In general the rules of the Confederate authorities in regard to the money belonging to the prisoners were simple. Gold was permitted to the prisoners—to be administered through General Winder—but Federal paper was not recognized as a legal currency by the Confederacy. However, this might be sold at the prisoner's option at the prevailing rates of exchange, and the Confederate money received might be given the prisoners or retained for their use.[53]

While Colonel Streight debated with the officials over the money which he had received as a result of his deal with General Forrest, the enlisted men suffered from the lack of many of the necessities of life. This was especially true of those prisoners who were confined on Belle Isle. The greatest hardship which the prisoners on the island had to undergo was the scarcity of tents or other shelter on the island.[54] The inevitable result of this scarcity of tents was an increase in the amount of sickness on the island. The prisoners were not allowed to visit the sinks at night and the crowded conditions of the camp prevented the proper police of the grounds during the day. The entire surface became saturated with putrid animal matter. The prisoners' carelessness of their

[50] *Official Records,* series 2, VI, 275.

[51] *Ibid.,* 414-15.

[52] *Ibid.,* 456-57, 469-70, 507-9.

[53] Seddon to Winder, *Official Records,* series 2, VI, 202.

[54] Page, *op. cit.,* 41-42. The first prisoners sent to the island after the cessation of exchange were supplied with tents but the increase in the number of prisoners soon surpassed the supply of tents that was available. The result was that about one-fourth of the five thousand prisoners on the island were without shelter while the others were crowded into the original tents. During the winter 1863-64, more tents were issued but there was at no time an adequate supply. Roach, *op. cit.,* 61-63. In the case of shelter on Belle Isle the writers of memoirs have given vent to so many abusive statements that the whole subject is clouded. Boggs, *Eighteen Months under the Rebel Flag,* 7-8, declared that there was not a shelter of any kind on the island. The Sanitary Commission in its propaganda *Narratives of Sufferings,* etc., declared there were no trees within the prison enclosure. Cf. 45 ff. Dufur, *op. cit.,* 45, says that Sybley tents were furnished but were badly crowded.

personal cleanliness added to the sickness of the camp. An additional factor in causing disease was the poor character of the food issued to the men. The bread was made of unbolted meal which was said to produce diarrhoea and dysentery in those who ate it. The prisoners were also poorly clad and without blankets despite the issues which they had received from the North. These had been sold by the prisoners to their guards. All of these factors combined to produce an unhealthy condition which was increased in extent and intensity by the refusal of the men to answer sick calls. Many died without having been seen by a surgeon.[55]

The hospitals for the prisoners in Richmond were located near the prisons. They all had been, like the prisons, tobacco warehouses before the war. They were kept clean and were ventilated.[56] The sick were given the same rations as were issued to the sick in Confederate hospitals.[57] The equipment, however, was inadequate,[58] although the prison surgeon reported that surgical instruments and medicines of good quality were issued by the surgeon-general.[59] The hospitals were crowded, and in March, 1864, the surgeon-general declared that this condition resulted in an excessive mortality. He also charged that the medical purveyor did not furnish medicines and the commissary-general did not give flour to the sick. General Winder, resenting the aspersions of the surgeon-general, declared that the mortality was the result of the inevitable conditions of prison life and not to crowding.[60] The worst cases of the sick who were still able to travel were sent home in exchange. Here their condition and the large number of deaths in the hospitals deepened the conviction that prisoners in Richmond were subjected to inhuman treatment.[61]

One of the charges brought against the South was that syphilis was deliberately spread among the prisoners through the use of impure vaccine. Smallpox being threatened in the

[55] Carrington to Winder, *Official Records*, series 2, VI, 1084-89.
[56] *Ibid.*, 262-63.
[57] *Ibid.*, 647.
[58] Roach, *op. cit.*, 64-66.
[59] *Official Records*, series 2, VI, 262-63.
[60] *Ibid.*, 1048-52.
[61] *Ibid.*, 512, 535-36, 843-44, 110-11.

hospitals and prisons, a number of the Federal surgeons confined there, acting as assistants to the Confederate medical officers, decided to vaccinate their fellows. The medical officer in charge of the hospitals advised against this course. The surgeons, however, took the matters in their own hands and proceeded with the vaccination. As it happened, they used pus instead of lymph for the vaccine and were further unfortunate in that they selected the virus from a subject who was affected with secondary syphilis.[62] Cases of smallpox were of frequent occurrence in the prisons, and the prisoners, who combined a natural dread of hospitals with the belief that their captors would take care that no prisoners should recover, suffered in silence until past the hope of recovery.[63] In December, 1863, General Butler, learning that the scarcity of vaccine was causing much suffering among the prisoners, sent a supply to Ould asking that his action should be considered either official or unofficial as the Confederate wished so long as the drug was accepted. Ould accepted the gift as an unofficial action of the Northern commander.[64]

Another factor adding to the unpleasantness of prison life, if not to disease and death, was the presence on Belle Isle of a gang of robbers and murderers, most of whom were bounty jumpers from New York who had been taken prisoners before they had the chance to desert and re-enlist. These recruits from the city's slums united under the lead of a prisoner who bore the pseudonym, "Captain Moseby," conferred on him by his fellow prisoners in recognition of his characteristics as a raider, and terrorized the camp. "Old men and young, the strong and the weak, the healthy and the sick were alike the sufferers; no place was sacred and no refuge secure, and day and night were equally auspicious," declared Colonel Sanderson who was forced to deal with the situation

[62] *Ibid.*, 262-63. McElroy, *op. cit.*, 109-10, attributes this entire matter to the medical ignorance of the Southern surgeons who, he declares, believed in the efficacy of charms and in witchcraft. The story of the impure vaccines and the spread of syphilis was told of other prisons.

[63] Davidson, *op. cit.*, 59-60.

[64] *Official Records*, series 2, VI, 658-59, 682-83.

while issuing the supplies sent from the United States. Although the raiders presented themselves guised in the rags of destitution to receive the dole from the government, they stole clothing which was issued to the needy prisoners.

An appeal to Lieutenant Bossieux, Commandant at Belle Isle, to remedy these conditions elicited the information that the limited guard force for the island prevented the authorities from any further duty than those connected with the police of the camp. Sanderson, in charge of issuing clothing, believing "that a little demoralization, more or less, among the troops of the enemy was not considered a cause of many tears" by the lieutenant, attempted to inspire the prisoners to organize against the raiders. Sanderson himself acted as the final judge of culprits arrested by the men and punished them to the extent of his power.[65]

These bad conditions in the prisons in Richmond had been foreseen by General Robert E. Lee as early as October, 1863. Learning from the papers that the Federal government had decided to make no further exchanges, Lee wrote to Secretary Seddon suggesting that prisoners should not be held in Richmond. He declared that the city was not a good place for prisoners since their retention there would increase the amount of supplies to be transported. The already inade-

[65] Sanderson, *op. cit.*, 39-43. As a result of these actions Sanderson gained a reputation for cruelty. He was even accused of aiding and sympathizing with the Confederacy. As a result of an enmity which he inspired in Colonel Streight, that officer caused Sanderson to be arrested when he was exchanged in March. The Indiana colonel accused Sanderson of revealing to the Confederates plans of the prisoners for escape. General Neal Dow, irritated because the hotel-keeper and chef refused to accept him in his mess when the prohibitionist arrived in Libby, added the charges of cruelty to prisoners on Belle Isle. Dow was doubtless envious of the officer who had succeeded him in the duty of issuing supplies to the prisoners. Sanderson was dismissed from the service without trial because of these charges. He demanded an investigation and an informal commission which sat upon the case found him innocent of the charges. The commission declared Sanderson justified for his actions in Belle Isle. "*My Record in Rebeldom*," published by Sanderson, gives the account of the hearing and the evidence. Actuated by an intense personal dislike for Colonel Streight and General Dow, Sanderson devoted himself to heaping calumny upon their heads while he gave what seems to be otherwise an honest and unprejudiced account of his prison experiences. For accounts of the "raiders" see Ransom, *op. cit.*, 16 *passim.* Stevens, *A Forlorn Hope*, 18, says "Moseby" began to organize his gang in Pemberton's prison.

quate transportation system, in his opinion, should be devoted entirely to the needs of the citizens. Prisoners would cause higher prices and consequent distress among the poorer classes. The prisoners were also a danger from a military standpoint in that they gave aid and information to the enemy and would endanger the city in case of an attack. He suggested that the prisoners be moved to Danville, Virginia.[66]

Before the order was given for the removal of the prisoners to Danville, an event occurred to confirm General Lee's fears of danger from the prisoners. Guards on Belle Isle overheard the prisoners state that they would soon have to escape as it was planned to plant cannon about them. The authorities, connecting this with the dispatch of a full division to the Federal commander at Newport News, believed that a movement against the city was planned and the prisoners would cooperate with the raiders. The cannon which the prisoners feared were immediately planted.[67]

The inadequacy of the guard at the prisons kept the people of Richmond in constant apprehension of an uprising of the prisoners. Early in 1864 it was reported that six hundred stands of arms were concealed among the prisoners on Belle Isle. This served to excite the citizenry despite the fact that double guards were immediately posted on the island.[68] An organization existed among the officers in Libby in prepara-

[66] *Official Records*, series 2, VI, 438-39, 455-56, 502. The prisoners sent to Danville found that their condition had not changed for the better, for the prison consisted of several warehouses about an open square. No preparations had been made to receive them, (Davidson, *op. cit.*, 66 ff. Hyde, *Captive of War*, 102. Eby, *Observations of An Illinois Boy*, 155) and the rations served here were even poorer than those they had received in the Confederate capital. Davidson, *op. cit.*, 72. The supply of water was so scanty it was necessary for detachments to carry water to their comrades from the river. *Ibid.*, 75-76. Sickness continued in Danville, but the prisoners seem to have had a somewhat better opinion of the hospitals here than of those in Richmond. *Ibid.*, 81-82. Wood was issued but the prisoners complained that the quantity was too small for their needs. Hyde, *op. cit.*, 106. Supplies, especially clothing, were issued to the prisoners from the shipments from the Northern government. Davidson, *op. cit.*, 80 ff.

[67] Jones, *op. cit.*, II, 92, 121.

[68] Ransom, *op. cit.*, 24-25. Richmond *Examiner*, January 4. The Richmond *Dispatch*, February 17, 1864, declared the prisoners were threatening to destroy the city; they complained because they didn't always have sugar in their coffee. "There is great

tion for the time when they would be able to break forth and take the city.[69]

Since the accommodations at Danville were inadequate for the Richmond prisoners, Captain W. S. Winder, a son of the general, was ordered by his father to go to Georgia toward the end of November, 1863, to select a location for a prison near Americus.[70] Andersonville was selected as the best location for the new prison, and in February the first prisoners were sent there from Richmond.[71]

Two events of importance for the prisoners occurred to hasten the removal of the Richmond prisoners to the new prison. The first of these was the escape of a hundred and nine officers from the Libby prison. A Colonel Rose, of Pennsylvania, and a Major Hamilton, of Kentucky, planned a prison delivery in conjunction with a raid by Federal cavalry. This original plan was abandoned, but the officers continued to devise schemes for escape and finally they succeeded in excavating a 57-foot tunnel to a shed near the prison. By February 9, 1864 the tunnel was opened and a hundred and nine of the prisoners made their escape during the night. Forty-eight of the hundred and nine officers, including Colonel Rose, were recaptured before they reached the Union lines. Among those who were successful was Colonel Streight, whose desire for sensation led him to give exaggerated reports of his sufferings while in prison. Streight was hidden by a Unionist in Richmond for over a week, although the first arrivals in the Union lines gave to the newspapers the statement that he had made the trip successfully. These statements deceived the Southern authorities who relaxed their vigilance and thereby enabled the wily colonel to make good his escape after the excitement had subsided.[72]

room for improvement in our mode of treating these invaders . . . . , we are not always going to have our prisoners murdered by inches and our homes burned over our heads without some attempt at retaliation. In the meantime, the sooner the Yankees now here are moved further South, the better for all parties."
    [69] Sanderson, op. cit., 31 ff.
    [70] Official Records, series 2, VI, 558.   [71] See Chap. VII.

The other event which hastened the removal of the prisoners was a raid directed against the city from the Federal lines. February 28 to March 4, two columns, under the command of General Kilpatrick and Colonel Ulric Dahlgren advanced upon the city with the avowed purpose of releasing the prisoners. Due to errors in direction Dahlgren was killed in an ambuscade and the failure of the two columns to unite saved Richmond. The inadequacy of the militia in the city for its defense and the terror which the citizens felt as a result of the prisoners being confined in Richmond was reflected in the action of the authorities. As the raiders approached the city the Libby prison was undermined and two hundred pounds of powder was placed in the hole. The prisoners were informed that any attempt to break out would result in the blowing up of the prison. When the immediate fear subsided the Confederate authorities made attempts to justify their action by alleging that the purpose was to frighten the prisoners into quietude. But the prisoners believed at the time and afterward that their destruction was only prevented by Dahlgren's failure. After these events the removal of the prisoners to Andersonville was rapid, four hundred a day being sent to the Georgia prison.[73]

[72] The best account of the tunnel is given by Moran, "Colonel Rose's Tunnel at Libby," *Century Magazine*, March, 1888, 770-90. See also Moran, *Bastiles of the Confederacy*, 112; Byers, *op. cit.*, 24-25; Glazier, *op. cit.*, 79-86; Jones, *op. cit.*, II 147; New York *Times*, February 17; Richardson, *op. cit.*, 404; Moore, *Rebellion Records*, VIII, 450-53; Domschcke, *op. cit.*, 77, 88; Rose, *Colonel Rose's Story*; Hamilton, *Story of the Famous Tunnel Escape*; Johnston, *Four Months in Libby*, 65-113; Hooper, "Twelve Days' Absence without Leave," *Overland Monthly*, V, 201-213. See also Richmond *Dispatch*, February 11.

[73] Jones, *op. cit.*, II, 152. For Kilpatrick's raid see *Official Records*, series I, XXXIII, 168-224; Moran, *Bastiles of the Confederacy*, 120, 133; Abbott, *Prison Life in the South*, 257-59; Glazier, *op. cit.*, 88-94; Jones, *op. cit.*, II, 164. New York *Times*, March 5, 12, 14, 19.

CHAPTER VII

ANDERSONVILLE

Andersonville—a name which has been stamped so deeply by cruelty into the pages of American history—is one of those miserable little hamlets, of a score of scattered and dilapidated farm-houses, which relieve the monotony of the wide and dreary level of sand plains, which, covered with immense forests, interspersed with fens, marshes, corn and cotton fields, stretch away in unbroken surface from Macon down to the Florida shores.[1]

Such was the place which Captain W. S. Winder, General Howell Cobb, and Governor Brown selected as the site for a prison when the scarcity of provisions and the danger to the city made it necessary to remove the prison from Richmond.[2] The site having been selected, Captain Richard B. Winder, a cousin of the Richmond prison commander, was ordered in December to repair to the spot and make preparation for the reception of ten thousand prisoners. Captain Winder was informed that he could get any amount of teams and labor which he might need for the work from the surrounding country, but the people objected to a prison in the neighborhood and he was forced to obtain permission from Richmond to impress the necessary aid. The delay entailed in waiting for this permission prevented the work of constructing the prison until January and even then the force under Winder's command was limited.[3]

This difficulty was but the beginning of the troubles which were to burden the captain. The distance of Andersonville from any source of manufactured supplies made it necessary to send to Columbus, Georgia, for all tools and equipment. February 16, Captain Winder was forced to send an agent to

[1] Hamlin, *Martyria*, 16.

[2] *Official Records*, series 2, VI, 558.

[3] *Ibid.*, series 2, VIII, 730-31. Winder to Church, explaining his connection with the Andersonville prison. This explanation was made after Winder's arrest in 1865. See Davis, "Andersonville and other War Prisons," *Belford's Magazine*, January, 1888. Spencer, *Narrative of Andersonville*, 15-21.

Columbus to obtain six-gallon kettles for boiling meat for the prisoners. Saddles, bridles, harness and horses, light wagons, and mules had to be impressed from the scanty population of the surrounding country. Captain Winder reported to General Winder that he had difficulty in procuring baking pans for the ovens, nails and padlocks for the doors, and glass for the windows.[4]

It was planned to construct barracks for the prisoners but the scarcity of lumber prevented the execution of the plan. Despite the fact that the prison was located in the midst of a pine forest, planks, which Captain Winder decided would be cheaper and superior to logs, could scarcely be obtained.[5] Lumber could not be purchased at less than one hundred dollars a thousand feet[6] and Winder was limited by his instructions to paying Georgia schedule prices. This schedule fixed the price of lumber at fifty dollars a thousand while the navy works at Albany and the hospital departments were paying seventy-five or eighty dollars. Under such competition lumber could not be supplied and Winder was given permission to impress such mills as were not needed by the railroads. The railroads had already protested that Winder's proposition to impress mills would cripple transportation. The result of this was that mill owners contracted with the railroads for a small part of their total output and, protected by this agreement, sold the greater portion of their work in the open market while Winder was forced to do without lumber.[7]

The duties of Captain Winder in making preparation for the prisoners at Andersonville included making the necessary arrangements for procuring supplies for them. Arrangements were made with the local mills to grind for the prisoners;[8] the commissary of Florida was instructed to furnish beef

---

[4] *Official Records,* series 2, VI, 962, 996, 1015, 1000.

[5] *Ibid.,* 965-66.

[6] *Ibid.,* 1043.

[7] *Ibid.,* series 2, VIII, 732. Stevenson, *The Southern Side of Andersonville Prison,* 21, says barracks were built.

[8] *Official Records,* series 2, VI, 972.

for the prison;[9] and Winder was required to purchase beef in southwest Georgia and Florida. There arose the difficulty of obtaining men to drive the cattle to the prison for slaughter, for, as the captain found, "all able-bodied men exempt from service are speculating" and would not give their time to driving beeves.[10]

In the midst of the preparations for equipping the prison, Captain W. S. Winder received word that the prisoners in Richmond were being removed to Andersonville at the rate of four hundred a day. The first detachment left Richmond February 18, and arrived at the new prison February 27,[11] and, of course, the prisoners arrived at Andersonville before the preparations for their reception had been completed. There were no buildings in the prison, which consisted of sixteen and a half acres of land enclosed by a stockade. The stockade was constructed of pine logs twenty feet in length, hewed to about twelve inches in thickness, and planted five feet in the ground. The logs were joined so closely that it was impossible to see through the wall. At intervals about the top of the stockade were sentry boxes, roofed, equipped with a ladder, and elevated so that the top of the stockade came to the waist of the sentinel. The stockade was longer east and west, and on the west side two gates, protected by a double stockade, opened into the prison. A stream of pure water about five feet in width ran through the prison yard dividing it roughly in half. The ground sloped gradually

---

[9] *Ibid.*, 976-77.

[10] *Ibid.*, 965-66. The nearest commissary was at Columbus, Georgia, fifty miles away, and upon him Winder called for beef, bacon, flour, sugar, molasses, rice, soap, and candles. With the exception of sugar and flour, which were only to be issued to the sick, he called for rations for 10,000 men. Since it was his intention to make candles at the prison, Captain Winder asked that the tallow be left on the beef. *Ibid.*, 914.

In addition to this difficulty were the troubles over transportation. *Ibid.*, 992-93. Later, when the prisoners were moved from Andersonville, General Winder reported that a load of supplies for the equipment of a prison had been unloaded by the railroad and the cars taken to transport cotton for speculators. *Ibid.*, series 2, VII, 955-56.

[11] *Official Records*, series 2, VI, 925-26. Richmond *Examiner*, February 18. New York *Times*, February 27. McElroy, *Andersonville*, 118-19. Page, *op. cit.*, 60-61.

to this stream.[12]   The stockade at the time of the arrival of
the prisoners was not yet completed, but two pieces of artil-
lery guarded the open side.[13]

The prisoners, finding themselves without shelter, set
about to utilize the lumber, logs, and branches remaining
within the enclosure from the building of the stockade. Huts
were thus constructed for the early arrivals. The logs for
the stockade had been taken from the enclosure, and no trees
were left to protect the prisoners from the Georgia sun. The
huts which they constructed were comfortable, but the
scarcity of materials for even such rude buildings rendered
the shelter inadequate. In addition, the huts were arranged
in accordance with the prisoners' fancy and police was rendered difficult after the prison became crowded.[14] Captain
Winder continued unable to get the necessary lumber for the
prison. In April he wrote to the quartermaster at Macon
that he was burying the dead without coffins because he did
not have lumber to supply the needs of the living.[15] Late in
the month Captain Winder reported that he had permission
to impress lumber, but again transportation difficulties stood
in his way. Nails and tools were almost impossible to procure.[16] Colonel A. W. Persons, commanding the prison
guard, had to leave the prison to go in search of picks,
shovels, and other necessary tools which could not be obtained
through Captain Winder's requisitions.[17]

Because the bakehouse which Captain Winder planned to
construct had not been completed, the first prisoners were
issued uncooked rations. For the purpose of issuing rations
and maintaining discipline within the camp, the newcomers
were divided into squads of two hundred and seventy men

[12] McElroy, op. cit., 128-29. Page, op. cit., 61-62. Boggs, Eighteen Months
under the Rebel Flag, 17-18. Davidson, Fourteen Months, 112-13. Ransom, Andersonville Diary, 40. Abbott, Prison Life in the South, 119. Sabre, Nineteen Months,
84-85. Stevenson, The Southern Side, 18 ff.

[13] Official Records, series 2, VIII, 731. Ransom, op. cit., 42.

[14] Official Records, series 2, VII, 124-25. Spencer, op. cit., 25-26, says there were
regular streets.

[15] Official Records, series 2, VII, 40.

[16] Ibid., 89.   [17] Ibid., 63-64, 169-70.

which in turn were subdivided into messes of ninety each.[18] The rations issued to the first prisoners consisted of a pound of meal, a pound of sweet potatoes, and a pound of beef or a half pound of bacon.[19] Iron bake pans were issued to the prisoners who first arrived but the later arrivals were not supplied with cooking utensils.[20] The rations issued at first suffered a reduction as more prisoners came into the camp. In April prisoners state that only a pint of meal was issued daily.[21]

In May the bakery for the prison was completed, and the prisoners received the same rations as were issued to the soldiers who were guarding them. The pound of beef or one-third pound of bacon, one and one-fourth pounds of meal, and occasional beans and rice were issued cooked.[22] At intervals mush[23] was issued to the prisoners, and on a few occasions soap formed a part of the issues.[24]

[18] Glazier, *The Capture, The Prison Pen, and the Escape*, 334. McElroy, *op. cit.*, 131, says they were divided into messes of twenty-five and squads of one hundred. This was in February before the arrival of Wirz. The peculiar division of ninety and two hundred and seventy seems to have been Wirz's idea. See Stevens, *A Forlorn Hope*, 25.

[19] *Official Records*, series 2, VIII, 731. This is Captain Winder's statement made after his arrest in 1865 and may therefore be expected to be exaggerated. However, his report of rations issued during the quarter ending March 31, 1864 seems to confirm his contention. He reported at that time having issued 7,119 pounds of beef, 6,150 pounds of bacon, 11,880½ pounds of meal, 15,103 pounds of potatoes, 13,460 pounds of beans or peas, and in addition regulation rations of hard bread, wheat, sirup, candles and salt. *Ibid.*, series 2, VI, 1125. Ransom, *op. cit.*, 41 states that he received a quart of cornmeal, one-half pound of beef, and some salt on March 15. This he declared to be an improvement on the rations issued in Richmond.

In general the subject of rations at Andersonville is as difficult to determine with accuracy as in the case of Richmond. The official reports are lacking, and the prisoner's accounts written after the event are either inaccurate or deliberately misleading. Forbes, *Diary of a Soldier and Prisoner of War in the Rebel Prisons*, was published in 1865, the writer having died at Florence, S. C., on February 1, 1865. Entries in the diary, which bears no evidence of having been edited in the light of war psychosis, indicate that rations were issued twice a day and were adequate, although limited to corn-bread and bacon. There are no entries in the diary complaining of the rations received. (Cf. pages 28 and 37.)

[20] Davidson, *op. cit.*, 124. [21] Ransom, *op. cit.*, 49.

[22] *Official Records*, series 2, VII, 124-25.

[23] Kellogg, *Life and Death in Rebel Prisons*, 109-10.

[24] *Ibid.*, 59. About the end of May there was a reduction in rations. Cf. Glazier, *op. cit.*, 340. Abbott, *op. cit.*, 198.

The cookhouse was located just outside the stockade on the banks of the stream which flowed through the prison. The result of this location was that all the refuse from the bakery passed into the stream to pollute the only supply of water in the prison. This situation was irremediable with the facilities at the command of the officers in charge of the prison; the only recourse was to allow the prisoners to dig wells to supply themselves with pure water.[25]

The small rations and the polluted stream were blamed by the prisoners, after their release, for the sickness and death at Andersonville. In the early months of the prison's history, however, the prevalence of disease was due to other causes. In the latter part of April, Surgeon Isaiah H. White, in charge of the hospital at the post, declared that the heavy mortality was the result of the long confinement of the prisoners before they arrived in Andersonville, although the inadequate hospital facilities at the post were also to be blamed.[26] Because of the lack of lumber, makeshift hospitals were early placed in the corners of the stockade. A few tent flies were used to protect the sick prisoners who lay on beds of pine needles on the ground.[27] None were admitted to the hospital who were able to help themselves,[28] and even then the accommodations were inadequate for the crowds of sick. The drainage from the sinks of the camp passed through the hospital grounds. To add to the hardships of the hospital administration, Surgeon White reported that the supplies for the hospital, since they had to be kept within the prison enclosure, were stolen by the well prisoners. He complained that the prisoners came into the hospital and annoyed the sick. To the twenty-fifth of April there were 2,697 cases of sickness in the hospital and 718 deaths. White recommended that a hospital should be constructed outside the stockade to remedy these evils and reduce the number of deaths.[29]

[25] *Official Records*, series 2, VIII, 733.   Mann, "On the Andersonville Circuit," 255.
[26] *Official Records*, series 2, VII, 89.
[27] McElroy, *op. cit.*, 166-67.   Davidson, *op. cit.*, 115.
[28] Ransom, *op. cit.*, 48.
[29] *Official Records*, series 2, VII, 89.

This recommendation was concurred in by General Howell Cobb who visited the prison in the early part of May. At that time there were twelve thousand prisoners in the stockade,[30] 1,026 prisoners having died in the stockades from February 23 to May 10.[31] Many of these deaths were due to respiratory diseases contracted by the prisoners en route from Richmond. The lack of barracks rendered these cases fatal. The other deaths and most of the cases in the hospital were due to diarrhoea and dysentery, and in most cases these diseases were combined with scurvy.[32]

The sick in the hospital and the stockade were visited by a Catholic priest from Macon, Father Hamilton, who went among them offering the solace of religion to Protestants as well as to communicants of the Roman church. Father Hamilton seems to have been the only representative of organized Christianity who regularly ministered to the prisoners at Andersonville.[33] Contacts with the outer world were few, and the prisoners grew despondent awaiting news of exchange. Mental depression aided in increasing the ravages of disease and death.[34]

In order to remedy the bad sanitary condition of the prison and decrease the number of deaths, it was planned to improve the police of the camp. The first step in this direction was to be the construction of two dams across the stream which flowed through the stockade. The upper of the dams was to be devoted to drinking and cooking purposes while the lower would permit the prisoners to bathe. Surgeon White believed that the men were so filthy in their habits that it would be necessary to force them to use the lower dam, but he was convinced that its use would improve the health of the prisoners. Along the banks of the stream below the dam, it was planned to construct sinks for the men. The opening of the flood gates of the two dams would thereby cleanse the

[30] Cobb to Cooper, *Ibid.*, 119-21.   [31] *Ibid.*, 135-39.   [32] *Ibid.*, 124-25.

[33] Ransom, *op. cit.*, 59.   Boggs, *op. cit.*, 46. The Masons rendered aid to the members of their order in the prison. Page, *op. cit.*, 64, says a rebel chaplain visited the prisoners occasionally.

[34] Stevenson, *op. cit.*, 28. *Official Records*, series 2, VIII, 588-632.

prison of the ordure which was now accumulating along the banks of the stream.[35] The completion of these plans was delayed by the scarcity of tools which were not received until early in May.[36] May 12, the work of planking the sides of the stream preparatory to constructing the sinks was begun.[37]

This plan, which, owing to the necessity of other work and the continual arrival of prisoners, was never carried to completion, was devised by Captain Henry Wirz. Wirz, whose connection with Confederate prisons dated from his assignment to duty with General Winder in 1861, had been sent from Richmond, March 27, and was assigned by Colonel Persons to the command of the interior of the prison.[38]

Concerning this man whose name was for a long time considered synonymous with cruelty, much has been written. Prisoners who were in his charge at Andersonville attribute to him most of the suffering which resulted from their imprisonment. In the imagination of the prisoners who survived the ordeal of a prison which was located where equipment and proper care were impossible, Henry Wirz stands as the cruel and inhuman author of all their sufferings, and their descriptions of him unite in assigning to his features the physiognomy of the brute. One prisoner whose literary ability surpassed his accuracy remembered Wirz as "an undersized, fidgety man, with an insignificant face, and a mouth that protruded like a rabbit's. His bright little eyes, like those of a squirrel or a rat, assisted in giving his countenance a look of kinship to the family of rodent animals—a genus which lives by stealth and cunning, subsisting on what it can steal away from stronger and braver creatures. He was dressed in a pair of gray trousers with the other part of his body covered with a calico garment, like that which small boys used to wear, called 'waists.' This was fastened to the pantaloons by buttons, precisely as was the custom with the

---

[35] *Ibid.*, series 2, VII, 170-71.

[36] *Ibid.*, 169.

[37] Kellogg, *op. cit.*, 85.

[38] *Official Records*, series 2, VII, 169-70. *Trial of Henry Wirz*, 221. Chipman, *The Tragedy of Andersonville*, 60.

garments of boys struggling with the orthography of words
in two syllables. Upon his head was perched a little gray
cap. Sticking in his belt, and fastened to his wrist by a strap
two or three feet long, was one of those formidable looking
but harmless English revolvers that have ten barrels around
the edge of the cylinder and fire a musket bullet from the
center. The wearer of this composite costume . . . stepped
nervously about and sputtered volubly in very broken English . . . 'py Gott, you don't vatch dem dam Yankees glose
enough! Dey are schlipping 'rount, and peatin' you efery
dimes.' "[39]

This description, while it conveys an erroneous impression
of the physical appearance of the prison commander, ade-
quately reveals the state of the prisoners' minds towards him.
The half-mocking respect which the officers in the Richmond
prisons had for the bustling efficiency of Sergeant Wirz in the
more palmy days of the Confederate prisons, was changed in
the new prison to bitter hatred. The fact that he was a for-
eigner and spoke with an accent militated against his making
a good impression. Rumors began to circulate within the
stockade concerning him. "What one suspected was recounted to the next as a fact."[40] A prisoner's diary records
the development of a psychosis to which Wirz was eventually
to fall a victim. Three days after Wirz's arrival he is described as a brute and the prisoners had begun to refer to
him as the "Flying Dutchman." Two days later it is recorded: "It is said that Wirtz (sic) shot someone this morning." A week later: "We hear stories of Captain Wirtz's
cruelty in punishing the men, but I hardly credit all the

[39] McElroy, *Andersonville*, 142-43. Most other writers agree with the purport of
this description but vary the details. Page, *op. cit.*, 80-81, varies from the usual description and denies that Wirz was the "short, thickset Dutchman, repulsive in appearance, besotted, ignorant and cruel" that other writers describe him. Page states that
Wirz was five feet, eight inches tall, slim, handsome, with an aquiline nose, even
features, and high forehead. His eyes were sad instead of ratlike. See also, Kellogg,
op. cit., 87; and Boggs, *op. cit.*, 14, for descriptions of the usual order. Goss, *A
Soldier's Experience*, 71 ff. Spencer, *op. cit.*, 55-62. Lyon, *In and Out of Andersonville*, 29.

[40] Page, *op. cit.*, 77.

stories." The next day: "Wirtz don't come in as much as
formerly. The men make it uncomfortable for him." May
2: "Wirtz is walking about the prison revolver in hand, cursing and swearing. The men yell out, 'Hang him up!' 'Kill
the Dutch louse.' . . . and every few minutes a handful of
dirt is thrown by someone." May 10 it was recorded that
Wirz was domineering and abusive: afraid to come into the
camp where a thousand men would willingly die if they could
kill him first. "Certainly the worst man I ever saw."[41]

Wirz's promotion from a private to a captain is evidence
that his superiors did not share the attitude of the prisoners
toward him. Undoubtedly his foreign accent and nervous
manner set him apart as peculiar in the eyes of the enlisted
men confined at Andersonville, but the officers who had been
subjected to him in Richmond, and his superiors in the Confederate service, were more competent to judge his worth.
Nine years in the armies of Europe before he came to America to practice medicine had made him a strict disciplinarian.[42]
This quality enhanced his value in the administration of the
prison system. Officers sent to inspect the prison at Andersonville united in commending the energy of the commander
of the interior of the prison. Wirz's request in May to be
promoted in order that he might more competently command
the officers associated with him was endorsed by General
Winder with the statement that Wirz's superior in diligence
and efficiency could not be found.[43] General Cobb declared
that he performed his duties admirably.[44] An inspector from
Richmond declared that he was firm and rigid in discipline
but kind to the prisoners.[45]

Only affairs relative to the prisoners within the stockade
were under the control of Captain Wirz. Colonel A. W.

[41] Ransom, op. cit., 43, 44, 45, 48, 49, 54, 55. Ransom dates Wirz's arrival March
25. His dates are usually inaccurate by several days. This is undoubtedly the result of
later editing. The story of Wirz walking about with a revolver before heckling prisoners is quite likely a later interpolation.

[42] See account by Major Hairston in Jeffrey, *Richmond Prisons 1861-1862.*

[43] *Official Records,* series 2, VII, 170.

[44] *Ibid.,* 119-21.   [45] *Ibid.,* 135-39, 167-69.

Persons commanded the guard force at the prison. Colonel Persons was popular with the prisoners as were the guards from Alabama.[46] As the number of prisoners increased the guard force came to be considered inadequate. General Howell Cobb visited the prison and concluded that there was little danger of escape from the stockade. However, he added two companies of Georgia reserves to the guard force[47] and requested that an officer of ability be sent to the prison. In response to these representations General Winder arrived at the post, June 8.[48]

Immediately upon his arrival Winder, whose experiences with the prisoners in Richmond had taught him the necessity of a competent guard force, noticed the paucity of the force at the Georgia prison. He had a command totaling 2,867 when all were present, but there were only 1,462 available for the duty of guarding 24,000 prisoners. Believing that the force should be doubled he appealed to General Cobb for more of the Georgia reserves.[49] But Cobb was unable to add as much as a single man to the guard force, whose effectiveness in the meantime had been considerably reduced by an epidemic of measles and whooping cough.

To overcome the defects growing out of the smallness of the guard, attempts were made to increase their efficiency. General Cobb on his visit in May addressed the guards to inspire them in the faithful performance of their duties. "Would you turn this horde of Lincoln's hirelings on the sacred soil of Georgia?" he is said to have asked them.[50] Winder issued orders in June that the guard would be held strictly responsible for all escapes and difficulties arising from the failure to perform rigidly their duties.[51] "The murders along the deadline increased," remarked the prisoner who quoted Cobb's speech.

Fifteen feet within the stockade a row of posts joined by boards nailed to their tops marked the limits of the space

[46] Page, op. cit., 70. [47] Official Records, series 2, VII, 92, 119-21, 142.
[48] Ibid., 192, 213, 377. [49] Ibid., 378.
[50] Boggs, op. cit., 31. [51] Official Records, series 2, VII, 393.

alloted to the prisoners. According to orders prisoners ven-
turing beyond this "deadline" were to be warned to leave,
and if they refused or failed to obey they were to be shot by
the nearest sentinel. The rigid discipline of the very young
and very old men who composed the reserve force on guard
had the effect of making them extremely cautious. Shots, it
seems, were sometimes fired without provocation and often
without warning. The prisoners believed that the guards
were encouraged to deliberate murder by receiving a furlough
of thirty days for each Yankee they killed.[52]

Because of the inadequacy of the guard force they could
do no more than endeavor to prevent the prisoners from
escaping. Internal discipline, essentially the function of the
captors, could not be administered. The band of bounty
jumpers who had terrorized Belle Isle arrived in Anderson-

[52] *Ibid.*, 403-4. Davidson, *op. cit.*, 113-14. Page, *op. cit.*, 85-88. Page, always a
defender of Wirz, declared that his hut stood three feet inside the deadline by permission of Wirz. Practically every writer of Andersonville experiences had a long
list of murders along the deadline. It is impossible from the very volume of the
allegations to select the true cases from the false. A few cases are given with sufficient
details to be convincing while the majority are based on prison rumors and have little
or no basis in fact.

One of the earliest cases of shooting a prisoner at the deadline grew out of the
suspicions of the prisoners that one of their number was reporting to Wirz the progress
of several tunnels which the prisoners were digging in hopes of being able to make
their way to freedom. Suspicion fastened itself on a garrulous cripple who had been
befriended by Wirz. A mob of prisoners assaulted the suspect on the night of May 14.
The next day, their anger increasing, they again sought to beat him, but the victim
eluding their chase, slipped across the deadline to obtain protection from the guard.
When ordered back he informed the guard that he would rather be killed by a rebel
than by his fellows. Wirz ordered the man back and attempted to quiet the irate
prisoners. After he had gone the guard was forced to shoot the demented prisoner
when he consistently refused to withdraw from the deadline. Most of the writers see
in this case only another evidence of the brutality of the guards and the intention of
the rebels to kill all of the prisoners. Charge 2, specification 8, in the charges brought
against Wirz cites a case on May 15, stating that Wirz ordered a guard to kill a
prisoner. On this charge he was found guilty. Page claims that Wirz left the enclosure before the prisoner sought refuge the second time across the deadline. The specification against Wirz declared that the name of the cripple was unknown. McElroy
gives it as Hubbard of Chicago, private in the Thirty-eighth Illinois Volunteers. See
Official Records, series 2, VIII, 784-91. Page, *op. cit.*, 95. Ransom, *op. cit.*, 56-57.
Glazier, *op. cit.*, 330-40. McElroy,, *op. cit.*, 156-58. Boggs, *op. cit.*, 25-26. Kellogg,
op. cit., 194-95. Abbott, *op. cit.*, 197-98. Dufur, *Over the Dead Line*, 77-78. Goss,
op. cit., 85 ff. Sabre, *op. cit.*, 10-31. Spencer, *op. cit.*, 82-83. Bullard, *Over the
Dead Line or Who Killed Poll Parrot?* passim.

ville about the first of April; and, under the leadership of
William Collins of Pennsylvania, who still bore his soubri-
quet of "Moseby," began anew its depredations. The majority of the "raiders" were from New York City and their
fellow prisoners described them as the scourings of the city's
slums. Their depredations were at first carried on under the
cover of darkness, but gradually growing in number and
boldness, they finally dominated the camp. Prisoners who
had money or other desirable possessions were robbed, and
murders were not unknown. The better class of prisoners
appealed to Wirz, but he was unable to handle the situation.
Finally a solution was arrived at in the decision to permit the
prisoners to organize in their own defense and to arrest and
try the suspected persons. Orders issued by General Winder
gave permission for this action. The early days of July were
spent in organizing and fighting with the result that the
"Regulators" succeeded in arresting twenty-four of the raider
gang. A jury of twelve, selected largely from the newer
prisoners sat at night to hear evidence and brought in a verdict of guilty with sentence of death against six of the leaders.
This sentence, approved by the Confederate officials, was
carried out on July 11. A scaffold was erected within the
stockade, and in full sight of all of the prisoners Wirz and
the guard brought in the condemned men. The six mounted
the gallows and the traps were sprung by the officers of the
regulators. The eighteen raiders who were not convicted did
not escape the vengeance of their fellow prisoners. They
were forced to run a gauntlet of prisoners armed with clubs
and three of them died from the effects of this beating.[53]

[53] A single adequate account of this episode is lacking. The story, however, em-
bellished with many details, is given in practically every account of the prison. For
Winder's order see *Official Records*, series 2, VII, 426. For description of the career,
arrest, trial and execution of the raiders see Ransom, *op. cit.*, 45-67, 71-72, 76, 77,
81-84; Boggs, *op. cit.*, 21-22, 29, 35-36; Abbott, *op. cit.*, 198; Glazier, *op. cit.*,
339; Urban, *In Defense of the Union*, 469-80; McElroy, *op. cit.*, 220-51; Mann,
op cit., 606-8; Kelley, *What I Saw and Suffered in Rebel Prisons*, 50-53; Kellogg,
op. cit., 155-57; Davidson, *op. cit.*, 168 ff. Hyde, *Captive of War*, 222 ff.; Dufur,
op. cit., 85-103; Stevens, *A Forlorn Hope*, 29-34; Goss, *op. cit.*, 150-58; Sabre, *op.
cit.*, 112-17. Creelman, *Collections of a Coffee Cooler*, 13, says General Sherman
approved the sentence of the raiders before they were executed.

Such disorders in the prison were inevitable. The prisoners were all enlisted men, and their utter demoralization was an outgrowth of a long prison experience during which they had lost the restraining influences of organization. Their officers were confined at Macon, Georgia, and the Confederate authorities were not able to provide, nor could they have wished for, a military organization among the prisoners.

Moreover, the crowded condition of the prison, in addition to giving the raiders a wide field for their depredations, increased the demoralization of the prisoners. In March the mean strength of the prison was seventy-five hundred. April saw the number increased to ten thousand. In May there were fifteen thousand; in June, 22,291; and during July the mean strength of the prisoners within the stockade had increased to 29,030 men. With such an increase in numbers, the guard, which did not increase, must necessarily have been limited to the functions of maintaining a vigilant watch against escape. The officers in charge of the prison could do little more than to secure the prisoners and make the often futile efforts to obtain sufficient food for them.[54]

In the latter part of June, the stockade, originally designed to hold ten thousand men, was enlarged by the addition of ten acres.[55] At this time the number of prisoners in the stockade was twenty-six thousand and the additional area brought the entire enclosure to twenty-six acres. This was a slight relief to the crowded conditions but the arrival of more prisoners soon brought a repetition of the former conditions. The end of July found 31,678 prisoners in the stockade.[56]

Limited though it was, not all of this area was available for the prisoners. The deadline cut off fifteen feet from the stockade walls while along the banks of the stream the constant milling of the men produced a swamp, which occupied three and a half acres in the center of the prison.[57] The

[54] *Official Records*, series 2, VII, 524-25.
[55] *Ibid.*, 426-27. Boggs, *op. cit.*, 42-43. Kellogg, *op. cit.*, 157. Urban, *op. cit.*, 484, 490. Davidson, *op. cit.*, 138. Goss, *op. cit.*, 166.
[56] *Official Records*, series 2, VII, 708.
[57] *Ibid.*, 546.

absence of proper sinks along the banks of the stream led the men to defecate in the swamp, which, becoming the depository of fecal matter from thousands of men, was rendered not only uninhabitable but a source of disease to the entire prison. Maggots bred in the swamps to a depth of fifteen or eighteen inches, according to one prisoner,[58] while another remembered that

The largest crawled out in the hot sand, shed their tail-like appendages; wings would unfold, and an attempt be made to fly; and thousands were clumsily dropping all over the camp. They tumbled into our mush, bedding places, and on the faces of the sick and dying.[59]

The rapid increase in number of prisoners rendered the bakehouse, in preparation when the first prisoners arrived, insufficient even before it was completed; rations were issued uncooked to part of the prisoners. Issued raw, the food was even more unsavory in appearance than when it had undergone the disguising processes of cooking. The meal was received unsifted from the mills and in this condition was issued to the prisoners. Wirz pronounced it unfit for use and declared that one-sixth of the whole was husk. He also complained that the lack of buckets prevented the prisoners from receiving rice, beans, vinegar, and molasses.[60] A serious difficulty faced Captain Winder in the utter lack of funds to make purchases of food. July 18, he asked for $175,000, stating that he had had for guards and prisoners but $75,000 since the first of April. The guards had not been paid.[61] A year later, during the last four months of the prison's existence, Captain Winder received no money from the government.[62]

On July 25, General Winder informed the adjutant general that he had 29,400 prisoners at the post, 2,650 troops,

[58] Kelley, *op. cit.*, 40.

[59] Boggs, *op. cit.*, 27. See also McElroy, *op. cit.*, 188. Sanitary Commission: *Narrative*, etc., 93. Kellogg, *op. cit.*, 56 ff. Urban, *op. cit.*, 536-37. Mention is made of the swamp in *Official Records*, series 2, VII, 524-25, 426-27. See also reports of Surgeon Jones. *Ibid.*, series 2, VIII, 588-632, and in Chipman, *op. cit.*, 83-97. Quoted also by McElroy, *op. cit.*, 298-320.

[60] *Official Records*, series 2, VII, 207.

[61] *Ibid.*, 473.

[62] *Ibid.*, series 2, VIII, 733.

and 500 negroes and laborers, and "not a ration at the post." He had ordered that ten days' supply be kept on hand, but he found that this was not being done. The commissary-general, upon hearing Winder's complaint, informed him that he did not have the right to issue orders to the prison commissary. Winder might appeal directly to the commissary-general, but he could not issue orders about food; he declared he would have countermanded Winder's order if the district commissary had not ignored it. The army was rationed only one day in advance and prisoners could not be given a ten-day issue. He promised to care for the prisoners until the army was pressed.[63]

In the early part of August Colonel D. T. Chandler was sent from Richmond to make an inspection of the Andersonville prison. He was told by the prison authorities of the efforts that they had made to provide the proper rations for the prisoners. Wirz pointed out the fact that tools had been difficult to procure; sheet iron for baking pans had not arrived, and wheelbarrows, lumber, and axes were lacking. Wirz informed him that the rations which the prisoners received were the same as those given to the guard. These rations, according to Wirz, consisted of a third of a pound of bacon or one-half pound of beef, one and one-half pounds of cornmeal, with occasional issues of beans, rice, molasses, vinegar, and soap.[64] General Winder pointed out that the cookhouse, designed for ten thousand, could not serve the thirty-two thousand who had been sent to the prison, but he assured the colonel that adequate cooking arrangements would soon be completed.[65] Surgeon White recommended that antiscorbutics—green corn, molasses, and vinegar—be issued to the men who were suffering from scurvy.[66]

Chandler, after making what seems to have been a casual inspection, reported to the war department that nothing had been done and little effort had been made to procure the proper food for the prisoners. He declared that the prison-

[63] *Ibid.*, series 2, VII, 499.   [65] *Ibid.*, 541.
[64] *Ibid.*, 521-22.   [66] *Ibid.*, 541-45.

er's ration consisted of a third of a pound of bacon, and one
and one-fourth pounds of unbolted cornmeal. Fresh beef,
rice, and molasses were seldom if ever issued. He declared
that he had seen men digging in the swamp for roots with
which to cook their raw food because wood was not issued to
those who received rations uncooked.[67]

This report also revealed the animus of the inspector to
General Winder. Colonel Chandler recommended that
Winder be removed and someone substituted who combined
energy and good judgment with some feelings of humanity
toward the prisoners. Winder advocated the retention of
the prisoners in the condition which Chandler found them
until death reduced them to a number which could be prop-
erly cared for. He believed that Winder could have improved conditions at the prison by the exercise of energy and
judgment. He recommended, however, that Wirz be promoted for his efficiency.[68]

Those who were so fortunate as to have money could sup-
plement the small rations by purchases from the sutler, whose
shop was established inside the stockade.[69] Prisoners who
had money in sufficiently large amounts bought in large
quantities from the sutler and retailed their purchases at a
profit to their more impecunious fellows. Others bought

[67] *Ibid.*, 546-53.

[68] Chandler's report in opposition to Winder doubtless reflected the opinion of him
which had been current in Richmond before he was ordered to Andersonville. The
report, wholly unfair to the prison administration, was made a subject of much importance after the war. It served the court which tried Wirz as proof that there was
a conspiracy on the part of the rebels to murder prisoners. The judge-advocate of the
court and Judge Holt, the most bitter men in the circles of administration, found proof
that this report had been seen by Jefferson Davis, who must therefore have been
informed of conditions at Andersonville. Writers of prison reminiscences cite this
report as evidence of the cruelty of their captors. Winder denied Chandler's statements, although he did not know the opinion which Chandler had expressed as to his
fitness for his office. The matter became a question of the truthfulness of the two
officers and a military court was ordered to settle the matter. The death of Winder
and the end of the war prevented this court from meeting. *Ibid.*, 755-62.

Chandler had been an officer in the United States Army and was surrendered by
Twiggs in Texas. He then resigned his commission in the army, and entered the
Confederate service. See page 4045. Also *Ibid.*, series 2, VIII, 527.

[69] Boggs, *op. cit.*, 24. Kelley, *op. cit.*, 37-38. Ransom, *op. cit.*, 71.

flour and baked bread to sell while some of the prisoners opened complete restaurants.[70] Prisoners were allowed to retain their money, although large amounts were held by the officers in charge of the prison and issued to them in monthly amounts, the prisoners receiving the benefit of the exchange premium.[71] They were permitted to receive boxes[72] from home. From July to November the Sanitary Commission sent to Andersonville 5,000 sheets, 7,000 pairs of drawers, 4,000 handkerchiefs, 600 shirts, 2,000 blouses, 4,000 pairs of pants, together with hats, overcoats, blankets, shoes, canned milk, coffee, farina, cornstarch, and tobacco in corresponding quantities.[73] But purchases and gifts, valuable though they were, could not overcome the deleterious effects of the crowded prison, the stinking swamp, lack of shelter and clothing, and improper conditions.

On May 22, because of the crowded stockade and the raiding propensities of the prisoners, who, Surgeon White declared, "refuse assistance to a dying comrade under the same blanket,"[74] the hospital was moved from the stockade to a site a few hundred yards away. Here in a parallelogram two hundred and sixty by three hundred and forty feet, with shade trees and good drinking water, there was room for eight hundred sick. Equipped with two hundred and nine small picket tents and flies, the accommodations were crowded with 1,020 of the worst cases. In addition to the crowds, White experienced considerable difficulty in procuring medicines. Requisitions had to be made to the medical director at Atlanta, while the medicines came from the government laboratories at Macon. The delay caused by this red tape resulted in hardship at the prison and led to White's making a request that he be allowed to requisition the medical purveyor at Macon direct. The only remedies obtainable at

---

[70] Hyde, op. cit., 218. Official Records, series 2, VII, 755-62. Davidson, op. cit., 157-65.

[71] Official Records, series 2, VII, 460-61, 198-99.

[72] Page, op. cit., 71. Davidson, op. cit., 178-79.

[73] Report on Treatment of Prisoners of War, 207.

[74] Official Records, series 2 ,VII, 170-71.

Macon were herbs; the blockade cut off all drug supplies.[75]

The principal diseases from which the prisoners suffered were bowel complaints, dysentery and diarrhoea, combined with scurvy.[76] Since only the worst cases could be admitted to the hospital, many prisoners suffered and died from these diseases within the stockade. The food which the prisoners received, particularly the cornbread made from unbolted meal, tended to increase these diseases of the digestive organs. The husks in the meal acted as an irritant to the bowels. Sick within the stockade were eventually housed in barracks but could receive no medical attention.

The stream which flowed through the hospital served as a sink and was loaded with excrement. "I observed a large pile of cornbread, bones, filth of all kinds, thirty feet in diameter and several feet in height, swarming with myriads of flies, in a vacant space near the pots used for cooking," reported Surgeon Jones. Mosquitoes infested the tents and "many of the patients were so stung . . . that they resembled . . . a slight attack of measles."

The police of the hospital was defective. The attendants, prisoners released on parole for this service, "seemed to have but little interest in the welfare of their fellow captives. I heard a sick and wounded Federal prisoner accuse his nurse, a fellow prisoner of the United States Army, of having stealthily, during his sleep, inoculated his wounded arm with gangrene, that he might destroy his life and fall heir to his clothing." The attendants neglected to clean their patients; rags used for bandage of wounds affected with gangrene were used several times without washing.[77]

[75] *Ibid.*, 386-87, 430. Hyde, *op. cit.*, 245.

[76] *Official Records*, series 2, VII, 426-27.

[77] "The manner of disposing of the dead was also calculated to depress the already desponding spirits of these men . . . . whose strength had been wasted by bad air, bad food, and neglect of personal cleanliness. The deadhouse is merely a frame covered with an old tent cloth and a few bushes, situated in the southwest corner of the hospital grounds. When a patient dies, he is simply laid in the narrow street in front of his tent, until he is removed by the Federal Negroes detailed to carry off the dead. . . . In the deadhouse the corpses lie upon the bare ground, and are in most cases covered with filth and vermin." Jones Report, *Official Records*, series 2, VIII, 588-632. Chipman, *op. cit.*, 83-97.

The hospital staff attached to the prison consisted of but thirteen surgeons at a time when there were twenty-six thousand prisoners at the post.[78] This deficiency in staff prevented medical attention to the sick within the stockade. Chandler reported that at sick call only the stronger were able to get to the physician and many were carried out daily who had died without ever having been seen by a surgeon. Those who died within the stockade were carried to a deadhouse similar to that in the hospital, their fingers, according to Chandler, having first been mutilated by the prisoners to remove their rings.[79]

With conditions such as these, it is not surprising that more than twelve thousand graves of Federal prisoners were dug at Andersonville during the year that it was occupied as a prison. In March, 1864, 283 prisoners died out of the 7,500 confined there. In April, 576 died; in May, 708; June, 1,201; July, 1,817; August, 2,993; September, 2,677; October, 1,595; November, 499; December, 165; January (1865), 197; February, 147; March, 108; April, 28.[80]

More impressive even than the number of deaths in the prison is the number of cases treated. During the six months from March 1 to August 31, 42,686 cases of disease and wounds were reported.[81] The only prisoners who were able to escape some sickness were those who were paroled for work in connection with the routine affairs of the prison. At the first, prisoners were detailed to work on the buildings about the post;[82] Captain Winder established a shoeshop to manu-

---

[78] *Official Records*, series 2, VII, 426-27.

[79] *Ibid.*, 546-53.

[80] *Official Records*, series 2, VII, 541-45, 708. The figures from September, 1864 to April, 1865 are taken from Chipman, *op cit.*, 375. These are possibly higher than the actual deaths as Chipman was trying to account for some two hundred and fifty prisoners whose records were lost and whom he supposed to have died and been buried without a record being kept. Every writer on Andersonville attempts to give figures and often they lose themselves in the mazes of their own guess-work. There are 12,912 graves at the National Cemetery at Andersonville of prisoners who died while in prison. See Ransom, *op. cit.*, 287-88. The list of names and graves was published by the New York *Tribune*, in 1865 and by the quartermaster's department as General Order No. 69½.

[81] Jones Report, above.   [82] *Official Records*, series 2, VI, 1028.

facture boots for the army from the hides of cattle killed for the prisoners.[83] Some prisoners were employed by citizens of the locality to work for them,[84] but some of the people objected to the paroled prisoners' being allowed to travel over the country, fearing that they would give information to raiding parties of the enemy.[85] Prisoners who did escape from the prison—paroled prisoners having the best chance of fleeing from their miseries—were hunted down by bloodhounds and generally recaptured by this means.[86]

On August 9 a severe rain caused the creek to rise and break away part of the stockade. The rain and rising water cleaned the ground of the accumulation of human excrement which polluted it and, while it caused the shelterless prisoners to suffer, produced a better sanitary condition within the stockade for a time. The stream, following the storm, was sluiced, which aided a more adequate drainage. The most important result of the storm, however, appeared on the morning of August 10. It was found that the rain had cut a channel beneath a stump, just inside the deadline, and this had developed a spring of pure fresh water, which, supplemented by several other and smaller springs which broke out as the result of the storm, gave the prisoners a better supply of water than had hitherto been obtained from the polluted stream and the few wells which had been dug.[87]

[83] *Ibid.*, series 2, VII, 56, 181-82, 402-3.

[84] *Ibid.*, 215.   [85] *Ibid.*, 436-37.

[86] Kellogg, *op. cit.*, 64 ff. Much was made of this use of dogs by the prison authorities. The owner of the dogs moved close to the prison and was paid for each prisoner whom he brought in. Wirz was convicted of killing escaped prisoners with these dogs.

[87] To the prisoners, whose need for water had been met in this way, the appearance of the spring bore all of the evidence of a miraculous intervention of superhuman agencies. The spring was named "Providence Spring." To a group of religious enthusiasts within the prison, led by "Boston" Corbett—later famous as the slayer of Wilkes Booth—the appearance of the spring was a direct answer to prayers which they had offered for water. *Official Records*, series 2, VII, 583-84. Urban, *op. cit.*, 210. Kelley, *op. cit.*, 61-62. Page, *op. cit.*, 140-41. These give the best accounts. Maile, *Prison Life at Andersonville*, has written to prove that the spring was a direct answer to prayer. Miss Mildred Rutherford says that the spring existed before the prison, but was clogged by washing rains and was opened by the storm. See "True History of Andersonville," in Miss Rutherford's *Scrap Book*, II, June, 1924.

This alleviation of the discomforts of prison life was accompanied by another. Despite Colonel Chandler's statements that Winder favored allowing the prisoners to remain in Andersonville until death diminished their ranks to a number which could be cared for, the General was fully aware of the conditions and was attempting to change them. Although General Winder continued to maintain, as he had maintained in Richmond, that the crowded condition of the prisons was not the cause of the heavy mortality, he attempted to move the prisoners from Andersonville. While considering several suggested sites a raid from Sherman's army, defeated before it reached Andersonville, impressed upon the prison officials the need for haste.[88] A few days after the raid, Winder commissioned his son, who had located Andersonville, and another officer, to seek a new prison site. They were ordered to rent the land, secure water privileges, and obtain the use of timber and near-by houses.[89] On August 5, these officers reported the selection of a site near Millen, Georgia, on the Augusta railroad;[90] and General Winder, again asking for the power to impress labor, teams, and sawmills, was instructed to hire the work done.[91] Winder sent an officer to begin the construction of a stockade.[92]

As it became obvious that Sherman's army would take Atlanta, Seddon urged Winder to hasten the preparations for removing the prisoners from Andersonville.[93] On September 5, orders came to send the prisoners away immediately. Since the prison at Millen was not completed, the prisoners were removed, despite the protests of the commanders at those places, to Charleston and Savannah.[94] Seddon explained that he was compelled to send the prisoners where he could, but promised that other arrangements would be made soon.[95]

[88] *Official Records*, series 2, VII, 463, 467, 469, 471, 473, 476. See Kelley, *op. cit.*, 59-61 for Stoneman's raid. *Official Records*, series 2, VII, 483.

[89] *Ibid.*, 509.   [91] *Ibid.*, 565.

[90] *Ibid.*, 546.   [92] *Ibid.*, 593.

[93] *Ibid.*, 678.

[94] *Ibid.*, 773. McElroy, *op. cit.*, 396. Kellogg, *op. cit.*, 210. Abbott, *op. cit.*, 205. Boggs, *op. cit.*, 46-47. Glazier, *op. cit.*, 347.

[95] *Official Records*, series 2, VII, 788-89, 805, 817, 795.

The prisoners in Charleston were crowded into the yard of the city jail where the ground soon became filthy with the overflowing sinks and the vermin which had shared the exodus from Andersonville.[96] The rations, however, were superior to any they had received for months. Wheat bread, rice, hominy, flour, beans, soap, salt, and molasses were issued to them, and after their release the prisoners looked back on Charleston as the "oasis" of their prison experiences. Aiding this sentiment were the visits of the Sisters of Charity of Charleston who came among them distributing gifts to the well and bestowing care and medicines upon the sick.[97] Many of the prisoners worked on the fortifications about the city and received better rations,[98] while the proximity to the Union lines led General Foster to send supplies of food and clothing to them.[99]

These conditions were not to last. Hardly had the prisoners arrived in Charleston than General Jones sent an officer to prepare a stockade at Florence, South Carolina, where the prisoners could be sent.[100] Yellow fever broke out in the city threatening the prisoners, and Jones protested that he had no guards.[101] September 13, Secretary Seddon ordered Winder to send no more prisoners to Charleston but to put them in the stockade at Millen.[102] The commissary officers sent to Florence reported that the accommodations there would not be sufficient for a large number of prisoners,[103] but Jones removed all of the prisoners from Charleston as fast as they arrived.[104] The last prisoners left Charleston October 8.

The prisoners found at Florence a prison which recalled to their minds their experiences at Andersonville. Twenty-three acres were enclosed by a stockade against whose outer side a mound of earth had been raised to form a guard walk.

---

[96] Glazier, op. cit., 146. Isham, Prisoners of War, etc., 67.
[97] Moran, Bastiles of the Confederacy, 101-2. Kellogg, op. cit., 297-99. McElroy, op. cit., 528. Goss, op. cit., 189-216.
[98] Boggs, op. cit., 48.
[99] Official Records, series 2, VII, 874-75, 886, 890, 900.
[100] Ibid., 817.
[101] Ibid., 805.
[102] Ibid., 821.
[103] Ibid., 825.
[104] Ibid., 837, 838, 846.

The ditch from which this earth had been taken was sufficiently deep to prevent tunnels. A bolder stream of water
flowed through this prison, but the Andersonville swamp was
duplicated here. Sickness and death continued at rates rival-
ing those of the former prison. October 12 there were
12,362 prisoners at Florence of whom eight hundred were
sick in the hospital. Diarrhoea and scurvy carried off from
twenty to fifty a day. The hospital, built of branches of trees
and situated within the stockade, gave protection from the
heat but not from the rain. Well prisoners and sick received
the army ration of one-fourth pound of meat or its equivalent in peas or rice, and three gills of molasses, but it was
impossible for the commissary to obtain the molasses. Meat
was seldom issued.[105]

The prisoners sent to Savannah were quartered in a stockade on the grounds of the old United States Marine Hospital.
As at Charleston the prisoners received treatment far excel-
ling their experiences in Andersonville. The food was better,
and their quarters were tents. There are but two graves of
Federal prisoners at this place. But Savannah was open to
the same objections as Charleston, and October 10, the prisoners were removed to the prison at Millen.[106]

The lack of a power to impress labor for the construction
of the prison at Millen and the more serious lack of funds[107]
prevented the occupation of the prison until early October.
All of the prisoners except those unable to travel were removed from Andersonville, which was stripped of its arma-
ment and equipment for the new prison.[108]

The prison at Millen followed the customary style in
prison architecture in the South. The stockade, 1,398 by

[105] Kellogg, op. cit., 312. Official Records, series 2, VII, 972-74, 854-55, 976-79,
1086-87, 1097-1100. Abbott, op. cit., 205 ff. Boggs, op. cit., 48-54, Kellogg, op. cit.,
310-16, 350. McElroy, op. cit., 547-48. Goss, op. cit., 216-29. Creelman, op. cit.,
17-30.

[106] Ransom, op. cit., 93-109. Report on Treatment of Prisoners of War, 164.
McElroy, op. cit., 420-30. Urban, op. cit., 573-79. Kelley, op. cit., 72-74.

[107] Winder to Cooper, September 21, asked for $250,000, declaring that Captain
R. B. Winder did not have a cent for materials and tools. Official Records, series 2,
VII, 854.

[108] Ibid., 869.

1,329 feet, enclosed forty-two acres which Winder declared
to be the largest prison in the world. The stream running
through was large, and there was no swamp. A ditch carried
water from the stream beneath the sinks and insured adequate
removal of the ordure. The ground was divided by streams
sixteen feet wide, into thirty-two parts, each of which was
designed for a thousand men and was further subdivided into
ten sections. This arrangement promised to obviate the disorder of Andersonville and render easier the police of the
camp.[109] Wood left within the stockade enabled the prisoners to construct comfortable huts for themselves.[110] Rations
received by the prisoners here were comparable to those received at Andersonville,[111] the baking and cooking arrangements not being completed when the prisoners arrived.[112]
The sick were poorly supplied with medicine and those who
were able to travel from Andersonville found their condition
only slightly improved.[113] The hospital arrangements were
hastened to completion, but the equipment was inadequate
for the seven hundred sick who came from the older prison.[114]
During the first month at Millen there were 486 deaths
among the 10,299 prisoners confined there.[115]

On November 17, a raid from Sherman's lines forced the
abandonment of the prison at Millen.[116] The prisoners were
removed to Blackshear, and Thomasville, Georgia, while
plans, not effected until January, were being made for returning them to Andersonville.[117]

With these migrations of the prisoners, searching always
for a place where they could be secure from raids, General

[109] Ibid., 881.
[110] McElroy, op. cit., 455-56. Kelley, op. cit., 75-76. Urban, op. cit., 583.
[111] McElroy, op. cit., 458. Urban, op. cit., 585. Kelley, op. cit., 76. Glazier,
op. cit., 317-18.
[112] Official Records, series 2, VII, 955-56.
[113] Kelley, op. cit., 77.
[114] Official Records, series 2, VII, 993-94.
[115] Ibid., 1113-14.
[116] Ibid., series 1, XLIV, 862, series 2, VII, 1140, 1144, 1148, 1155. Urban,
op. cit., 600-601.
[117] Urban, op. cit., 603. McElroy, op. cit., 490-500, 532 ff. Official Records,
series 2, VII, 1204, 1220, 1238-39, 1258, 1262, 1286. Hyde, op. cit., 327.

Winder eventually grew tired and recommended that all officers and men whose terms had expired should be sent on parole across the lines. He believed that the laws of war would authorize such an action.[118]

Late in January the commander of the prison at Florence announced that the rations of the prisoners were barely sufficient to prevent starvation. There had been but two issues of meat in two months. The commissary-general endorsed this report with the statement that he could get no money from the treasury and the rations of the prisoners would have to be subjected to a further reduction.[119] General Beauregard recommended that the Florence prisoners be removed to southwest Georgia,[120] but Winder pronounced this impractical because he did not have the troops with which to guard the prisoners while moving them.[121]

Happily, before a new movement began, news came of the success of Ould in arranging an exchange; so the prisoners were sent to Wilmington to be handed over to the Federal commander at that place.[122]

[118] *Official Records*, series 2, VII, 1304.   [121] *Ibid.*, 184.
[119] *Ibid.*, series 2, VIII, 137-39.   [122] *Ibid.*, 449-57.
[120] *Ibid.*, 172.

CHAPTER VIII

OTHER SOUTHERN PRISONS
1864-1865

Although after the war Andersonville came to be regarded as the typical Southern prison—so much so that the other prisons were lost from sight—it was not the only place within the Confederacy where prisoners of war were confined in 1864-65. Prisoners were held at Danville[1] and in a cotton warehouse at Cahaba, Alabama,[2] until April, when they were removed to Andersonville. The prison at Salisbury continued in existence throughout the war, mostly for political prisoners and Yankee deserters, although prisoners of war were sent there in October, 1864.[3]

Aside from Andersonville, the most important of the Southern prisons, however, was the officers' prison at Macon and its successors elsewhere. Officers remained in Richmond after the noncommissioned officers and enlisted men were removed to Andersonville. Early in May they were sent to Macon, Georgia, where General Howell Cobb had prepared a prison for them.[4] The stockade constructed here was built of twelve-foot planks and enclosed three acres on the banks of a stream. Outside the stockade a plank walk enabled the guards to survey the prisoners while five cannon commanded the interior of the prison. In the center of the area a small

[1] See Boggs, *Eighteen Months under the Rebel Flag*, 11 ff. Davidson, *Fourteen Months*, 82-105. Hyde, *Captive of War*, 113 ff. *Official Records*, series 2, VI, 888-90.

[2] *Official Records*, series 2, VI, 1124. An excellent account of this prison, from the standpoint of an inmate, is Hawes, *Cahaba, A Story of Captive Boys in Blue*, New York, 1888. See also Walker, *Cahaba Prison and the Sultana Disaster*.

[3] Glazier, *The Capture, the Prison Pen, and the Escape*, 323-28. The experiences of the two correspondents of the New York *Tribune* confined in Salisbury during these months are related in Richardson, *The Secret Service, the Field, the Dungeon, and the Escape*, and Browne, *Four Years in Secessia*. Cf. also "History and Tabular Statement of Salisbury Prison" in the archives of the war department.

[4] *Official Records*, series 2, VII, 106, 168. Byers, *What I Saw in Dixie*, 31-34. Roach, *Prisoner of War*, 123-24. Glazier, *op. cit.*, 101-5. Cooper, *In and Out of Rebel Prisons*, 48 ff. Drake, *Narrative of Capture*, 6-8.

building was left standing and this served as a hospital and as quarters for the generals who were among the officers.[5] The prisoners were permitted to build shelter for themselves from refuse boards left from the building of the stockade, and the officers in charge of the prison brought into the enclosure lumber and building material from which the prisoners constructed other shelter. However, the supply was inadequate, and many of the officers were forced to burrow in the ground or to make tents from their blankets.[6]

The rations which the prisoners received at Macon were superior to those which had been issued to them in Richmond. The customary issues of cornmeal which retained the husks, bacon which the prisoners agreed was both rancid and full of maggots, and beans which they averred to be mostly bugs, together with salt, vinegar, and "watery" soup were given them. The amounts, always too small in the prisoners' eyes, were the same as those received by the guards. In addition, the customary sutler's stand was opened where the prisoners with money could purchase vegetables.[7]

One of the greatest defects in the rations resulted from the lack of vessels in which they could be received. Since the rations were issued for five-day periods to squads of one hundred men a considerable problem ensued in finding proper containers. To each squad of one hundred was issued five iron skillets with covers, fifteen without covers, ten tin pails of six-quart capacity, ten smaller pails, and five wooden buckets. Despite an equipment which at Andersonville

[5] *Official Records,* series 2, VII, 169. Abbott, *Prison Life in the South,* 61. *Report on the Treatment of Prisoners of War,* 162. Isham, Davidson, and Furness, *Military Prisons and Prisoners of War,* 41-43. Glazier, *op. cit.,* 110-11. Cooper, *op. cit.,* 51. Roach, *op. cit.,* 127. Domschcke, *Zwanzig Monate,* 112 ff.

[6] Glazier, *op. cit.,* 114. Cooper, *op. cit.,* 78-79. Abbott, *op. cit.,* 62.

[7] Isham, etc., *op. cit.,* 43. Cooper, *op. cit.,* 57-58. Roach, *op. cit.,* 129. New York *Times,* July 22. Prisoners were allowed to draw from Captain R. B. Winder, quartermaster here as well as at Andersonville, money which had been in their possession at the time of their capture. This money was transferred from the quartermaster at Richmond to Winder when the prisoners were removed. *Official Records,* series 2, VII, 416. A monthly limit of one hundred dollars in Confederate currency was placed on such issues, but the prisoners were allowed the premium accruing in exchanging United States for Confederate money. *Ibid.,* 158-59. Also series 2, VI, 962.

would have appeared princely, the prisoners were obliged to receive their rations of rice and cornmeal in the legs of drawers while soap was received on chips. A few axes were available at the camp, and two prisoners from each mess of twenty were permitted daily to go out to cut and carry in an armload of wood.[8]

As the officers confined in Macon were not more than fifteen hundred in number, they escaped the unhealthy condition of Andersonville. Scurvy and diarrhoea were present to some extent, but never to the extent that hospital facilities greater than those available in the small building within the stockade had to be provided.[9]

If the prisoners could not complain overmuch of their rations, of crowding and sickness, they were, nevertheless, able to develop a firm conviction that the Confederate authorities sought to hasten their early demise. The platitude that no prisoner loves his jailor was exemplified in the attitude of the prisoners toward Captain W. Kent Tabb, the commandant of the prison. After Tabb had discovered several tunnels, he mounted cannon where they could command the interior of the stockade.[10] In addition to this evidence of the cruel intentions of Captain Tabb, he was convicted by public opinion within the prison of deliberate robbery. The story went the rounds of the prison of how a Captain Frank Irich of New York entrusted to Tabb a watch to be sold for four hundred dollars. No reports of the sale having been obtained by the owner, the prisoner accosted Tabb with a demand for the watch or the money. Tabb told him that he had sold the watch for two hundred dollars. Then when Irich asked why Tabb was wearing the chain he was told that the purchaser had given it to the commander.

[8] Abbott, *op. cit.*, 62 ff. Roach, *op. cit.*, 129. Ferguson, *Life Struggles in Rebel Prisons*, 92 .

[9] Glazier, *op. cit.*, 124, 127, related that he had scurvy and that it was quite prevalent. Few other writers mention sickness at Macon. As for the number of prisoners confined here Captain Gibbs mentioned, June 16, that there were a thousand (*Official Records*, 2, VII, 372-73) and June 26 he formally reported 1400. (*Ibid.*, 418-19). Domschcke, *op. cit.*, 131 ff., reported much scurvy.

[10] Cooper, *op. cit.*, 85 ff.

The result was that Irich threatened to expose the commandant and was bucked and gagged for his words—but the watch
was returned.[11] Occasional shots were fired at prisoners near
the deadline and the prisoners here as at Andersonville believed that the sentinel who killed a prisoner was promoted
and given a furlough.[12] The suffering of their men at Andersonville, reported to the officers by Father Hamilton, convinced them that their own sufferings were but a part of a
deliberate policy of cruelty adopted by the Confederacy.[13]
When General Winder took control of the prison, he became
to the prisoners the arch-fiend who directed all of the sufferings which they experienced.[14]

The removal of the prisoners from Richmond and their
location in scattered posts brought the Confederate authorities to a sense of the need of a unified control over the prisoners. As long as they were in Richmond, General Winder,
acting in charge of the department of the Henrico, and the
secretary of war, to whom they were consigned by law, had
the control over the prisoners. When they were removed to
Georgia, General Winder continued in control but without
general control over the confinement and treatment of prisoners. Because Ould, commissioner of exchange, kept the
records of his office apart from those kept by Winder, conflicts
arose between the two officers.[15] Though suggestions were
made that a commissary-general of prisoners be appointed,
with a bureau in which both Ould and the commissary-
general could use the same records,[16] no steps were taken
toward this end, but Winder, having charge also of the prison
at Macon, was ordered to Andersonville. Brigadier General

[11] Practically every account of the Macon prison relates this story. See Glazier,
op. cit., 118-19. Abbott, *op. cit.*, 70. Byers, *op. cit.*, 34. Cooper, *op. cit.*, 61. Roach,
op. cit., 128-29 Domschcke, *op. cit.*, 127-28. Ferguson, *op. cit.*, 98. Langworthy,
Reminiscences of a Prisoner of War, 21 ff., has Lieutenant Davis take the watch.
Prutsman, *A Soldier's Experience.*

[12] Glazier, *op. cit.*, 113-20. Drake, *Narrative*, 8.

[13] Abbott, *op. cit.*, 72 ff. Drake, *Narrative*, 9.

[14] See for example Byers, *op. cit.*, 77 ff. Abbott, *op. cit.*, 172. McElroy, *Andersonville*, 561-66. Domschcke, *op. cit.*, 195. Spencer, *Narrative of Andersonville*, 44.

[15] *Diary of a Rebel War Clerk*, II, 154. See Jones.

[16] *Official Records*, series 2, VII, 172-74.

William M. Gardner assumed control over affairs in Richmond and received the reports on prisons which were formerly made to Winder.[17] General Gardner, however, was unable to learn what his duties were, what authority he exercised, or even where the prisons were located.[18] Late in July orders were issued assigning General Winder to the control of prisons in Georgia and Alabama, and Brigadier General Gardner to all of the prisons east of the Mississippi.[19]

Prior to Winder's arrival in Georgia, General Sam Jones, commanding at Charleston, requested that he be allowed to take fifty prisoners, including a general, from the prison at Macon and confine them in Charleston. Since the enemy were shelling the city from Morris Island and property was being destroyed, he thought that by placing the prisoners in the exposed part of the city the property might be saved. Secretary Seddon approved this action, and June 9, orders were issued to General Cobb to furnish Jones with the prisoners he requested.[20] When General Foster on Morris Island protested against this use of prisoners, Jones declared that they were not sent to be fired upon. After this assurance Jones and Foster arranged to exchange the officers for hostages who had been sent to the latter on Morris Island.[21]

Within a month after Winder's arrival in Georgia, he became convinced of the necessity of removing the prisoners from Macon. In June a riot of the prisoners was frustrated by the inadequate guard only because a secret warning had been given the commanders.[22] The prison at Macon was within a few hundred yards of three railroad depots and several workshops. The already inefficient guard was rendered worse by their post in a large town. The location was

[17] *Ibid.*, 213-14, 400.   [18] *Ibid.*, 490-91.

[19] *Ibid.*, 501-2. Camp Ford near Tyler, Texas, the principal prison west of the Mississippi, seems to have been completely outside the control of the Richmond authorities.

[20] *Official Records*, series 2, VII, 185, 216-17.

[21] A long correspondence between the generals over the subject of the confinement of the prisoners in Charleston is given in *Official Records*, series 1, XXXV, Part ii, 135, *passim*. See *Ibid.*, series 2, VII, 371.

[22] *Ibid.*, 372-73.

unhealthy for both guard and prisoners.[23] Winder urged that the prisoners be sent to Charleston where Jones had already taken some of the officers.[24] A raid by Stoneman settled matters, and, despite the protests of Jones, six hundred were sent to Charleston late in July,[25] while the remainder of the Macon prisoners were sent to Savannah.[26]

The prisoners found Savannah the best prison of their experience. Here, confined in the yard of the United States Marine Hospital, tents were issued to the men, shade trees protected them from the sun, and rations of one pint of cornmeal, one pound of beef, one gill of rice, and occasionally flour were issued and cooking utensils supplied.[27]

The prisoners moved from Savannah to Charleston in September believed that they, like the first who had been sent to the city, were designed for hostages to protect the city,[28] and this belief was shared by General Foster who requested that six hundred prisoners from Fort Delaware be sent to Morris Island to be treated exactly as were the prisoners in Charleston.[29] Placed at first in the yard of the city jail, which the prisoners described as the filthiest place of their experience,[30] the prisoners were offered a better prison if they would give paroles not to attempt to escape. Most of them accepted this proposition and were moved to the Roper Hospital from which they might obtain passes to the town.[31] Here the Sisters of Charity, later to prove ministering angels to the men from Andersonville, cared for the sick among them.[32]

[23] *Ibid.*, 418, 472.   [24] *Ibid.*, 463.

[25] Isham, etc., *op. cit.*, 60-61.

[26] *Official Records*, series 2, VII, 60-61. Abbott, *op. cit.*, 84 ff. Byers, *op. cit.*, 49-51. Cooper, *op. cit.*, 107-8.

[27] Isham, etc., *op. cit.*, 61 ff. Glazier, *op. cit.*, 132-33. Abbott, *op. cit.*, 86-87. Domschcke, *op. cit.*, 139-52. Ferguson, *op. cit.*, 113-22. Drake, *Narrative*, 10-12.

[28] Glazier, *op. cit.*, 150 ff.

[29] *Official Records*, series 2, VII, 597-98, 625, *passim*. See Dunkle, *Prison Life During the Rebellion,* and for an account of the treatment of these hostages on Morris Island, Murray, *The Immortal Six Hundred.*

[30] Abbott, *op. cit.*, 104 ff. Cooper, *op. cit.*, 115. Ferguson, *op. cit.*, 128 ff.

[31] Abbott, *op. cit.*, 112 ff. Byers, *op. cit.*, 52.

[32] Cooper, *op. cit.*, 119-20.

The arrival of the first detachment of prisoners had been opposed by General Jones, but when in September there arrived also the officers who had been at Savannah and the men from Andersonville, he determined to remove the prisoners on his own responsibility. When moved to Charleston the prisoners came under the control of General Gardner,[33] but Jones planned to remove the men to Florence and the officers to Columbia, South Carolina, furnishing for the latter prison four or five hundred reserve troops as a guard. It was his intention to use an island near the state capital for the confinement of the prisoners.[34] The threatened epidemic of yellow fever in the city hastened action;[35] Winder was ordered to remove the men to Millen, and, while no mention was made of the officers,[36] Jones dispatched an officer to Columbia to select a site for the officers' prison.[37]

Early in October the officers were moved to Columbia where for a night they were kept in an open field exposed to a drenching rain. The next day they were asked to give their paroles not to escape from the prison to which they were to be moved. Despite the glowing descriptions of the proposed place, which the officers of the inefficient and inadequate guard held out to them, the prisoners wisely decided to see the location before making any promises.[38]

The wisdom of the prisoners' decision became apparent when they arrived at the site of the prison. It consisted of an open field without trees or buildings. Wood, water, and the sinks were outside the lines of the guards which marked the boundaries of the prison. The prisoners were furnished with eight axes and ten shovels to build their quarters. Since there were twelve hundred of them this supply of tools was not sufficient. The sutler had axes for sale at fifty dollars each. A few weeks after their arrival a beginning was made

[33] *Official Records*, series 2, VII, 782-83.
[34] *Ibid.*, 817.
[35] *Ibid.*, 825.
[36] *Ibid.*, 866.
[37] *Ibid.*, 894.
[38] Roach, *op. cit.*, 140-41. Byers, *op. cit.*, 62. Abbott, *op. cit.*, 124-32. Cooper, *op. cit.*, 126. Ferguson, *op. cit.*, 143 ff.

in building barracks for the winter.[39] Rations here were chiefly distinguished by large issues of sorghum molasses and the prison became known as "Camp Sorghum."[40]

The wisdom of the prisoners in declining to give paroles not to escape was further proved by the large number of escapes from Columbia. The guard force was notoriously inadequate for securing the prisoners, who did not even have a fence about them, and escapes were easily accomplished. The most common method of escape was to pass out of the guard line with a group who had given their paroles to go after wood or water,[41] although others passed out by bribing the guards or rushing the lines.[42]

The prisoners who escaped generally started for Knoxville once they were beyond the lines of the guards. This route, although longer, was deemed safer than to turn towards the Union lines at Augusta.[43] The problem of finding food for their journey as well as that of finding their way was solved by the negroes of the region who undertook to guide the prisoners and to furnish them with supplies. The fleeing men were passed from hand to hand by the negroes who guided them over obscure trails, hid them from white eyes during the day, and shared with them not only their food but the rude comfort of their cabins. "It would have been impossible . . . to make an escape without the aid of negroes, . . ." declared one prisoner.[44] In addition to the negroes' aid, help was received from Unionists in the country who hid the fugitives in their houses and furnished encouragement, clothing, food, and negro guides to take them to other citizens farther along the route whose sympathies were with the prisoners' cause. Conscripts hiding in the mountains from the agents of the conscription bureau welcomed the Yankees and

[39] Abbott, *op. cit.*, 132 ff. Glazier, *op. cit.*, 180-81. Hunt, "My Escape from Camp Sorghum" 2 ff. Roach, *op cit.*, 171. *Report on the Treatment of Prisoners of War*, 199. Ferguson, *op. cit.*, 144-47.

[40] Glazier, *op. cit.*, 178-79. Isham, etc., *op. cit.*, 74-75.

[41] Hunt, *op. cit.*, 5. Isham, etc., *op. cit.*, 79-81.

[42] Cooper, *op. cit.*, 130 ff.

[43] Glazier, *op. cit.*, 202-3.

[44] *Ibid.*, 219.

gave them directions for passing out of the country. Members
of the "Loyal League" in Charleston and other cities hid
escaping prisoners, and Richardson and Browne, correspondents of the New York *Tribune*, escaping from Salisbury, discovered that the "Sons of America" was an organization
especially formed to assist Union men, prisoners, and refugees in escaping to the North. In the mountains of North
Carolina and Tennessee guides made a regular business of
conducting such persons to Knoxville.[45]

Although it was estimated that 75 per cent of the 373
prisoners who escaped from Columbia were recaptured,[46] the
great number of escapes gave force to the protests of Governor Bonham against the prisoners' being sent to his capital.
As early as Stoneman's raid, General Gardner had recommended that a prison be established at Columbia,[47] but feeble
efforts, blocked by the lack of labor and supplies, had resulted in no actual progress. In the latter part of September
Gardner was ordered to begin the construction of a prison
there.[48] When Governor Bonham had protested against this
establishment, Gardner referred him to an engineer officer
who had been sent to Columbia to select the site of the
prison.[49]

This difficulty with Bonham was complicated by the action
of General Jones in hastily removing the prisoners from

[45] *Ibid.*, 194-310. Abbott, *op. cit.*, has chapters entitled "Among the Negroes,"
207-19, "In Search of Liberty," 219-39, "Escaped and Recaptured," 260-96, "Five
Weeks Among the Loyal League at Charleston," 296-303, "My Escape from Belle
Isle." See also Cooper, *op. cit.*, 150 ff., Hunt, *op. cit.*, and the chapters in Rich-
ardson's and Browne's accounts of their prison life. Other writers dealing with
escapes from Columbia and other prisons are: Dufur, *Over the Dead Line*, 164 ff.;
Johnson, *The Sword of Honor: From Captivity to Freedom*, 23 ff.; Bliss, *Prison
Life of Lieut. James M. Fales*, 53 ff.; Sabre, *Nineteen Months*, 150-62; Drake,
Narrative, 15-90; Hadley, *Seven Months a Prisoner*; Kellogg, *Capture and Escape*;
Langworthy, *op. cit.*; McCowan, *The Prisoner of War*, 43-55; Newlin, *Account of the
Escape of Six Federal Soldiers from Danville*; Doble, *Reminiscences of Prison Life
and Escape*; Drake, *Adventurous Escape*.
[46] Roach, *op. cit.*, 143, estimates that three hundred escaped. Winder reported
that 373 had escaped to December 6, *Official Records*, series 2, VII, 1196.
[47] *Ibid.*, 490-91.
[48] *Ibid.*, 870-72.
[49] *Ibid.*, 930, 975.

Charleston without consulting either Gardner or Bonham. It was a month after the establishment of the prison at Florence before Gardner knew that such a prison existed. When he learned of it and of Jones's interference he asked that he be relieved of all duties connected with prisoners. He alleged that his health was not good, the duties of the post of Richmond consumed all of his time, and the prison administration was of such a scope that it should be under the exclusive control of a competent man.[50] In addition to objecting to the interference of local commanders in the disposition of the prisoners, Gardner complained that the prisoners were relieved of their property at the time of their capture and the property turned over to the quartermaster. Then the prisoners were moved so often that their property could not keep up with them; often they were exchanged without their possessions accompanying them.[51]

This complaint led to instructions being given to draw up a scheme for the organization of the prison system.[52] Accordingly, November 21, General John H. Winder was made commissary-general of prisoners charged with the care of all prisoners east of the Mississippi. Departmental and army commanders were ordered not to interfere with his orders and arrangements. The commanders of prisons, responsible to General Winder only, were placed in command of the guard at their several posts.[53] Winder immediately took charge of the prisons, establishing his headquarters at Augusta, and ordering semimonthly reports sent from all of the prisons in the Confederacy.[54]

Winder immediately turned his attention to the construction of a prison at Columbia, where in spite of instructions from Davis to stop the work,[55] Gardner had used some impressed negroes to continue his preparations. He had decided on a location on the railroad between Columbia and Charlotte, North Carolina.[56] Winder, using Bonham's com-

[50] Ibid., 963-64, 972-74.
[51] Ibid., 986-87.
[52] Ibid., 1086-87
[53] Ibid., 1150.
[54] Ibid., 1193.
[55] Ibid., 1151.
[56] Ibid., 1188.

plaints of the large number of escapes from the prison in the field as an argument, received permission to use the grounds of a lunatic asylum as a temporary prison.[57] He continued the construction of the prison located by Gardner and planned to move the prisoners from Salisbury to the new prison which, with Andersonville and Millen, would make sufficient accommodations for all of the prisoners in the Confederacy.[58]

The crowded condition of the prison at Andersonville and the migrations of the prisoners from Macon had made it necessary for the prisons in Richmond to be reoccupied. By the end of September six thousand prisoners had accumulated on Belle Isle. The suffering of these prisoners because of the lack of shelter led to efforts to procure tents or building materials. The utmost endeavors of the authorities could locate but seventy-five tents, and lumber was not to be had. Such lumber as was already cut, together with all the products of the sawmills about Richmond, was needed to build and repair hospitals in the city. As a result of this failure to provide shelter, five hundred of the prisoners were sent to Danville [59] bringing the number in that prison to twenty-four hundred, its maximum. Early in October seventy-five hundred prisoners were sent to Salisbury, where there were already about eight hundred political and military prisoners. Hence Richmond held only a few hundred prisoners from recent captures and those awaiting special exchanges.[60]

Salisbury on a smaller scale reproduced all of the defects of Andersonville: there was a scarcity of water in the few wells which supplied the prison; no stream ran through the prison to carry off the ordure, and the stench became unbearable. The prison was within the town and could not be guarded without endangering the property and lives of the citizens; three shots struck a hotel during an attempted outbreak of the prisoners in November.[61] Wood was distant

[57] *Ibid.*, 1179-80, 1184.   [58] *Ibid.*, 1196-97.   [59] *Ibid.*, 870-72.
[60] *Ibid.*, 986-87. Cf. Booth, *Dark Days of the Rebellion*, 106 ff.
[61] For this outbreak see the Richmond *Enquirer*, November 28, and the *National Intelligencer*, December 2.

and the thirty-nine wagons impressed for the service could not bring in an adequate supply, while the one hundred cords needed daily for troops and prisoners cost a depleted treasury sixty thousand dollars a month. The eleven acres in the prison was insufficient room, and the red clay soil soon became a sea of mud. The rations—soup and twenty ounces of bread without meat or sorghum—were the same as issued to the troops on guard. The prisoners suffered also from the lack of clothing and quarters. Blankets and clothes received from the North were sold to the sutler for food; the failure of the wheat crop in the surrounding country made it impossible for the commissary to obtain flour; "muggers" among the prisoners robbed their fellows. The result of these conditions was disease and death. From October, 1864 to February, 1865, 3,479 prisoners died out of a total of 10,321 confined there.[62]

Because of these conditions General Winder planned to remove the prisoners as soon as he could obtain a safe place for them.[63] News of a fresh raid from East Tennessee contemplated by General Stoneman[64] hastened action, and on February 17, it was reported that there were but 5,476 prisoners there.[65] In March the need of the government for workshops led to the evacuation of the prison,[66] but at the same time a new site was sought where the expected prisoners of Johnston's army could be retained.[67] The failure of Johnston to make captures obviated the necessity for the new prison.

In the meantime General Winder at Columbia abandoned the original site chosen for a prison and planned a new one fourteen miles from the city. His plan was to purchase the site, so on January 1, 1865 he moved his headquarters to

---

[62] Citizens of Salisbury to Seddon. *Official Records, series* 2, VII, 1128-30. Winder to Cooper, *Ibid.*, 1219-21. Report of Major Hall, *Ibid.*, series 2, VIII, 245-55. See also Glazier, *op. cit.*, 324-26. Browne, *op. cit.*, 200 ff. Booth, *Dark Days of the Rebellion*, 106-350. McCowan, *The Prisoner of War*, 26. History and Tabular Statement of Salisbury Prison. War Department Archives.

[63] Official Records, series 2, VII, 1251; VIII, 11-12.

[64] *Ibid.*, series 2, VIII, 158. [66] *Ibid.*, 403, 411.

[65] *Ibid.*, 245. [67] *Ibid.*, 412-13.

Columbia.[68] But before the title to the site was reported upon, General Winder, February 7, succumbed to a heart attack before the tent of the sutler of the Florence prison.[69] In the place of General Winder, General G. W. Pillow was appointed commissary-general of prisoners; but he was almost immediately relieved,[70] and General Daniel Ruggles was appointed late in March.[71] Although exchanges of the prisoners were being made at Wilmington, Ruggles continued the construction of the new prison at Killian's Mills, fourteen miles from Columbia.[72] This prison was not built, but as late at April 7, 1865 Ruggles was preparing at Danville to receive the prisoners whom he expected from Lee's army near Appomattox.[73] The military collapse of the Confederacy prevented this prison from being used and put the builder, Ruggles, into a prison himself.

[68] *Ibid.*, series 2, VIII, 5, 83, 86.

[69] *Ibid.*, series 1, XLVII, part ii, 112. Prisoners who hated Winder, believing him the author of their sufferings, rejoiced at the news of his death. His last words, according to the prisoners, were: "Cut off the molasses, boys." See Byers, *op. cit.*, 77-78; Abbott, *op. cit.*, 172; McElroy, *Andersonville*, 561-66, with customary accuracy dates the death January 1, 1865. See also Domschcke, *op. cit.*, 195.

[70] *Official Records*, series 2, VIII, 205, 224, 421; series 1, XLVII, part ii, 1174, 1284, 1313.

[71] *Ibid.*, series 2, VIII, 427.

[72] *Ibid.*, 463-64.

[73] *Ibid.*, 478-79.

CHAPTER IX

WAR PSYCHOSIS AND THE
NORTHERN PRISONS

Apparently an inevitable concomitant of armed warfare is the hatred engendered in the minds of the contestants by the conflict. The spirit of patriotism which inspires men to answer the call of their country in its hour of need breeds within those men the fiercest antagonism toward that country's enemies. Such enmity finds its natural expression not only on the battlefield in the heat of conflict but also in the lives of the soldiers and the sentiment of the community from which they come, both of which have been thrown out of their accustomed peace-time routine by the outbreak of the war. The attachment to an ideal, a cause, or a country, when such attachment calls for the sacrifice of security and life, blinds the person feeling that attachment to whatever of virtue there may be in the opposing ideal, cause, or country. Seemingly, it becomes necessary for the supporters of one cause to identify their entire personality with that cause, to identify their opponents with the opposing cause, and to hate the supporters of the enemy cause with a venom which counterbalances their devotion to their own.

To a people actuated by such a devotion to a cause, it is inevitable that their opponents appear to be defective in all principles which are held dear by that people. The enemy becomes a thing to be hated; he does not share the common virtues, and his peculiarities of speech, race, or culture become significant as points of difference or, better, sins of the greater magnitude. The critical faculties, present to some degree in times of peace, atrophy on the approach of national catastrophe.

With such a state of mind coming as the natural result of the upheaval of the social order which the war produced, it was not difficult for credence to be gained for stories of atrocities committed by one or the other side in the Civil War. Immediately after the battle of Bull Run newspaper correspondents, on or near the field, sent accounts of the battle to their home papers. Throughout the loyal portion of the United States the defeat of the Union armies produced a depression which was fed by the stories of barbarities accompanying the correspondents' accounts. "Most shocking barbarities begin to be reported as practiced by the rebels upon the wounded and prisoners of the Union that fall into their hands. We are told of their slashing the throats of˙some from ear to ear; of their cutting off the heads of others and kicking them about as footballs; and of their setting up the wounded against trees and firing at them as targets or torturing them with plunges of bayonets into their bodies," commented the editor of an administration journal as he characterized the Confederates as "brutal robbers," "fighting as outlaws of civilization."[1] An illustrated weekly carried a full-page picture of rebels plunging their bayonets into the bodies of wounded soldiers.[2] "The Southern character," remarked the first paper, "is infinitely boastful, vainglorious, full of dash, without endurance, treacherous, cunning, timid, and revengeful."[3]

So far as prisons and prisoners of war were concerned, the attention of Northern newspapers, the fomenters and agents for the dissemination of this psychosis, was first directed toward obtaining an exchange for prisoners held in the Confederate prisons. The position of the government, that exchange would be tantamount to recognition, was characterized as absurd by the newspapers, whether they in general supported or opposed the administration.[4] However, the tendency of some papers to support the administration by saying, "In a war of this kind words are things. If we must

[1] New York *Times*, July 25, 1861.

[2] *Harper's Weekly*, August 17,. 1861, 525.

[3] New York *Times*, May 1, 1861. Cf. *National Intelligencer*, August 15 for denial of such stories.

[4] New York *Times*, August 1, 21; September 30; October 3. New York *News*, August 2, 19, 20. Cf. Ely, *Journal of Alfred Ely*, 50 ff, 68, 135.

address Davis as president of the Confederacy, we cannot exchange and the prisoners should not wish it,"[5] led the papers advocating exchange to advance a humanitarian argument. The sufferings of the prisoners in the South were emphasized,[6] and how prisoners were confined in close rooms, "whose poisoned atmosphere is slowly sapping their strength hour by hour," was often related.[7] The more sensational press gathered stories of bad food, cruel treatment, and utter destitution and predicted in the first months of the war that the Richmond tobacco warehouses would "rank with the British prison ships and the dungeons of the Revolution."[8]

Secretary Stanton, unwilling to give up the position of the administration in regard to exchanges and unable to resist the tide of opposition to the established policy, as his first official act as head of the war department, determined to send Bishop Ames and Hamilton Fish to Richmond to relieve the prisoners' sufferings.[9] This action had for the moment the desired effect of quieting opposition to the administration although it was believed that Mr. Ely should have been sent. Since there was some doubt that supplies which Ames and Fish might send would be delivered to the prisoners, the opinion was expressed "that the best way to supply the wants of our captive soldiers is to bring them home, even at the cost of releasing as many rebels." With this attitude of mind prevailing, the failure of the commissioners to get admission to Richmond was hailed as an "unexpected and most splendid success," and exchange was promised immediately.[10]

As this mission did not consummate the promised exchange, the organs of public opinion returned to their policy of exciting sympathy for the prisoners. Although it was declared that the treatment of prisoners in the South was not due to a vindictive spirit on the part of the Confederate

[5] *Harper's Weekly*, November 30, 1861.

[6] New York *News*, August 20.

[7] New York *Times*, September 30, 1861.

[8] *Harper's Weekly*, November 2, 1861.

[9] *Official Records*, series 2, III, 192, 213, 222-24, 236. See above, page 20.

[10] New York *Times*, January 25, 28, 1862, also January 30, February 15.

authorities, it was stated that they were unable to control the passions of the "drunken and ignorant hordes" of their army, and it was admitted that they did not possess the means to maintain a war prison. Under such conditions exaggerated accounts of outrages on unarmed prisoners by their brutal keepers were legion.[11]

In July an escaped quartermaster of an Iowa regiment reported to the governor of his state an account of his experiences in Montgomery and Selma, Alabama, and Macon, Georgia, which revealed that not everyone was willing to clear the rebels of vindictive feeling. He said that the two hundred and fifty officers who shared his confinement received less than one-fourth the rations of a private in the United States army "and are subjected to all the hardships and indignities which venomous traitors can heap upon them." The prisoners were confined "in a foul and vermin abounding cotton shed." At Tuscaloosa they were forbidden to leave the crowded room to go to the sinks at a time when diarrhoea was prevalent; at Montgomery the prisoners were destitute of clothing; and at both places the hospitals were denied medicines. Cornbread issued to the prisoners was made of unsifted meal and the meat at Montgomery was spoiled. Men were killed for looking out the window—"prohibiting them the poor privilege of looking at their mother earth."[12]

In the East, public opinion of rebel vindictiveness underwent a modification with the beginning of exchanges under the cartel. "It would not be fair to blame the rebels' vindictive spirit entirely," declared a newspaper correspondent, "but partly from that and partly from a lack of foods and medicines" the prisoners were suffering. A surgeon told a newspaper correspondent that in the wounds of many of the men there were enough maggots to fill a wine glass."[13]

As the vindictive spirit of the Confederates came to be more emphasized, the corollary proposition was developed that prisoners in the Northern prisons were accorded excel-

[11] *Harper's Weekly*, February 22 (picture on page 117).
[12] *Official Records*, series 2, IV, 230-32.
[13] New York *Times*, July 23, 1862.

lent treatment. "How different an example of humanity the North is setting," remarked this correspondent; and his paper, demanding exchange, declared that the rebel prisoners were growing stout. They were fed on capital food, given medicines, and fanned with cool breezes in the summer. Its readers were called upon to "think of the crowded and filthy tobacco warehouses, the brutal keepers, the sanguinary guards, the rotten food, the untended wounds, the unmedicined diseases, the miserable marches through the blazing South!" "What horrors has death on the battlefield to this?"[14] Under such pressure as this, the cartel was negotiated and prisoners began to be exchanged.[15]

Clinching evidence of the vindictiveness of the rebels came as a result of Davis' proclamation against General Pope and his officers. "The rebels won't let the United States think good of them," it was declared. "For a full year they have maintained a systematic bedevilment of Union prisoners and now," although Pope had made no arrests, the rebels, "gloating in cruelty, make haste to oppress."[16] During the period that exchanges were carried on under the cartel the attitude of mind already created by the stories from the Southern prisons was not allowed to die. Instead, by a process of accretion, there developed a firm belief in the mind of the Northern people that the Confederacy deliberately sought to torture the prisoner who fell into its hands. This development took place despite the fact that both Colonel Corcoran and Congressman Ely published accounts of their prison experiences which contradicted the prevailing beliefs. Mr. Ely's account, published in the spring of 1862 before the formation of the cartel, related his experiences without any manifestation of the cruelty of Southern keepers. He revealed an opposition to the administration's policy of not exchanging prisoners, and, although reciting several murders of prisoners at the windows, insisted that such acts of brutality could not have been known to General Winder or the secretary of war.

[14] New York *Times,* July 9, 1862.
[15] Cf. *Ibid.,* July 24.
[16] *Ibid.,* August 18, 1862.

Ely borrowed money from the prison commissary, received gifts from sympathetic friends, and admired General Winder. The only moral which he pointed out in his book, *The Journal of Alfred Ely*, was that his insight into Southern character was not worth the "sufferings, privations, indignities and discomforts" which he underwent as a result of the unfortunate curiosity which led him to be a spectator at the battle of Bull Run.

Colonel Corcoran, returning with the first of the prisoners to be exchanged under the cartel, also published an account of his experiences. More critical than the work of his fellow prisoner, *The Captivity of General Corcoran* declared the rebel secretary of war to be "one of those disgraces to mankind with which the world is anything but blessed," but he had no harsh words for General Winder. Although "the Hero of Bull Run," as Corcoran described himself in his book, had suffered indignities unbecoming a hero, his account as a whole did not serve to confirm the stories which were current at the time.

More in accordance with the prevailing sentiment was a book from the pen of a Methodist Protestant minister of abolitionist leanings; James J. Geer, of Cincinnati, in *Beyond the Lines; or, a Yankee Loose in Dixie*, related his experiences in Montgomery, Alabama, and Macon, Georgia. He escaped from the latter prison, was recaptured, and finally exchanged. Throughout these experiences he developed a decided antipathy toward the aristocratic and the "clay eating" classes of the South. Negroes who helped him in his escape and shared his confinement in various jails were revealed as oppressed and kept in ignorance by their white masters. The tone of the book was bitter and stories of rebel barbarities filled its pages.

The influence of such accounts was widespread and tended to make each prisoner feel that he was being oppressed. The inevitable reaction of the prisoners and the people of the North was to demand that the prisoners in the Northern prisons should be given a similar treatment. Late in 1862 a committee in the Ohio Senate, investigating conditions at Camp Chase, found that the prisoners were accorded the best of treatment. Negro slaves accompanied their masters to the prison and were confined with them as servants. Officers were paroled to visit the city of Columbus:

> Is it a wonder that the loyal people of Ohio, both in the field and at home, knowing all these things and remembering how our prisoners were confined in loathsome slave pens and tobacco sheds, and the bodies of our dead barbarously desecrated by the rebels, should feel outraged by this misguided sympathy—this mistaken clemency toward the perpetrators of all these foul wrongs?[17]

A returned prisoner expressed the same sentiment when he voiced the hope that the rebel prisoners in the North would be put on an allowance similar to the coarse cornbread, bad meat and cold water that he had experienced in Richmond.[18]

Such suggestions created an attitude of mind among the Northern people which was destined to cause distress to the prisoners held by the Federal Government. The first prisoners to be confined in any considerable number in Northern prisons after the cartel were the captives who were taken at the fall of Arkansas Post in January, 1863. Because of the inadvisability of delivering these prisoners at Vicksburg, as provided in the cartel, they were sent to Camps Douglas, Butler, Morton, and Chase.[19] At Camp Chase, where the officers from Arkansas were sent, was first revealed the new attitude of the Federal authorities toward the prisoners. A private of the guard, affected by the prevailing psychosis, reported to General Rosecrans that the orders which Rosecrans had given forbidding prisoners to purchase supplies from sutlers were ignored at the camp.[20] Even the com-

[17] *Ohio Senate Journal*, 1862. Appendix, 155-56.

[18] *Official Records*, series 2, V, 267-68.

[19] *Ibid.*, 201, 203 ff. Some hesitancy was experienced in regard to Camp Morton as there was only a small force available for guard duty (*Ibid.*, 221) and the number of anti-war and anti-administration politicians was felt to render it injudicious to confine a large number of prisoners at Springfield. (*Ibid.*, 227-28.) However, necessity overruled these prudential considerations and repairs were made so that four thousand prisoners could be cared for (*Ibid.*, 239-40, 258-59), although by the last of March, there were but six hundred and twenty-two prisoners confined there. (*Ibid.*, 391-92.)

[20] *Ibid.*, 265-66.

mander of the post wrote to Captain Lazelle about conditions. He reported that the officers had large amounts of money, much of it received from friends, which they expended lavishly. They wished to purchase clothes of expensive cloth which could be easily converted into uniforms when they went South. They also purchased good boots which they could not procure at home. The commander suggested that one suit and a change of underclothing was all the prisoners needed. In addition, he asked instructions concerning delicacies which the prisoners bought or received from friends, who were reported as sending daily large boxes, trunks, and packages of clothing. Commissary-General Hoffman answered this letter with the order that the officers could have only such clothing as they required for immediate use, and the clothes of a quality which would not last them any considerable time after exchange. Boots, if purchased, must be of the poorest quality, and the prisoners could not be allowed to buy uniform clothing. Reasonable amounts of food and delicacies might be received from friends or bought from the sutler.[21] In the future, gifts of clothing above the allowance which Hoffman had declared permissible were to be confiscated by the commandant.[22]

Prisoners sent to Camp Butler were not so well supplied with material wealth as their officers, and General Wright, commanding the department, issued clothing and supplies to them. He ordered straw, blankets, and stores supplied to the prisoners who he noticed were suffering from exposure. Colonel Hoffman, however, ordered Captain Freedley to take charge of the prisoners at Camps Butler and Douglas and informed General Wright that the prison fund would supply the indispensable needs of the prisoners; blankets and clothing were to be issued only when absolutely necessary. Freedley reported that the prisoners were furnished rations surpassing those of the Confederate army and were cheerful and contented. Their good treatment had rendered them so indolent that they had no desire to escape, although the

---

[21] *Ibid.*, 305-6, 317-18.   [22] *Ibid.*, 462-63.

guards were equally indolent and the camp was filthy. The prisoners were quite content to remain in filth and vermin.[23]

It was not the intention at this time to retain the prisoners, and they were confined in the various posts only because military necessity prevented their delivery at Vicksburg. Plans were made for moving them to City Point for delivery; the last of March the prisoners at Camp Chase were ordered sent to Fort Delaware and those at Delaware were ordered to Fort Monroe for delivery by Ludlow.[24] But preparations were being made to retain the prisoners in case the difficulties in the execution of the cartel should not be resolved by the "friendly representations" provided for in that document. Quartermaster-General Meigs examined Pea Patch Island upon which Fort Delaware was situated and reported that there was room for five thousand within the fort and space on the island for barracks for ten thousand.[25] Hoffman recommended to Stanton that these barracks be built, although he stated that only rarely would accommodations for such a number be needed. Stanton gave the necessary orders for the construction of barracks for five thousand prisoners.[26]

As the prisoners left Camp Chase for Fort Delaware, they reported that their extra clothing had been taken from them by their guard.[27] One of them informed Hoffman that he had been subjected to the "grossest and most inhuman treatment. My person insulted, the clothing torn from my back, my baggage robbed of all it contained. . . ." The commander at Delaware vouched for the destitution of the officers when they arrived, stating that he had to issue four hundred and twenty-two blankets to as many prisoners from Chase. In reply to this report and complaint, Hoffman, who might have been expected to take steps to punish the guard for such depredations, further revealed that he too had become a victim of the war psychosis. He declared that such acts were wholly unauthorized by the United States; "for it is a

[23] Ibid., 250, 272, 379-82.
[24] Ibid., series 2, V, 403.
[25] Ibid., 425-26.
[26] Ibid., 457, 267.
[27] Ibid., 444.

well-known fact that clothing and blankets have been issued to the many destitute who have fallen into our hands . . . but if I am rightly informed, it has by no means been so with our troops when they have been captured. . . . So far from receiving clothing it has frequently happened that they have been stripped of all their outer garments and then crowded into prisons inconceivably filthy, so much so that it would be shocking to humanity to confine in such a place even the most abandoned criminals." The complainant to Hoffman's mind had merely "been made to suffer an unauthorized retaliation for innumerable outrages which have been committed on our people . . ."[28]

Although Hoffman continued to state that there would be no need for permanent prisons, he continued throughout the spring of 1863 to make preparations for the confinement of large numbers of prisoners. The necessity for a sewer at Camp Douglas, recommended so strongly by President Bellows of the Sanitary Commission the year before, was again brought to the attention of the quartermaster's department. The Sanitary Commission returned to the project and made a report showing that the hospital at the post was in bad condition. The inmates were without a change of clothing, covered with vermin, without proper beds, and the death rate was mounting; two hundred and sixty prisoners out of eight thousand died between January 27 and February 18. The commission pointed out that at this rate the camp would be emptied by death in three hundred and twenty days. They recommended the abandonment of the site because of the lack of drainage.[29] As a result of this renewed pressure, the sewer was authorized in June.[30]

The prisoners at Fort Delaware, instead of being sent in exchange, remained in the camp. Permanent arrangements were put under way,[31] and Delaware was declared to be a regular prison depot. In July, when the new barracks were occupied, they immediately began to sink in the mud so that

---

[28] *Ibid.*, 477, 487.
[29] *Ibid.*, 492, 587-89.
[30] *Ibid.*, series 2, VI, 4.
[31] *Ibid.*, 501-2.

there was danger of their falling over.[32] The dampness did not serve to mitigate the unhealthy condition of the prison and the mortality became a subject of newspaper comment.[33]

The complete failure of the commissioners of exchange to agree on the execution of the cartel, and the events of the early days of July, 1863, led Hoffman to prepare two new prisons. At Rock Island, Illinois, barracks were ordered built, but they were to be "mere shanties," put up in the roughest and cheapest manner."[34] The other prison, designed at the same time, to hold eventually ten thousand prisoners, was located at Point Lookout, Maryland. Since old tents were to be used instead of barracks, the prison was ready to be occupied by the middle of August, and by the last of the month eighteen hundred had been sent there.[35]

The officers who were confined on Johnson's Island after the failure of the cartel were not subjected to the same lack of shelter as were the enlisted men at Rock Island and Point Lookout; prison accommodations had already been prepared for them. They were, however, restricted in clothing. Late in July, Hoffman instructed the commander of the post, Colonel Pierson, that the prisoners were to be limited to one outer suit and a change of underclothing. If they had this much they were not to be permitted to buy more. If they made these purchases of clothing, the suits must be of gray cloth with plain buttons and no trimming. Shoes were to be of poor quality and under no conditions were they to have boots. Pierson informed Hoffman that the prisoners wrote to friends for clothing and gave their measurements, and good clothes were sent them. Hoffman ordered that clothes not of the required quality and color be returned to the sender.[36] Pierson accordingly directed all orders for clothing stopped, but declared that unless the prisoners received clothes from some quarter, many would not have a change of underclothing and many others would be nearly naked.[37]

[32] Ibid., 538, 88.
[33] New York Times, July 11.
[34] Official Records, series 2, VI, 115, 196.
[35] Ibid., 132-33, 206, 243.
[36] Ibid., 161, 184, 192-93.
[37] Ibid., 201-214.

The kindness of friends in sending gifts to the prisoners did not meet with general approval on the part of those affected with the general psychosis. At Camp Morton, where visitors were permitted to talk with prisoners, a citizen of Indianapolis informed Hoffman:

> I am a loyal man and love my country and her free institutions and cannot consent to see such favors extended to rebels as are constantly done at Camp Morton and remain silent. . . . when I remember the cruel treatment our own brave soldiers have always received from the rebels . . . it makes my blood boil to see the extreme privileges granted to Morgan's thieves.

Although the indignant citizen did not give his name, Hoffman recommended an investigation.[38]

The lack of clothing at Johnson's Island led the prisoners to complain to their own government. A prisoner there wrote to Secretary Seddon revealing the destitution of the prisoners in the face of the coming winter and asked for a month's pay in United States money for the officers.[39] Such information of the cruel treatment of prisoners in the North conformed with the psychosis which had developed among the Confederate authorities. The Confederates believed as firmly as did the citizens of the United States that their soldiers in prison were the victims of barbarous treatment. Just before this report from Johnson's Island was received, the surgeon-general of the Confederate army informed Secretary Seddon of the sufferings of the prisoners at Fort Delaware because of the crowded condition, "pestilential cells," unwholesome food, and bad water of the prison. This, the surgeon-general declared to be an "unworthy attempt to subdue or destroy our soldiers by pestilence and disease."[40] The condition at Fort Delaware had become involved in the warfare of recriminations which Ould and Meredith were waging at this time, and Ould lost no opportunity to inform his opponent of the "anguish" of the prisoners in "your horrible prisons."[41]

[38] *Ibid.*, 162-63.
[39] *Ibid.*, 200.
[40] *Ibid.*, 181.
[41]*Ibid.*, 182-83.

As Ould, who had received complaints from Confederate prisoners, continued to protest against the treatment of prisoners at Fort Delaware,[42] Hoffman denied that the prisoners were badly treated.[43] This denial was made in the face of the report of the surgeon-general who referred to Hoffman a proposition to remove one tier of bunks from the barracks and make windows reaching to the floor to relieve the crowded conditions. Despite the fact that the surgeon believed that this would decrease the mortality, Hoffman refused to permit the removal of the bunks, although he did send the excess prisoners to Point Lookout.[44] The surgeon-general, however, insisted that Fort Delaware was not a suitable place for a large depot of prisoners; the ground was wet and marshy and in a malarial country. The crowding of eight thousand prisoners, sick and well, into the barracks, without facilities for cooking and without proper police, produced typhoid fever.[45]

The unwillingness of Hoffman to remedy these conditions at Fort Delaware was paralleled by the attitude of Secretary Stanton. Hoffman recommended that the buildings at Camp Douglas, burned by the paroled troops, should be rebuilt. Stanton informed the commissary-general of prisoners that the Secretary of War is not disposed at this time, in view of the treatment our prisoners of war are receiving at the hands of the enemy, to erect fine establishments for their prisoners in our hands. Whatever is indispensable, however, to prevent suffering . . . will be provided . . . by the use of the prison fund. . . . Nothing more will be authorized.[46]

Secretary Stanton's decision in this case revealed his reaction to the conditions which had developed in Richmond. The lack of clothing and the shortage of meat had been met by shipments of blankets, money, and rations from the North. At the same time, however, more serious reports of the conditions in Richmond began to come north. Returned prison-

[42] Ibid., 250-51.
[43] Ibid., 310.
[44] Ibid., 235, 244-45.
[45] Ibid., 281. For conditions at Fort Delaware as seen by a political prisoner see Handy, United States Bonds.
[46] Official Records, series 2, VI, 314-15.

ers at Annapolis, sent north in the exchange of sick, were reported as arriving "in a pitiable condition of mind and body, having experienced extreme suffering from a want (apparently) of proper food." The surgeon-general was informed that these exchanged sick wore

the visage of hunger, the expression of despair, and exhibited the ravages of some preying disease within, or the wreck of a once athletic frame . . . Their hair was disheveled, their beards long and matted with dirt, their skin blackened and caked with the most loathsome filth, and their bodies and clothing covered with vermin. . . . Their pinched features, ghastly cadaveric countenances, deep sepulchral eyes, and voices that could hardly be distinguished (some could not articulate) presented a picture which could not be looked upon without its drawing out the strongest emotion of pity.[47]

In addition to these conditions which could be seen at Annapolis came Dow's report of fearful mortality and utter destitution on Belle Isle.[48]

Following upon these reports, General Hitchcock stated that measures were in progress and some means "are not distant to remedy or punish the evil."[49] To remedy conditions Meredith sent rations to the prisoners through Ould and coupled this with an offer to take the prisoners off the Confederate hands and hold them on parole.[50] Although Hitchcock recognized the inability of the South to feed the prisoners,[51] he did not allow this to prevent his attempt to "punish" the evils. Newspapers demanded that the suffering prisoners be exchanged regardless of the merits of the Ould-Meredith controversy,[52] but Hitchcock was not inclined to yield his position on paroles. More in accordance with the prevailing sentiment was the request of Dow that the rebel prisoners in the North be treated in the same way the Confederacy treated its captives. An agent of the Sanitary Commission who had spent three days in Richmond prisons added a refinement of the suggestion by recommending that retaliation be put into effect against the Confederate officers

[47] Ibid., 474-76. Cf. also National Intelligencer, November 20.
[48] Official Records, series 2, VI, 482-83.
[49] Ibid., 446-47.
[50] Ibid., 503.
[51] Ibid., 604.
[52] New York Times, November 10.

rather than against all prisoners from the South.[53] Preparations for carrying out this recommendation were put under
way at once. General Fitzhugh Lee, confined in Fort Monroe
awaiting Davis' action in the case of Flinn and Sawyer, was
ordered sent to Johnson's Island where, in case the government ordered "special treatment similar to that which the
rebels extend to Union prisoners in Richmond prisons, General Lee will be in a right position for sharing it."[54] Secretary
Stanton gave his sanction to the steps being taken and ordered
Hitchcock to ascertain the treatment of prisoners in Richmond and to "take measures for precisely similar treatment
toward all the prisoners held by the United States, in respect
to food, clothing, medical treatment, and other necessities."
Hitchcock had Meredith ask Ould about the reported conditions, and Meredith added the threat that the North would
act on the best information it possessed if Ould did not
reply.[55] General Halleck added his agreement by stating
that "this atrocious conduct is applauded by the people and
commended by the public press of Richmond as 'a means of
reducing the Yankee ranks.'" This, he believed, justified
retaliation.[56]

To Meredith's request for a statement of the treatment of
prisoners in the South,[57] Ould replied that the prisoners in
Richmond were given the same rations as the troops and
declared that if the supply was scanty it was because of the
destructive warfare which the North waged. He attacked
the stories of the treatment of prisoners as "infamous." In
addition, Ould sent a report of the provost marshal of Richmond on the condition of the prisoners.[58] This report, being
an official reply to Meredith's inquiries, should, on strict
legal principles, have been deemed sufficient by the Northern

[53] *Official Records*, series 2, VI, 510-11, 513-14.

[54] Hitchcock to Hoffman, *Ibid.*, 484-85. Lee was sent to Lafayette instead of to
Johnson's Island. *Ibid.*, 515-16.

[55] *Ibid.*, 485-86.

[56] *Ibid.*, 524. Annual Report.

[57] See Jones, *War Diary*, II, 98.

[58] *Official Records*, series 2, VI, 537-38, 544-48. See above page 121.

authorities. General Hitchcock, however, was not satisfied to act on strictly legal principles. He declared that while Ould's report of rations might be correct, they were contradicted by every report from the South, and these contradictions were confirmed by the condition of the sick returned to Annapolis. He maintained that Davis' proclamation was still in effect, chaplains of negro regiments were held in prison, negro soldiers were confined in separate prisons, two negro soldiers had been sold into slavery in Texas, and Ould had been generally dishonest in connection with paroles. Ould's sense of right, he concluded after this enumeration of Confederate sins, was so obtuse that no trust could be placed in anything he said. When Ould refused to receive this diatribe because of its insulting tone, Hitchcock declared that it was because he was convicted of improper conduct.[59] The report of surgeons returning from Richmond was so vehement in denunciation of conditions in Richmond that it convinced Hitchcock and Meredith of the complete falsity of the report of the Confederate commissioner.[60]

The return of Hitchcock to the negro issue led him to write, with the approval of Stanton, a letter to the New York *Times* in explanation of the sufferings in Richmond and why no exchanges had been made. Although he recited the entire list of Northern grievances on the subject of paroles, he declared that the vital question was that of the negro troops. He cited the case of a Lieutenant Coleman, who with his men had been killed by the rebels when captured with a colored command.[61] Fearing that this letter would not prove his point sufficiently well, especially since the negro troops played only a minor role in the published correspondence between Meredith and Ould, Hitchcock, a week later, indited a postscript citing laws of the Confederate congress and Ould's

[59] *Ibid.*, 552-54.

[60] *Ibid.*, 569, 572-75. See above page 122. Although the surgeons reported that a cook and a carpenter said the supplies sent South were directed to Lee's army, Meredith decided to stop sending supplies. Hitchcock directed that unless he had positive, confirming information he should continue to forward them. *Ibid.*, 607.

[61] *Ibid.*, 594-600. New York *Times*, December 2.

statements in regard to the negro prisoners.[62] These letters had one unlooked-for effect. The Lieutenant Coleman referred to as having been shot wrote from Libby prison that he had not suffered that penalty. Hitchcock so informed the *Times;* but he asserted that since Coleman did not refer to the soldiers, it was proof that they had actually been executed.[63]

This willingness to believe the worst side of the stories which circulated about the treatment of prisoners led to more definite steps being taken to carry out Hitchcock's determination to "punish" the evils in accordance with Stanton's order. On December 1, orders were issued to the commander of all the prisons to withdraw the sutlers from the prisons and to permit no more purchases by the inmates.[64] In September, prisoners at Johnson's Island had received permission from Hoffman to purchase overcoats and winter underwear, and Pierson was instructed to issue clothes to the destitute among them on the advice of the post surgeon.[65] Pierson gave the sutler permission to sell coarse gray overcoats to the prisoners, and some of the prisoners wrote to friends for clothing, Pierson directing the friends to send only suits of the proper color.[66] When Pierson received the order to stop the sutler, he immediately protested on the grounds that someone should be permitted to sell stamps and tobacco to the prisoners.[67] At the other prisons clothing had been issued, but they had other difficulties: Fort Delaware continued to be unhealthy. Three hundred and thirty-one out of the seven thousand prisoners died there in the month of September and the surgeon declared that "mere humanity" should dictate the selection of a more healthful spot. Smallpox broke out at the post in October and increased suffering and death.[68]

[62] *Official Records,* series 2, VI, 615-18.

[63] New York *Times,* January 1, 1864. A resolution in the House of Representatives, December 16, praised the United States and condemned the rebels for their treatment of prisoners. *Congressional Globe,* December 17.

[64] *Official Records,* series 2, VI, 625.

[65] *Ibid.,* 330.   [67] *Ibid.,* 654.

[66] *Ibid.,* 353, 500.   [68] *Ibid.,* 359, 422, 440, 476-77, 607, 525.

At Camp Douglas the lack of clothing led Hoffman to permit prisoners to receive clothing from relatives but not from friends.[69]   The same instructions were given to the commander of Camp Morton who was informed that "so long as a prisoner has clothing upon him, however much torn, you must issue nothing to him, nor must you allow him to receive clothing from any but members of his immediate family, and only when he is in absolute want."[70]

Only at Point Lookout were the prisoners without barracks, but Hitchcock pointed out that tents, "as every soldier knows," "are easily made comfortable, and are always thankfully received by the troops in the field."[71] Stanton had refused to permit barracks to be built at the prison, and tents for ten thousand were issued. Gifts of edibles were refused to the prisoners on the grounds that they were well supplied, although scurvy was reported to be prevalent.[72] The middle of November a committee of the Sanitary Commission reported a large number of sick prisoners, suffering from many diseases with diarrhoea prevailing. The sick were filthy and received no attention. Their rations consisted of four ounces of beef or pork, four ounces of potatoes, and three ounces of hardtack for dinner; for breakfast and "tea" they received a pint of tea, two gills of rice, one gill of molasses, and three ounces of hardtack. Some of the sick were on half rations. The well prisoners lacked wood and clothing and suffered from the cold. The committee reported deaths of thirty per cent but agreed that the rebels, since they received the same as the soldiers of the guards, were too well treated.[73] Hoffman ordered the commander to issue clothing and not let the men go naked "though it is the desire of the War Department to provide as little clothing for them as possible."[74] The commander branded the report of the Sanitary Commission a lie and declared that the prisoners received thirteen ounces of bread, eight ounces of meat, and coffee or soup daily. An

[69] *Ibid.*, 525-26, 602.
[70] *Ibid.*, 503-4.
[71] *Ibid.*, 613.

[72] *Ibid.*, 390, 489, 473.
[73] *Ibid.*, 575-81.
[74] *Ibid.*, 585.

inspector sent to the prison reported that bad water caused intestinal disorders; but with the exception of admitting that the men were a dirty lot, he cleared the officials of the prison of the charges of the Sanitary Commission.[75]

These conditions in Northern prisons produced a reaction in the South. As it was believed in Richmond that the stories of Southern atrocities were told "to fire the war spirit,"[76] a counter attack began. A Doctor Pallen, writing from Canada, asked Stanton for permission to go to Richmond to get supplies for the prisoners in the North. He reported that he had learned of the nakedness at Johnson's Island, Point Lookout, Chase, and Douglas. At Point Lookout he charged that the men were in tents and half of the nine thousand prisoners there slept on the ground without blankets; some had frozen to death.[77] Hitchcock ordered Hoffman to get conclusive proof of the falsity of these charges and the commanders of the prisons agreed in denying them *in toto*. At Camp Chase clothing had been issued and few were sick.[78] Pierson admitted the need of clothing at Johnson's Island but denied that prisoners were suffering. At Douglas the prisoners were reported to be clothed but to lack the full regulation ration of meat.[79]

A more violent and far-reaching reaction to the Northern stories and conditions came in December from Ould. Northern papers continued to publish accounts of the sufferings of prisoners in the South and illustrators portrayed the skeletons on Belle Isle who once had worn the Federal Uniform.[80]

[75] *Ibid.*, 644-45, 740-45.

[76] Richmond *Inquirer*, November 16. New York *Times*, November 21.

[77] *Official Records*, series 2, VI, 718. A letter to the *National Intelligencer*, November 21, cites the Montreal *Commercial Advertiser* as saying that the rebel officers on Johnson's Island were suffering from the cold. The writer declared this to be false and contrasted the treatment on Johnson's with that given to prisoners in the South. Cf. also the Richmond *Dispatch*, November 30, which speaks of this "diabolical" treatment at Johnson's. Soldiers were called upon to remember on the battlefield the "hellish" treatment of their comrades.

[78] *Official Records*, series 2, VI, 746-47.

[79] *Ibid.*, 758-61, 778-800.

[80] See New York *Times*, December 5, 1863; *Harper's Weekly*, December 5, 779-81; *National Intelligencer*, November 11.

Southern papers stated that the South was forced by circumstances to admit its poverty and accept gifts from the Yankees for the prisoners whom the North would not exchange. It was pointed out that they accepted supplies which liars were willing to swear were diverted to the Confederate armies. If the South refused to receive supplies, they would be accused of deliberate cruelty; but the United States should be informed, it was advised, that the Confederacy treated the prisoners as well as the conditions of the country permitted while the soldiers and citizens of Richmond drank the same muddy waters of the James as the prisoners.[81] Either this presentation of the situation, or the belief that the North would not consent to an exchange so long as supplies could be sent to their soldiers, led Ould to inform Meredith that the assent of the Confederate government to gifts of food and clothing to the prisoners had been made the subject of so much abuse and vilification that it had been decided to withdraw the right. Clothing and provisions already at hand were to be given the prisoners until the supply was exhausted after which they would receive the same rations as the soldiers in the field.[82]

Before Ould's letter was received, Secretary Stanton had informed the President that retaliation would be resorted to when it became necessary, but not so long as the rebels allowed the United States to send supplies to the prisoners.[83] Despite the implication of this statement, no immediate effort was made to subject prisoners in the North to any extraordinary treatment. The South's action was declared to be "childish and unworthy" of a civilized people. Some consolation was derived, however, from the number of rations reported as having been sent south—one hundred and ten thousand full rations being the figure stated—which would suffice for the prisoners for many months. The newspapers demanded that the prisoners be exchanged.[84] But when, on

[81] Richmond *Examiner*, November 28.   New York *Times*, December 5.
[82] *Official Records*, series 2, VI, 686.
[83] *Ibid.*, 647-49.
[84] *Philadelphia Inquirer*, December 17 and 18.

December 13, Butler was appointed an agent of exchange, the South refused to deal with him on the grounds that he was an outlaw.[85] This resulted in a proposal from Butler to allow him to subject the prisoners at Point Lookout to the same treatment that prisoners received in Richmond,[86] but it was understood that Lincoln doubted the propriety of such action, while Stanton was reported as favoring it. The press, however, opposed the policy, and no attempts at the time were made to carry it out.[87]

Instead of attempting retaliation after Ould's letter, Stanton gave his permission to allow sutlers at the Northern camps to sell pipes, tobacco, and a few other articles of a similar nature. Hoffman had already given this permission to the commander at Fort Delaware and had advised Stanton that the lack of tobacco would be provocative of attempts to escape.[88] Stanton was quoted as believing that the prisoners in Richmond were being given better treatment. For several months there was no change in the routine affairs of the Northern prisons.

In the early part of December, 1863, the prison at Rock Island being reported ready for occupancy, prisoners were ordered sent there from Camp Douglas.[89] The prisoners had suffered from exposure and brought smallpox with them.[90] There was a swamp on the island, the drainage was poor, and the water for the prisoners was pumped from the river. In January a hundred and seventy-three prisoners out of a total of 7,149 died; three hundred and thirty-one prisoners died in February. Fortunately, the smallpox decreased in violence and in number of cases,[91] so by March the number of deaths was reduced to one hundred and thirty-two.[92]

[85] See below page 211.
[86] *Official Records*, series 2, VI, 771.
[87] Philadelphia *Inquirer*, January 5, 6, 1864. New York *Times*, January 21.
[88] *Official Records*, series 2, VI, 774, 706, 701-2.
[89] *Ibid.*, 626, 634.
[90] *Ibid.*, 848.
[91] *Ibid.*, 1001-4. In addition to smallpox there was much scurvy on Rock Island. See Minnich, *Inside of Rock Island*, 8.
[92] *Official Records*, series 2, VII, 23-29.

During these months Camp Chase and Fort Delaware also had cases of smallpox, although not to the extent that Rock Island endured. At Delaware the disease, which had raged during the summer and autumn, was reported in December, 1863 as being on the decline,[93] and by the first of March as having completely disappeared, thus making room at the prison for four thousand more prisoners.[94] This number immediately was ordered sent to the prison.[95]

Despite these conditions, Quartermaster-General Meigs came to the conclusion that the prisoners were too well treated by the Federal authorities and suggested to the New York *Times* that they be put to work. "We are killing them by treating them as southern gentlemen until they die of gout."[96]

The conditions in the prisons, however, combined with a suggestion from Butler that Ould would refuse to receive gifts even from individuals unless the North accorded better treatment,[97] led to a relaxation of the rules instead of an increase in discipline. Orders were issued to all commanders directing them to receive for the prisoners any boxes which contained no military equipment, uniforms, liquors, or excess clothing.[98] A threat from Ould in December that the Confederacy would retaliate,[99] combined with protests from the prisons and suggestions that the list of permitted articles be extended,[100] led to orders from the commissary-general of prisoners permitting sutlers to sell tobacco, writing materials, clothing, groceries, toilet accessories, and cooking utensils.[101]

This relaxation of the rules concerning prisoners was destined not to last long. An exchange of sick prisoners, carried out between Butler and Ould, brought into the North an

---

[93] *Ibid.*, series 2, VI, 735-36; see also 825 (January 10, 1864).
[94] *Ibid.*, 1000-1. For smallpox at Chase see *Ibid.*, 819.
[95] *Ibid.*, 1015-16.
[96] *Ibid.*, 893-94. New York *Times*, February 3, 1864.
[97] *Official Records*, series 2, VI, 954-55, 973-75, 983-84, 985, 1027.
[98] *Ibid.*, 1036.
[99] *Ibid.*, 919.
[100] *Ibid.*, 966-67.
[101] *Ibid.*, 1014-15. March 3, 1864.

increasing number of those who had suffered the worst at the hands of the Confederacy. Added to the stories which these prisoners told, was the report that powder had been placed under Libby prison at the time of Kilpatrick's impending raid. This, combined with the reports of the captured raiders, who were placed in cells, the alleged mutilation of the body of Colonel Dahlgren, and the approval of these actions by the Richmond newspapers, who called upon their government to give up its timid policy in regard to prisoners, served to revive the belief in deliberate Southern cruelty.[102] On March 4, Colonel Streight arrived in Washington and gave an account of the horrors of Libby to the congressional committee on the conduct of the war.[103] "Only slavery could so harden a man," declared one paper as it related how the Confederates put prisoners into gloomy cells, fed them on mouldy bread, and subjected them to petty persecutions and brutal indignities. The North had been too cool to these barbarities, it was asserted, and, as the rebel prisoners had received better fare than in their own homes, been given cleaner clothes, and had been imprisoned in an invigorating climate, they returned to the South with improved constitutions and ready for service. "Retaliation," stated one paper, "is a terrible thing, but the miseries and pains and the slowly wasting life of our brethren and friends in those horrible prisons is a worse thing. No people or government ought to allow its soldiers to be treated for one day as our men have been treated for the last three years." It was also pointed out that these conditions checked enlistments and enfeebled the armies in the field.[104]

An exchange of prisoners, mostly sick and wounded, in the middle of March brought to Annapolis Lieutenant Colonel James M. Sanderson, who had quarreled with Colonel Streight in Libby. To representatives of the press Sanderson

[102] New York *Times*, March 5, 12, 14, 19. The Washington correspondent believed that the attempt was made to scare the prisoners by telling them that powder had been placed under the prison.

[103] New York *Tribune*, March 5.

[104] New York *Times*, March 31, 1864.

deplored the reports which had circulated in the North. He believed that such stories as those which told that mule meat had been given to the prisoners tended to bring the whole subject into ridicule and materially interfered with humane efforts to mitigate the real evils. Of Major Turner, commander of Libby, he spoke highly, and he even found bright spots in the character of one Dick Turner, an attache of the prison, who was hated by the prisoners for his alleged cruelty.[105] But Colonel Streight, carrying old enmities with him, had preceded Sanderson and had brought reports more pleasing to the public ear. Streight charged that Sanderson had informed the rebels of a plot to escape, and Sanderson, immediately after his arrival in Washington, was placed under arrest.[106]

A boatload of sick prisoners arriving in the latter part of April gave an added impetus to the demand for retaliation. "We've not heard as much lately as formerly of the maltreatment of prisoners in Richmond," commented the New York *Times*, "but it has not abated. Nay, their diabolism will never abate as long as it is in their power to exercise it. The slaveholder is born to tyranny and reared to cruelty." The paper, with this diatribe, went on to give an account of the sufferings of the newly arrived prisoners.[107] Hoffman made a trip to Annapolis to see the condition of the men and came away filled with the stories of their confinement on Belle Isle without shelter and with insufficient food. He urged upon

[105] *Ibid.,* March 12. Concerning mule meat the Richmond *Dispatch* of March 2 asked "Well, what of it? It was vastly too good for men who have essayed to bring starvation on the people who captured them, and they would have no right to complain if they were forced to that fate they designed for us. . . . Better men have eaten mule meat, and thought it very good. Even that Northern patriot Fremont has supped so full of it that he has been braying ever since. But the Yankees lied. The mule has not come to that fate yet. He is one of our institutions. He is cousin german to the negro, and too important to be fed to Yankees. The anatomist who detected the mule bones in the meat sent him was a charlatan, as Yankees generally are. He knows nothing of bones and makes no bones of lying."

[106] New York *Times,* March 14. Sanderson, *My Record in Rebeldom,* is the defense Sanderson made against these charges. The commission which tried him praised his conduct.

[107] New York *Times,* April 22.

Stanton the adoption of a policy of retaliation against the Confederate officers who were held by the United States. Stanton, however, sought to prepare the way for retaliation by calling upon the House Committee on the Conduct of the War to visit Annapolis. He made the statement that

the enormity of the crime committed by the rebels toward our prisoners . . . is not known or realized by our people, and cannot but fill with horror the civilized world when the facts are fully revealed. There appears to have been a deliberate system of savage and barbarous treatment. . . . the result of which will be that few, if any, of the prisoners that have been in their hands during the past winter will ever again be in a condition to render any service or even to enjoy life.[108]

As a step toward carrying out this policy, although making no distinction between officers and men, Hoffman ordered a reduction of rations in all of the camps. The commander of Fort Lafayette reported that for the few prisoners confined at his post these rations were insufficient, while the commander of Camp Douglas asserted that the new rations were too large. The prisoners at Douglas wasted hominy, did not need tea, and used candles to light them in digging tunnels. He recommended a still further reduction in the rations.[109] This suggestion appealed to Hoffman on the ground of economy as well as retaliation, and, May 6, he wrote to the commanders to prepare for further retaliation by increasing the guard force in case the prisoners rebelled at the reduced rations.[110] Hoffman then embodied the reduced ration proposed from Camp Douglas in a memorandum to the secretary of war. Obtaining the concurrence of the commissary-general of subsistence, the surgeon-general, and General Halleck, Stanton approved the proposed reduction.[111] Only

[108] *Official Records*, series 2, VII, 110-11.

[109] *Ibid.*, 72-75, 134, 192-93.

[110] *Ibid.*, 123-24.

[111] *Ibid.*, 73, 150-51. The new rations were hard bread, 14 ounces; soft bread, 16 ounces; cornmeal, 16 ounces; beef, 14 ounces; bacon or pork, 10 ounces; beans, 6 quarts per hundred; rice and hominy, 8 ounces per hundred; sugar 12 pounds per hundred; Rio Coffee, 5 pounds ground or 7 pounds raw per hundred; tea, 1 pound per hundred; soap, 4 pounds per hundred; candles, 5 pounds per hundred; salt, 2 quarts per hundred; molasses 1 quart per hundred; potatoes, 15 pounds per hundred.

at Camp Morton was there serious danger of rioting when the new rations went into effect, and there the guard force was increased.[112]

The committee on the conduct of the war visited the camp at Annapolis and at Baltimore to examine the condition of the returned men. They took pictures of the prisoners to accompany the report of their inspection.[113] The printed report was a document of thirty pages and contained eight pictures of prisoners in the worst state of emaciation. With sunken and unshaven cheeks, hollow and glassy eyes, protruding bones, and an expression of utter despondency, the pictures were striking confirmation of the story of cruelty which the report related. Two of the pictures, according to the dates given, were of men who had died before the committee arrived, two died immediately after their visit, and the other four were reported as convalescent. The testimony taken by the committee and embodied in the report was sufficient evidence to the Congressmen that there was a fixed determination on the part of the rebels to kill the Union soldiers who fell into their hands. The testimony related how the prisoners were robbed at the time of their capture and carried to the fearsome tobacco warehouses of Richmond or to Belle Isle. Here, without food, shelter, fire, or provision for cleanliness, the men died. The readers of this report were assured that the men were patriotic and resisted the blandishments of their fiendish captors, who tried by offers of better conditions to induce them to espouse the Confederate cause.[114]

[112] *Ibid.*, 193.

[113] New York *Times*, May 7, 1864.

[114] *Report No. 67.* House of Representatives, 38th Congress, first session. The appalling pictures which lent such proof of cruelty to this report were later explained away by the Confederates. Jefferson Davis stated in 1876 that he sent the report to Ould who reported that these cases were the worst in Richmond. Since the prisoners were beyond hope, their own desire to be sent home overruled the advice of the prison surgeon. Moreover, Davis asserted that a Catholic priest informed him that the worst case had not been a prisoner but had been left at Annapolis as his regiment passed through the city en route to the battle field. See Davis to James Lyons, in *Southern Historical Society Papers*, I (1876). The report of the committee on the conduct of the war is also in Moore, *Rebellion Records*, VIII, 80-98.

Shortly after the publication of this report, Hoffman received a request from a committee of the Sanitary Commission to permit them to make a similar inspection and report. Hoffman referred the request of these men to Stanton, who, on the grounds that the House Committee had made a full report "under circumstances more favorable for eliciting the full facts of the case," refused to sanction the proposal.[115] The committee, headed by Dr. Ellerslie Wallace of New York City, proceeded, however, to make a report on prisoners in North and South, and toward the end of June presented to Hoffman a list of questions concerning treatment in Northern prisons. They asked what rations, blankets, and clothing were received by the prisoners, if they had fire in cold weather, if orders had been issued at any time to shoot prisoners at windows, and if shelter had at any time been "denied" them.[116] Hoffman returned favorable answers to these questions and sent a copy of the rations he had ordered issued April 20, without mentioning the further reduction which Stanton had already approved. He also sent a list of articles sold by sutlers and added the pious hope that the Sanitary Commission would be convinced that captives in the North were well treated, while in the South the lives of prisoners were deliberately destroyed.[117]

Several months after the report of the House Committee, the report of the Sanitary Commission's committee was published and revealed the state of mind of the committee, for it contained all of the stories of atrocities told of the treatment of prisoners up to that time.[118] Their treatment in the

[115] *Official Records*, series 2, VII, 188-89.   [116] *Ibid.*, 387-88.   [117] *Ibid.*, 398.

[118] October 7, 1864 the report was reviewed in the *National Intelligencer* by one who declared that the report came to him in "connection with his official duties." This is the earliest notice found for the publication. The last testimony taken bears date of July 5. While accepting the truth of the report, the reviewer deplored the tendency to stir up feeling which was attempted. An editorial in the *Intelligencer* of October 19, pointed out that the committee had been gullible, denied that the South was able to feed the prisoners, and declared that prisoners had been shot for looking out the windows of the Old Capitol prison. If slavery was the cause of the barbarities cited by the report, the editor asked how the committee accounted for the raiders in the Southern prisons? Cf., for the complete acceptance of the report, *Harper's Weekly*, October 29.

South was served up to readers by eight colored pictures, without names, dates, or supporting data. Two of the pictures were borrowed from the report of the congressional committee. The account of the treatment began with the statement that all of the prisoners were robbed of money and stripped of clothing at the time of their capture. The bleak tobacco warehouses of Richmond were described in lurid detail; the lack of furniture, the unheated rooms with broken windows, the crowds confined within each room were dwelt upon. Prisoners were shot at windows, the men were without food, and many became insane. Boxes from home were stolen and sold to the prisoners. Men were brutally punished for trivial offenses; the naked bodies of the dead were placed in heaps awaiting burial and were eaten by hogs, dogs, and rats. The officers of the prisons, General Winder, Major Turner, and Dick Turner were described as brutes; the latter was declared to have been a negro whipper by profession, "whose savage nature vented itself in frequent acts of personal insult and physical violence toward the prisoners."

As for Belle Isle, the committee recounted the absence of shelter, the huddled men who were fed like swine on cornbread made from unbolted meal, soup with worms and bugs —and mule meat! Rats were eaten by the starving men— once a dog was eaten—and men were grateful for the scraps thrown to them from the surplus supplies of their guards. The sick were not sent to the hospitals until past recovery, were mistreated by surgeons, and died.

The general conclusion was obvious. The entire program of mistreatment was to be charged to "a predetermined plan, originating somewhere in the rebel counsels, for destroying and disabling the soldiers of their enemy, who had honorably surrendered in the field." This fact was proved by the abundant resources of the Confederacy and by the excellent condition of the Southern soldier.

From the treatment of prisoners in Richmond the committee turned its attention to Northern prisons. Fort Delaware was defended as well built and ventilated; the pris-

oners were allowed money, urged to bathe in the river, given
sufficient and varied diet, and clothed. The sick were cared
for in clean hospitals. No deadlines were to be found in
Northern prisons, and only five had been shot by the guards
at Fort Delaware. The prisoners had so much food that a
surplus went into a fund to buy them luxuries. "So great
was the abundance of food, that the prisoners hid loaves of
bread, crackers, and meat under the bunks." The dead were
decently interred, the Episcopalian service being read over
their bodies. In the Northern hospitals, which were so clean
that the visitors sat upon the beds while taking testimony,
the prisoners were waited upon by female nurses and "one
of them was seen carrying a waiter of iced porter to the
wounded, and holding the glass to lips of the more helpless."
There was no robbery in the North; the prisoners were supplied with ice water in the summer. At David's Island hospital a library of two thousand volumes of religious works
met the eye of the entering prisoners. To cap all of this, the
testimony of Dorothea Dix, nationally famous humanitarian,
was added to show that the prisoners at Point Lookout were
given the best of treatment, and in the hospitals the facilities
were superior to those in the hospitals of the guard.[119]

Under the prevailing psychosis this publication must have
been a considerable stimulant to gifts to the Sanitary Commission. The press hailed the account as a truthful portrayal
of conditions and prophesied that it would have a beneficial
effect not only at home but in Europe.[120]

Before the attention of the Sanitary Commission was directed to the condition of the prisons, a problem developed as
a result of the crowded state of the eastern camps and the
pressing necessity for more prisons. In May the war department learned that there were vacant barracks at Elmira,

[119] The full title of the committee's report referred to in the preceding note (118)
was: *Narrative of the Privations and Sufferings of United States Officers and Soldiers while Prisoners of War in the Hands of the Rebel Authorities, Being the Report of a Commission of Inquiry Appointed by the United States Sanitary Commission,
With an Appendix, Containing the Testimony.* Philadelphia, 1864. Issued also as
Loyal League *Pamphlet,* No. 76.

[120] *Harper's Weekly,* October 29. Cf., however, note 118.

New York, where a draft rendezvous had been established.[121] An officer was sent to build a fence about the camp, and the first of July prisoners were ordered transferred there from Point Lookout.[122] The new prison revealed a serious sanitary defect immediately; the sinks, located upon the banks of a stagnant pond which ran the length of the enclosure, threatened to become a source of disease. A plan for the drainage of the pond was proposed in August.[123]

Because of the crowded condition of the prisons at this time, some improvements were made at the various camps. At Point Lookout tents were sent to provide shelter for the prisoners,[124] and a new hospital was built.[125] The water at the prison was brackish and regular boats were employed to carry a supply of drinking water.[126] At Johnson's Island tents were used to shelter the excess prisoners,[127] and at Douglas a new arrangement of the barracks increased the rooming space and obviated some of the more serious sanitary defects. Tents were also provided here for the excess.[128] A new prison provided at Camp Chase made room for seven thousand inmates.[129]

The crowding of the prisoners into inadequate prisons combined with the reduction of rations produced sickness in the various camps. In June protests came from Point Lookout against the issue of salt pork, and the commander demanded that vegetables be issued. Much scurvy was reported existent among the prisoners.[130] Hoffman informed the commander that on the certificate of the surgeon in charge tea, coffee, and sugar might be issued to the sick and antiscorbutics might be purchased from the prison fund if the

[121] *Official Records,* series 2, VII, 146.

[122] *Ibid.,* 424. For an account of the Elmira prison see Holmes, *The Elmira Prison Camp;* Keiley, *In Vinculis;* and King, *My Experiences in the Confederate Army.* Cf. *National Intelligencer* for July 25, for the wreck of a train carrying prisoners to the prison.

[123] *Official Records,* series 2, VII, 465-66, 603-5, 676-77. Holmes, *op. cit.,* 43-57.

[124] *Official Records,* series 2, VII, 440, 448-50; series 1, XXXVI, part iii, 739. Keiley, *op. cit.,* 113.

[125] *Ibid.,* series 2, VII, 162.

[126] *Ibid.,* 182-83, 200.

[127] *Ibid.,* 184.

[128] *Ibid.,* 184-85, 369.

[129] *Ibid.,* 382.

[130] *Ibid.,* 399-400, 448-50.

surgeon deemed them necessary. The commissary-general of subsistence sent dried vegetables to be issued.[131] An inspector reported scurvy and poor water at Johnson's, adding the demand that the sutler be permitted to sell sugar to the prisoners.[132] Hoffman issued a circular stating that sugar for the sick and vegetables for the prisoners generally might be purchased from the fund whenever the surgeons of the prisons recommended them.[133]

Hoffman was unwilling to add to the list supplies which the sutlers at the posts might sell. The adjutant general of Ohio, horrified at the permission being given to the prisoners to purchase from sutlers, demanded that the "sleek fat rebels" be strictly limited to the rations of the Confederate army. Hoffman approved the idea, stating that Stanton on the advice of Butler[134] had passed the rules for sutlers over his veto. On October 10, Hoffman ordered that the sutlers should be limited to the sale of paper, tobacco, stamps, pipes, matches, combs, soap, tooth brushes, hair brushes, scissors, thread, needles, towels, and pocket mirrors.[135] To this list Hoffman was willing to add but one article; the commander at Camp Chase asked that buttons be added, and Hoffman permitted sutlers to add suspender buttons to their meager stock.[136]

The lack of vegetables was the greatest defect in the prisoners' diet. An inspector urged the necessity for issuing vegetables at Camp Morton for two months in order to counteract the scurvy.[137] At Elmira seven hundred and ninety-three cases were reported at the end of August, and so strong was the pressure to give the sutlers permission to sell vegetables, especially as the fund was not sufficient to buy them, that Hoffman reluctantly gave his assent to the sale during the prevalence of the disease.[138] The commissary-general of prisoners informed the commander of Point Lookout, however, a few weeks later, that potatoes and molasses could not be issued under the law, but that any saving which

[131] Ibid., 439.
[132] Ibid., 484-87.
[133] Ibid., 521.
[134] Ibid., 528-30.
[135] Ibid., 573-74.
[136] Ibid., 672.
[137] Ibid., 554-56.
[138] Ibid., 682-83, 785.

might be effected by reducing the rations of soap and salt might be applied to the purchase of extra rations of food.[139]

In October reports from Camp Douglas showed an alarming increase in mortality; out of approximately seventy-five hundred prisoners the number of casualties rose from thirty-four deaths and one hundred and sixty-seven sick in June to one hundred and twenty-three deaths and three hundred and seventy-three sick in September. Nine hundred and eighty-four were sick at the end of the first week in October; this was due to the long confinement, inefficient medical attendants, and the refusal to allow the sutler to sell vegetables, declared the commanding officer.[140] From Elmira came the assertion that if the death rate of August and September continued for a year the prison would be depopulated.[141] This was partly the result of the stagnant pond which had not been drained. Though Hoffman approved a plan to lay a pipe from the nearby Chemung river to create a circulation of water, he suggested that the fall rains would obviate the necessity of beginning the work before the spring of 1865.[142] To the commander of Camp Douglas, Hoffman sent orders to reduce the meat ration in order to issue vegetables, but the commander objected on the grounds that meat was as essential in winter as were vegetables.[143] Even when Hitchcock recommended allowing the sutlers at Johnson's Island to sell vegetables, Hoffman refused his assent.[144]

These conditions in regard to rations lasted throughout the winter of 1864-1865 and until the end of the war. Everywhere the prisoners suffered for the lack of a proper vegetable diet.[145] In January, 1865, despite these conditions,

[139] Ibid., 835.
[140] Ibid., 954-55.
[141] Ibid., 996-97.
[142] Ibid., 1003-5, 1025.
[143] Ibid., 1006, 1058-59.
[144] Ibid., 1025-26, 1051.

[145] See Ibid., 1091-95 for conditions in November at Elmira, also 1133-36, 1167, 1173-74, 1180; Holmes, op. cit., 88-89. Cf. Mary W. Rhodes to the National Intellingencer, October 19, for description of bad conditions. Dorothea Dix reported to General Hitchcock, November 25, that the prisoners received all necessary care and adequate provisions; the health of the camp was good and there were few sick. Official Records, series 2, VII, 1159. For Johnson's Island see Ibid., 1168-69, series 2, VIII, 4-5; Hundley, Prison Echoes of the Great Rebellion, 115, 121, 131. For Camp Douglas see Official Records, series 2, VIII, 76.

orders were issued for a further reduction of rations. By this ration bread was placed at sixteen ounces; soap, two pounds to a hundred men; vinegar, two quarts per hundred rations; and only beans or peas, rice or hominy were allowed the prisoners.[146]

Exchanged generals in August took occasion to point out that the prisoners in the North were still much better treated than their enemies in the South. Only in the matter of food was treatment similar. They admitted that the Confederate soldier and his prisoners received the same ration, but they asserted that the inmates of almshouses in the North were never fed so poorly as the average Southern family. Hence the food which the prisoners in the North received was enough for the prisoners. But only in the matter of rations were the two sides equal. In the South there was no water, no soap, no shelter, no clothes, and men died daily at Andersonville without medical care. These officers suggested that the prisoners recently exchanged at Charleston should draw up a code of treatment for the Northern prisons, adding that such treatment would be "a measure of economy if not of justice." Hoffman, to whom these suggestions were submitted, gave his whole-hearted approval.[147]

General Sickles pointed out to President Lincoln that it would be impossible to obtain any effect from such a method of retaliation, as the South was clearly unable to furnish its prisoners with adequate supplies. He suggested that General Foster at Charleston be permitted to send supplies through the lines to the Federal prisoners. General Hitchcock, who approved the suggestions of the exchanged officers, declared that the sending of supplies to Richmond had been a failure, as the rebels had sent the supplies to the army and the prisoners had seen the guards eating from their boxes.[148]

At the time of these conflicting suggestions in regard to retaliation, a delegation of prisoners, released from Ander-

[146] *Ibid.*, 62-63.
[147] Wessels to Thomas and Seymour to Hoffman, *Ibid.*, series 2, VII, 570-72.
[148] *Ibid.*, 574-75.

sonville and Charleston to lay a petition before the President, arrived in Washington. From Andersonville one Prescott Tracy bore a petition signed by the sergeants of messes begging to be exchanged. Officers at Charleston added a plea for their own release to an account of the sufferings of their men at Andersonville.[149] The press reported the arrival of these petitions, which were not acted upon by the President, and gave accounts of the prisoners' life. Pointing out that exchange was stopped by a profitless quarrel over paroles and negro soldiers while the prisoners were allowed to suffer, the press called upon the government to perform its clear duty to exchange the prisoners,[150] and citizens wrote to the president begging that the prisoners be brought home.[151]

The demand of the Northern press that exchanges be carried out led Halleck to instruct General Foster, on Morris Island, to attempt to send supplies to the prisoners in Charleston and Andersonville. This was done by the order of the secretary of war, Halleck explained, despite the fact that the prisoners in Richmond had received but a small portion of the supplies sent them.[152] Foster, accordingly, requested permission from General Jones to send ten wagon loads of Sanitary Commission Stores to Andersonville, but Jones refused on the ground that Foster had told a prisoner that supplies sent to Richmond had been taken by the Confederates.[153] This information had come from Halleck who had stated: "We have the best of evidence that the greater part of the supplies sent to our men at Richmond never reached them. A deserter has testified very recently that a

[149] Ibid., 616-23. See also Ransom, Andersonville Diary, 89 and Abbott, Prison Life in the South, 72 ff.

[150] New York Times, August 23, 24, September 5; New York Tribune, August 26; the National Intelligencer, September 12, cited the Augusta (Ga.) Constitutionalist as saying that one hundred and twenty-seven prisoners instead of three hundred died in one day at Andersonville. However, on the twenty-fourth the Intelligencer copied a statement from the Meridian (Miss.) Daily Clarion of August 25, repeating the story of three hundred deaths in one day.

[151] Official Records, series 2, VII, 767.

[152] Ibid., 623.

[153] Ibid., 622-23, 678-79, series 1, XXXV, part ii, 257; series 2, VII, 800, 828.

portion of the clothing so sent is now stored in Richmond for issue to their troops."[154] Foster refused to allow this to turn him from his purpose but sent forward the supplies to be delivered by a Confederate officer.[155]

At the same time General Sherman called upon the head of the Sanitary Commission in St. Louis for clothing and other articles to be sent through General Hood to Andersonville. He stated to the sanitarian that he knew that the Confederates were really unable to supply such articles but "they are as proud as the devil and hate to confess poverty." Hood accepted the offer and the supplies were sent.[156]

In the meantime efforts had been made by Northern citizens, aroused by the reports of suffering which came from the South, to secure some arrangement by which the prisoners could be relieved. W. H. Winder of New York, a brother of General Winder, suggested to Secretary Stanton that the rebel prisoners be given all necessary supplies and the accounts presented to the Confederate government to be paid in cotton. General Hitchcock declared that this would require the consent of the rebel authorities, who had "systematically refused to relieve or to suffer us to relieve" the prisoners.[157] A more tenable suggestion came from a Mr. Broadwell who suggested that he be allowed to go south for the purpose of issuing blankets and clothing to the prisoners and to make arrangements for allowing the Confederates to supply their men in the North, payment to be made in cotton. Grant expressed his willingness to pass Broadwell through the lines on this mission.[158]

But before Broadwell was passed through the lines, Ould suggested to Mulford that each side should be allowed the privilege of forwarding articles of food and clothing to its

---

[154] *Ibid.*, 808-9.

[155] *Ibid.*, 848. When Ould learned that Jones had accepted articles from Foster, he immediately demanded information of the transaction, pointing out that the Sanitary Commission had been prohibited from sending supplies to Richmond because of their vilification of the Confederacy. *Ibid.*, 890.

[156] *Ibid.*, 857-58, 883-85.

[157] *Ibid.*, 582.

[158] *Ibid.*, 814-15. See also 920.

prisoners. The articles were to be made the subject of agreement. In order for the Confederates to perform their part of the agreement, it would be necessary to sell cotton outside the Confederacy and to ship the articles purchased after selling the cotton, to one of the ports of the United States. This proposal, sent also to Stanton, was referred to General Grant, who was given full control over the subject by the secretary of war.[159] General Hitchcock refused to assent to the arrangement, declaring that if the South could not feed its prisoners it should release them on parole,[160] Grant, however, saw no objection to the arrangement and so informed General Lee, declaring also that there was no objection to the sending of cotton to Northern cities and suggesting that an officer be paroled on each side to receive the goods sent through the lines.[161]

On October 31, Butler gave Mulford instructions to lay a proposition for the mutual supply of prisoners before Ould. The United States would agree to deliver food at designated points, the Confederates to furnish transportation beyond. The United States would furnish food, clothing, hospital stores, shelter, and fuel to their soldiers. The Confederacy was to be allowed to make the same arrangements, cotton being sent to New York and the purchases made there. Tents, however, could not be taken from the North into the Confederacy if such were purchased from the proceeds of the cotton. A board of three officers, who were to be paroled to issue and account for the supplies,[162] was to be appointed by each side from among their prisoners at each prison.

Ould accepted this arrangement and General W. N. R. Beall was appointed the agent for the South.[163] Although Beall made preparations for the arrival of the cotton,[164] delay

[159] *Ibid.*, 926, 929.

[160] *Ibid.*, 965-66.

[161] *Ibid.*, 1008-9.

[162] *Ibid.*, 1070-73, 1107-8. The correspondence relating to the arrangement to supply prisoners is given in the *National Intelligencer*, November 16.

[163] *Ibid.*, 1117-18, 1131, 1148-49. General Joseph Hughes and Colonel S. M. Weld were appointed the Federal agents in the South. *Ibid.*, 1198.

[164] *Ibid.*, 1206-7, 1217, 1260-61, 1246-49, 1263.

occurred in getting it out of the harbor of Mobile,[165] and it was not until January 23, that nine hundred and ninety-seven bales arrived in New York.[166] Much of the cotton was of poor quality and one hundred and seventy bales were late in arriving.[167] Ould immediately asked Grant for permission to send fifteen hundred more bales,[168] and Beall made a similar request, stating that he had received .8248 cents a pound for his cotton and had bought 16,930 blankets, 16,216 coats, 19,888 pairs of pants, 19,000 shirts, 5,948 pairs of drawers, 10,140 pairs of socks, and 17,000 pairs of shoes. General Halleck noticed that all of the money had been spent for clothing which fitted the men for the field and stated that Stanton was not inclined to sanction the admission of any more cotton on the same terms.[169] Halleck declared that the suits bought for the prisoners were the Confederate uniform in all but buttons.[170] With the first issue, therefore, Beall's work ceased; the exchange of prisoners and the end of the war removed the necessity for making further issues to the prisoners.[171]

The end of the war did not arrive before the Confederacy took an opportunity to strike a blow for its own defense in the field of propaganda. A senate resolution in the Confederate congress appointed a joint committee to investigate the treatment of prisoners by the two sides.[172] Early in March this committee presented a preliminary report which began with

[165] *Ibid.*, 1200-1, 1247, 1276-77, 1281, 1290, 1292; series 2, VIII, 2, 27; VII 1293-94, VIII, 67-68.

[166] *Ibid.*, 114, 123-24.   [167] *Ibid.*, 199-200.

[168] *Ibid.*, 202.   [169] *Ibid.*, 241-42.

[170] *Ibid.*, 227.

[171] *Ibid.*, 257, 289. Grant suggested that the prisoners who did not receive an issue of clothing might be sent in exchange, but Hoffman pointed out that there was no chance that those prisoners who were willing to take the oath would be given any of the supplies from the South. Since the number of oath takers about balanced the excess that the North held, this scheme would be impracticable.

More pleasant in its aspects was the work of General Hughes in distributing supplies from the North. Blankets were sent to Richmond, Danville, and Salisbury. Hughes supervised the issue at these places of some 5,000 blankets and corresponding amounts of shirts and trousers. The Confederate authorities, he reported, afforded him every facility. *Ibid.*, 220-21.

[172] *Ibid.*, 49. January 9, 1865.

an examination of the charges made in *House Report No. 67* and the Sanitary Commission's *Narrative*. The spirit and intent of these publications, it was asserted, was to inflame the evil passions of the North. The photographs were cited as evidence of this spirit; such cases, the committee believed, could have been found in every Northern hospital and even in homes. The committee then proceeded to describe the sufferings of the prisoners in the North. They denied the charge of robbery, although they admitted that in the heat of conflict, without the knowledge of the officers, some robbery may have taken place on the battlefield. Countercharges were made to the charge that prisoners were killed at the windows of the Libby prison. Other charges were either met with similar countercharges or absolutely denied. Finally the North was declared to have been totally responsible for the sufferings of prisoners in the South since they had refused to exchange. Only the powder under Libby prison was admitted, and that was justified by the necessity for intimidating the prisoners.[173]

[173] *Ibid.*, 337-53. March 3.

CHAPTER X

EXCHANGE UNDER BUTLER
1 8 6 4 - 1 8 6 5

On December 17, 1863, General Hitchcock made a trip to Fort Monroe to appoint General Benjamin F. Butler a special agent of exchange. Butler was authorized to make exchanges on the basis of equal numbers, with negro troops and their officers on the same plane as white. All questions of paroles and the release of the excess prisoners were to be waived for a time.[1]

The appointment of Butler was a concession to the demand of the people of the North that something should be done to obtain the release of the prisoners in the South. The reports of the scarcity of provisions in Richmond, which had necessitated the sending of supplies by the government and by private citizens, combined with the repeated stories of the Confederates' brutality to their unhappy charges, produced a feeling in the country that the technical question of the validity of certain paroles in Tennessee was not a sufficient reason for permitting prisoners to suffer in the South. Butler had sensed this popular agitation and had brought himself to the foreground by sending vaccine to the Confederate commissioner for the use of the prisoners. At the same time he had pressed on the administration his request to be allowed to try his hand at the exchange of prisoners. Butler was too prominent a politician to be lightly dismissed, and the secretary of war had consented to allow him to make the attempt which would, at least, quiet the people for a time.

Butler immediately informed Ould of his appointment[2] and prepared to send a load of prisoners to City Point. On December 25, he sent a boat load of five hundred and five

---

[1] *Official Records*, series 2, VI, 711-12; *National Intelligencer*, December 21, 1863.
[2] *Official Records*, series 2, VI, 752.

prisoners from Point Lookout. All of them were serviceable men, and Butler requested the Confederate commissioner to return a like number, leaving all controversial matters in abeyance.[3]

This turn of affairs in relation to the prisoners took the Confederate authorities by surprise. Butler was still under the declaration of outlawry proclaimed by President Davis in the previous year. Since this had not been removed, the question whether the new agent should be recognized became one of considerable moment. Ould immediately addressed a protest to General Hitchcock, pointing out the fact that Butler was *persona non grata* to the Confederates and asking for his removal.[4] Richmond opinion divided on the issue, one newspaper adopting the attitude that Butler was as good as any whom the Yankees might select. Hitchcock and Meredith were "scurvy fellows—falsifiers and tricksters" and well gotten rid of. It was also noted that Butler had disapproved of their policy and had favored a liberal plan of exchange.[5]

The Confederate authorities could not, however, allow a punctilio to stand in the way of an exchange of prisoners. In return, Ould sent five hundred and twenty prisoners from Richmond, addressing himself, however, to Colonel Mulford, in charge of the truce boat. Although the cartel had not been mentioned in Butler's letter, Ould hoped that this was the beginning of exchanges under that instrument. But if it were not the intention of the Federal authorities to return to the cartel, the Confederates, Ould declared, could not consent to a further release.[3]

To General Butler, who had expected thus easily to revive exchanges, the Confederate action appeared a deliberate insult. Highly incensed, he informed Stanton that he had sent prisoners in the belief that the Confederates would accept

[3] *Ibid.*, 754-55.
[4] *Ibid.*, 768.
[5] Richmond *Whig*, December 28. New York *Times*, December 31. Richmond *Dispatch*, December 29.
[6] *Official Records*, series 2, VI, 769. Cf. Jones, *A Rebel War Clerk's Diary*, II, 121.

a fair, just, and honorable proposition for the exchange of prisoners actually in custody. In reply he had received more prisoners than he sent but had also received letters which

.... assert in substance that unless the United States give up every claim that they have made in behalf of their soldiers who are prisoners of war; consent to sacrifice the colored soldiers the Government has enlisted; turn over their officers to the cruel punishments imposed by the pretended law of the Confederate Congress; and last, and much the least, consent officially that the person whom the Government has intrusted the command of this department shall be executed immediately upon capture. . . . no exchange can be effected while our soldiers, prisoners in their hands, are to be maltreated, starved, ironed, or hanged, as suits their caprice.

Butler therefore recommended that retaliation should be resorted to and asked that rebel officers be sent him so that he could insure the safety of every prisoner in the South.

If such orders shall be given me, I will see to it that under no possible circumstances shall there be doubt upon the point. . . . When I was sending medicines to prevent the spread of a loathsome disease among their citizens I was not so "obnoxious" to Jefferson Davis but that the medicine was received and the usual official courtesies passed between his agent and myself.[7]

Butler followed this letter to Washington and there urged his proposition before the officials. President Lincoln was understood to doubt the propriety of adopting Butler's proposals.[8] It was reported, however, that the United States would not allow Butler to be outlawed, and Stanton determined to confirm his agency by sending prisoners to Point Lookout. It was believed that this would have the desired effect on Jefferson Davis, who was said to be in favor of dealing with Butler.[9] The course of the government was generally approved. "If the rebels dread his severity," it was said, "they will be less likely to provoke it by additional cruelties to our prisoners."[10]

On his return to Fort Monroe, Butler informed Ould that

[7] *Official Records*, series 2, VI, 769-71.

[8] New York *Times*, January 4, 1864. Philadelphia *Inquirer*, January 5.

[9] *Ibid.*, January 6. This paper stated that Stanton planned to send thirty thousand prisoners to Point Lookout.

[10] New York *Times*, January 21.

the United States would appoint anyone it chose as agent of exchange and would not recognize a declaration of outlawry by the Confederacy. Butler asserted that the agents of the United States should be allowed all of the rights of a flag of truce—which was forbidden to him by Davis' proclamation—or all communications would be cut off. He renewed his application to exchange all prisoners man for man until one side was exhausted.[11]

While waiting for some definite answer from the South, Butler came into conflict with the secretary of war and with General Hitchcock. On January 24, Butler declared all prisoners, civilians, officers, and soldiers received to that date, exchanged. Stanton no sooner learned of the declaration than he ordered its execution suspended until Butler explained his action. Hitchcock proceeded to inform Stanton that Butler was following the precedent established by Ould and was therefore giving the Confederate a justification for his own illegal exchange.[12] Since Butler had exchanged the men at the time of their delivery, he could see no reason for not making the declaration, but Hitchcock informed him that instead of there being only the seven hundred and fifty prisoners whom Butler had received since his appointment, there had been delivered 2,921 since the last declaration of

---

[11] *Official Records*, series 2, VI, 836. When the boat which carried Butler's communication arrived in Richmond, it was found that there was no one authorized to negotiate for an exchange whom the Confederacy could accept, and the boat returned without any arrangements being effected. Jones, *op. cit.*, II, 130. No reply to Butler's messages was vouchsafed from the Confederacy, but a package of papers arrived, relating to the business of exchange. None of them was addressed to General Butler. Stanton, stating that he did not want anything to happen to compromise the position of the government in its right to select its own agents, referred the papers to Butler to ask if they were to be accepted without the proper address. *Official Records*, series 2, VI, 867. Butler, declaring that these papers were the "debris" of the exchange business, none of them of any importance, explained that the business was conducted by his sending inquiries which Ould endorsed. Butler refused to become excited over the papers and informed Stanton that he was attempting to manage affairs so as to avoid any collision, especially of a personal nature, so long as it could be avoided and still maintain his personal respect and the honor of the government. "I don't mean to make difficulties about personal matters. When a difference arises it will be a perfectly distinct one, which will justify me in taking the issue." *Ibid.*, 897.

[12] *Ibid.*, 871-74.

exchange in September, 1863. To support his argument, Hitchcock presented figures from Hoffman showing that deliveries to the value of 3,008 privates had been made since September.[13]

The discussion of Butler's declaration lasted through the month of February, 1864, growing in bitterness as the two generals alternately complained and defended their actions to the secretary of war. Hitchcock was so completely committed to his unpopular position in regard to paroles that any action which he could interpret as a surrender of that position was certain to obtain his enmity. The quarrel developed into a personal one, each of the generals appealing to Stanton to uphold his arguments. Hitchcock declared to Stanton that Butler showed an overweening anxiety to parade his name before the public in connection with exchange in order that the people might think he was doing something. Hitchcock recalled that he had recommended the appointment of Butler; "no vulgar love of newspaper notoriety tyrannizes over my disposition to impede its action in behalf of suffering humanity." He had supported Butler when the Confederates refused to accept him as agent, but "I now do not hesitate to express my deep regret that Butler was ever appointed because difficulties have increased and the country feels his appointment an embarrassment." In this vein the quarrel continued throughout the month of March, 1864.[14]

With no reply from Ould and no further deliveries of prisoners, the people of both sides gave up hope for an immediate exchange. In Richmond it was declared that the appointment of the "Beast" reduced the question of exchange to a matter of endurance. The country supported the president in sustaining his proclamation against Butler.[15] In the North the people were told that they must give up hope for an exchange. The question had become one of national honor, and, in addition, a general exchange would restore to the South an army as large as or larger than that which Lee had

[13] *Ibid.*, 898-99.   [14] *Ibid.*, 1007-13, 1092, 1097.
[15] Richmond *Whig*, January 19. New York *Times*, February 2.

under his command. It was the hope of the rebels to force the government to exchange, but the Northern people were called upon to sustain the administration by "an enlightened patience."[16]

In the meantime Ould informed Hitchcock that he would declare exchanged the prisoners received since September, 1863, and gave his permission for Hitchcock to make a similar declaration.[17] The declaration, made February 4, added to those delivered at City Point all of the Vicksburg prisoners who had assembled at a parole camp at Enterprise, Mississippi.[18] Following this declaration Ould addressed to Mulford a reply to Butler's proposition for a man-for-man exchange. Ould told Mulford to inform Butler that the Confederacy had always admitted and insisted upon the obligation of the cartel; especially its "cardinal" feature of delivery within ten days. Since the South was willing to resume its execution, the United States had only to begin sending prisoners according to the cartel and the exchange would begin.[19]

This letter, which was free from any mention of the matters in controversy between the agents, was probably the result of an agitation in Richmond to have the barrier of Butler's recognition removed from the exchange question. On February 8, resolutions passed the Virginia house of delegates which declared that Davis should withdraw his objections to Butler as an agent of exchange. The resolution also thanked the people of the commonwealth for their support of their president in the matter. The legislators, however, disclaimed any intention of advising the president to withdraw his proclamation against Butler.[20]

[16] New York *Times*, February 3.
[17] *Official Records*, series 2, VI, 884.
[18] *Ibid.*, 920.
[19] *Ibid.*, 921-22.
[20] *Ibid.*, 934-35. The *Daily Examiner* of Richmond opposed this action of the Virginia delegates, as it was the recognition of a "negro and a felon." It was claimed that Davis asked for and pushed the resolution. "Never will we admit negro negotiators" proudly boasted the journal. "This is a disgrace which the Yankees heap upon us." It was also pointed out that the retention of the prisoners would decrease enlistments in the Northern armies while the Confederates would fight even under such harsh conditions. *Ibid.*, 958-60.

Under these conditions of a more conciliatory tone from the South and its agent, Stanton instructed Butler to send up the river an experimental boat load of two hundred officers with an offer to exchange them. Hitchcock approved this action and believed that the rebels would feel compelled to accept the men. This scheme had been suggested to him by two exchanged prisoners who believed that the plan would work.[21]

Before Butler sent the officers, Mulford went up the river with a flag of truce. Ould met him at City Point and informed him that the only difficulty in the execution of the cartel was that the Confederacy would insist upon the delivery of the excess prisoners.[22] At the same time Mulford informed Ould that Butler was in favor of a general exchange and was able to consummate it. Ould told his secretary of war of this development, stating that Mulford had never deceived him. Ould interpreted the negotiations to mean that Butler had set his heart on securing the release of prisoners and that failure to accomplish this end would hurt him more than a refusal to recognize him. As Southern opinion was opposed to the recognition of Butler, Ould suggested that he go to Fort Monroe to obtain a definite statement on the matter of a general exchange. The only difficulty which Ould could see was that Butler might require some pledge as to slaves. If, however, Butler were recognized as agent, Ould felt sure that he could avoid the difficulty.[23] Ould and Seddon met in secret conference to determine their future action.[24]

The decision to which Ould and Seddon had come was revealed when the truce boat came from Fort Monroe. Butler had not only sent the two hundred officers but had also sent on the same boat six hundred privates. For these eight hundred prisoners, forty-eight officers and six hundred privates were delivered.[25] This number was based upon the propor-

[21] Ibid., 978-79.
[22] Ibid., 995.
[23] Ibid., 996.
[24] Jones, op. cit., II, 160.
[25] Official Records, series 2, VI, 1025.

tions of men and officers in prison on the two sides and emphasized the determination of the Confederates to exchange only on condition the excess prisoners were delivered on parole. But Butler was willing to overlook the fact that this was not a man-for-man exchange and called upon Hoffman to send to Point Lookout two thousand a week whom he could forward to Richmond.[26] In order to receive the fullest popular support for his actions, Butler requested Ould to send him officers from Texas and other distant prisons to refute the assertion in the North that only the prisoners at Richmond could be exchanged.[27]

But the popular approval which Butler sought was not forthcoming. Southern papers defended Ould's sending prisoners to Butler by revealing to their readers the fact that only a proportionate number had been sent. The Northern papers, copying this defense, informed their readers that if they reckoned the difficulties had been arranged, the negro soldiers and General Butler recognized, and the "sham" paroles rescinded, their conclusions were contradicted by the Confederate press and by the unequal deliveries.[28] Stanton called Butler's attention to such an article in the *National Intelligencer* and asked for an explanation. Butler denied that he was exchanging on a proportionate basis but declared that he would do so if he could not obtain the prisoners otherwise. Moreover, he accused Hitchcock of sending such information to the newspapers.[29]

Toward the last of March Butler notified Stanton that he had received altogether from Ould nine hundred and sixty-five men and sixty-five officers, a number larger than he had delivered. "I have now got the matter of exchange to such a point that I think we may go through upon a proper basis." Whereupon Butler called upon Ould to meet him at Fort

[26] *Ibid.*, 1033.
[27] *Ibid.*, 1034.
[28] New York *Times*, March 10, 12.
[29] *Official Records*, series 2, VI, 1038. See also the New York *Times*, March 14, 15, 16, stating that Stanton had ordered exchange stopped. The *National Intelligencer*, March 11; cf. March 15.

Monroe, informing Stanton that if exchange should not go through upon an honorable and fair basis the United States was in a position to work "such proper and thorough retaliation as will bring these rebels to their senses." He asked that all prisoners possible be sent to Point Lookout where they could be exchanged before the spring campaign began.[30]

On March 29, in a communication addressed to Butler as "U. S. Agent for Exchange," Ould announced that he was at Fort Monroe and ready for a conference.[31] Two days later in a meeting between the agents, the question of the negro soldiers was discussed, and Ould agreed that all free negroes could be treated as prisoners of war. Slaves, however, were not to be accorded such treatment, since, he contended, the Confederacy had the right to return them to their former owners. On the vexed question of paroles Ould asserted his former position that they were to be counted in accordance with the general orders of the United States, prior to July 3, 1863, the date of General Orders 207. Since this order provided that paroles should be legal only when granted by the commanding officer, it became necessary to decide what individual in a given case should be considered in command. Ould agreed to extend the definition to include the commander of a besieged fortress and commanders of detailed forces when acting independent of headquarters.[32]

Butler submitted to Stanton a memorandum of these points with an explanation of each. With the exception of the one relating to slaves, Butler declared that he could perceive no reason why some agreement could not be secured. Butler believed Ould's proposition in regard to counting paroles under the general orders of the United States to be fair;[33] he advised that the propositions be accepted. "The cartel was a hard bargain against us, but still it is our compact, and I

---

[30] *Official Records,* series 2, VI, 1082. [31] *Ibid.,* 1111. [32] *Ibid.,* 1121-22.

[33] Butler explained the necessity for defining the commander in the field by pointing out that General Pemberton surrendered to Grant at Vicksburg although General Johnston, a few miles away, was the commander of the department. The same was true of Port Hudson where General Gardner gave paroles while Johnston was near by. Both of these cases would be illegal under a strict interpretation of General Orders 207.

suppose that it is to be stood by." Regarding the right of the South to return slaves to their former masters, Butler was unwilling to make any concessions. He requested that the other questions, paroles and commanders, be settled in order that the issue of the negro should stand out in full justification for the failure of the North to abide by the cartel. Accepting the position that a slave was property, Butler declared that the position of the South was untenable. Under the laws of war, captured property became the property of the captor, who might exercise full control over it. It was an exercise of this right of ownership when the United States government set the negroes free. If such a piece of property should be recaptured, it would not, according to the laws of war, revert to the original owner but would become the possession of the capturing government.[34]

This report was submitted to General Hitchcock for his opinion. On the matter of the slaves Hitchcock refused to make any comment, stating that the question could be settled only by the president. The matter of paroles, however, was to Hitchcock of supreme importance. Hitchcock lost no opportunity to inject his interpretation of the parole controversy, and at this opening he again began an enumeration of the prisoners whom Ould had exchanged by declarations alleged illegal. Butler, Hitchcock asserted, had been completely deceived by the wily Confederate. As for Order 207, it was not intended to, and could not, affect the cartel. The laws of war were in effect before the cartel, and Order 207 was in harmony with those laws. Further, the order was intended only as instructions for the Federal troops and could not be cited by the South, nor was its interpretation a subject for the agreement of the agents.

This communication, together with Butler's report, was submitted to General Grant, who ordered Butler to suspend action until he could examine the question.[35] Hitchcock then followed up his letter to Stanton by reviewing his side of the

[34] *Official Records,* series 2, VII, 29-34.
[35] *Ibid.,* 46-50.

parole controversy to Grant.[36] The result was that Grant informed Butler to make no arrangements for the exchange of prisoners which did not recognize the validity of the Vicksburg and Port Hudson paroles, and provide for the release of a number sufficient to cancel the balance which the South owed. Until this release was made Grant ordered that not another prisoner of war should be paroled or exchanged by the North. In addition, Grant asserted that no distinction was to be made between the white and colored soldiers. Nonacquiescence in either of these propositions by the Confederate authorities was to be regarded as a refusal on their part to agree to a further exchange of prisoners.[37]

In a personal interview Grant explained to Butler his views on the question of exchanges. Grant believed that if exchanges were to cease, the tendency to desert to the enemy, manifested by bounty jumpers and conscripts, would be done away with. Since these soldiers were lost to the army unless tempted back by offers of larger bounties, a soldier in prison was worth two in the rebel lines. Butler, always a politician, pointed out to Grant that if the prisoners were not exchanged simply because they were more valuable in prison than in the army, the proposition could not be sustained before popular clamor. The government could not stand the pressure of the people, and the Copperheads could use such a statement to good advantage in the coming election. Butler suggested that the basis for stopping the exchange should be declared to be the Confederates' refusal to repeal the act of their congress against the negro troops. Furthermore the negro question should be pressed because, since the draft could not be enforced during the election, the negro soldiers would have to die in prison. Pressing of the question would aid the administration in the election and in exchange of the sick, which, Butler suggested, would serve to still some of the popular outcry.[38] Grant permitted him to accept all of the sick whom the Confederates sent but strictly ordered him to send none in exchange for them.[39]

[36] *Ibid.*, 53-56.
[37] *Ibid.*, 62-63.
[38] Butler, *Butler's Book*, 594-95.
[39] *Official Records*, series 2, VII, 69.

After this, the business of exchanges between the commissioners closed by declarations of exchange on both sides. On April 20, Ould declared exchanged, without having consulted Butler, all prisoners delivered to that date. Since these men would be sent into the field, Butler recommended that a declaration be issued by the adjutant general which would place the men whom the United States had received in the field in opposition.[40] A declaration was accordingly issued May 7, exchanging all prisoners received to that date and asserting that Ould owed the United States 33,596 prisoners from his "illegal" exchange of the Vicksburg prisoners.[41]

To the Richmond authorities the developments in the North were inexplicable.[42] Ould asserted that he was not hopeful of a general exchange. Aside from the obstacle created by the retention of Butler as agent of exchange, there was the totally inadmissible claim of the enemy that the recaptured slaves should be treated as prisoners of war. The best Ould hoped for was that a general delivery should be made for all except hostages held for the negroes. Eventually, he foresaw, this would lead to such difficulties as would force the complete abandonment of the cartel. But

. . . . as yet the Federals do not appear to have found any well-authenticated case of the retention of a negro prisoner. They have made several specific inquiries, but in each case there was no record of any such party, and I so responded. Having no especial desire to find any such case it is more than probable that the same answer will be returned to every such inquiry.[43]

The only real solution which Ould saw to the difficulties was for the South to obtain possession of an excess of prisoners. When that happened, he averred, "I shall give the Yankees successive doses of their own physic."[44]

---

[40] *Ibid.*, 108.
[41] *Ibid.*, 126. Ould declared that this declaration was in excess and issued another, June 6, See *Ibid.*, 216.
[42] See Davis' message to Congress, *Ibid.*, 103.
[43] Ould to Seddon, *Ibid.*, 103-6.
[44] Ould to Szymanski, *Ibid.*, 189-91. Secretary Seddon had even more radical ideas as to the proper avoidance of the negro problem. To Howell Cobb, who wrote from Georgia that he was having difficulty feeding the prisoners and advised an exchange

The opening of the campaign against Richmond in the early summer cut off communication between the agents of exchange. On June 8, the Federal agent was informed of the unwillingness of Richmond authorities to allow flag-of-truce boats to come up the river; torpedoes were planted in the channel.[45] The Confederates even refused to deliver to Mulford a load of sick prisoners.[46]

During the summer of 1864 there were no communications between the agents of exchange, although some exchanges took place between commanders in the field.[47] With the prolonged cessation of negotiations between the agents, the prisoners in the Confederate prisons began to feel that their government had deserted them. The prisoners at Andersonville, Macon, Charleston, and Savannah drew up petitions to their government to release them from their unhappy confinement. Some of the prisoners were dissatisfied with the mild tone of the petitions which accused the rebels of poverty rather than cruelty, but the prisoners were many and the petitions were sent.[48] Among the prisoners a bitter

if it could be arranged so that recaptured slaves should not be surrendered, Seddon wrote: "I doubt, however, whether the exchange of negroes at all for our own soldiers would be tolerated [by the 'Southern people.] As to the white officers serving with negro troops, we ought never to be inconvenienced with such prisoners." *Ibid.*, 203.

[45] *Ibid.*, 211, 216.

[46] *Ibid.*, 215, See also series 1, XXXVI, part iii, 717.

[47] Generals Canby and Kirby Smith, opposing each other in the southwest, arranged an exchange for the prisoners at Camp Ford, near Tyler, Texas. (For details see *Ibid.*, series 2, VII, 471, 481-82, 493-94, 508-9, 538-39, 588.) At Charleston General Sam Jones and General Foster arranged an exchange of prisoners. Jones had received fifty officers from the prison at Macon to be exposed to the fire of the Union batteries shelling the city; fifty officers were sent by General Halleck to be similarly exposed to fire in retaliation. An agreement between the generals resulted in the exchange of these officers early in August. (*Ibid.*, 371, 378, 447, 463, 520-21, 603. Also series 1, XXXV, part ii, 132 *passim*, especially 161, 212-13.) Six hundred prisoners were sent to Charleston while the negotiations were in progress, and Jones offered to exchange them for the six hundred who were immediately sent in retaliation. (*Ibid.*, series 2, VII, 502, 567, 602-3).

[48] See above page 205; also Glazier, *The Capture, the Prison Pen and the Escape*, 121-22, who claimed that the petitions were not sent; Davidson, *Fourteen Months*, 176 ff. Kellogg, *Life and Death in Rebel Prisons*, contends that the Andersonville prisoners refused to sign, 182, 188. See also the *Official Records*, series 2, VII, 618-20.

antagonism developed against the secretary of war, and one prisoner asserted that there were organizations among the prisoners at Andersonville and Macon to assassinate Stanton upon their release.[49]

The arrival of petitions from the prisons and the increasing fund of stories of the barbarities of the Southerners led the officials responsible for the prisons to adopt a policy of retaliation while the people of the North clamored for exchange.[50] Taking advantage of this popular demand and despairing of hope for obtaining an excess of prisoners in order to be able to retaliate on the North for their refusal to exchange, Ould decided to accept the Northern proposition to exchange man for man. On August 10, he addressed Mulford stating that for the purpose of relieving the sufferings of prisoners on both sides he assented to the proposition.[51]

The news of this offer was communicated to Butler, whose preparations to send a flag-of-truce boat up the river to meet the Confederate commissioner became known to Grant. Butler informed Grant that the boat was going to arrange a meeting with Ould in regard to the treatment of prisoners in retaliation. Grant, not satisfied with this explanation, informed Butler that he was opposed to any exchange until the whole matter was placed on a footing giving equal advantages to the North. Meanwhile he ordered that no flags of truce be sent unless he was advised of what was being done and gave his consent. Butler could state that no exchange would be made which did not give an equal advantage to the North. This satisfied Grant, who then approved of the expedition. Hitchcock had declared that an exchange was desirable, but Grant informed Butler, "On the subject of exchange, however, I differ from General Hitchcock. It is hard on our men held in Southern prisons not to exchange them, but it is humanity to those left in the ranks to fight our battles. Every man we hold, when released on

[49] Isham, *Military Prisons and Prisoners of War.* See also Page, *The True Story of Andersonville,* 106 ff. for the hatred of Stanton.
[50] See above pages 205 ff.
[51] *Official Records,* series 2, VII, 578-79.

parole or otherwise, becomes an active soldier against us at once either directly or indirectly. If we commence a system of exchanges which liberates all prisoners taken, we will have to fight on until the whole South is exterminated. If we hold those caught they amount to no more than dead men. At this particular time to release all rebel prisoners North would insure Sherman's defeat and would compromise our safety here."[52] Grant followed up this opinion by asking Stanton to forbid Foster to exchange the prisoners at Charleston. He contended that the enemy received the benefit of the exchange at once, while the poor condition of the men prevented any use being made of them by the North for two or three months.[53] Halleck ordered Canby not to carry out his arrangement with Kirby Smith, but he told Grant

.... to exchange their healthy men for ours, who are on the brink of the grave from their hellish treatment of course gives them the advantage. Nevertheless it seems very cruel to leave our men to be slowly but deliberately tortured to death. But I suppose there is no remedy at present.[54]

To Butler fell the task of presenting this decision to the Confederate commissioner in such a way that no odium would be cast upon the administration. This was particularly necessary in view of the approaching presidential election. In a letter to Ould, Butler requested to be informed if the proposal to exchange man for man applied to the negro soldiers. Davis' proclamation and the resolution of the Confederate congress still stood, and Butler asked if the United States was to understand that they had been nullified.

One cannot help thinking, even at the risk of being deemed uncharitable, that the benevolent sympathies of the Confederate authorities have been lately stirred by the depleted condition of their armies, and a desire to get into the field, to effect the present campaign, the hale, hearty and well-fed prisoners held by the United States in exchange for the half-starved, sick, emaciated, and unserviceable soldiers of the United States now languishing in your prisons.

[52] *Ibid.*, 605-7. See also Grant to Seward, *Ibid.*, 614-15, in which he expresses the same idea.

[53] *Ibid*, 662

[54] *Ibid.*, 685.

Citing the argument that slaves, as property, became the possession of the United States when captured—an argument which he had formerly presented to Stanton—Butler declared that the Confederates could not restore recaptured slaves to their owners after the United States, exercising its right as owner, had set them free. Mules, rushing across the lines, were the property of the side which captured them, and slaves fleeing to the army of the Federal government were in the same classification.[55]

This letter, of which Butler was exceedingly proud, was sent for publication to the New York *Times* in order that the people might be convinced that the government was upholding the rights of the negroes.[56] But Butler was not led astray by his own legal ingenuity and feared that the Confederates might in their turn believe that the release of prisoners would defeat Sherman and imperil Grant. In case the South accepted his argument, Butler was prepared to raise still other obstacles in the way of an agreement to exchange. He planned to insist that the declaration of outlawry against him should be rescinded and apologies made before he would enter further negotiations for an exchange. Grant approved this course, but it was never necessary to resort to these means to block exchange. "The Confederates never offered to me afterward to exchange the colored soldiers," Butler later declared.[57]

Popular opinion, however, had again become aroused to demand that the government exchange the prisoners. Before Butler's letter was received, Ould published a letter to the Southern people stating that he had made the offer.[58] It was to counteract the effects of this that Butler published his letter in the New York *Times*, which was already urging the government to make exchanges and which, after Butler's letter, declared that if the negro issue could be settled, no mere

[55] *Ibid.*, 678-91.
[56] *Ibid.*, 768-69. Published New York *Times*, September 6. This letter was also published by the government as a leaflet for general distribution.
[57] Butler, *Butler's Book*, 605.
[58] *Official Records*, series 2, VII, 794-96.

technical difficulty should be allowed to stand in the way of an exchange of prisoners.[60] Citizens wrote to Lincoln calling upon him to relieve the prisoners in the South who were "sickening, dying, rotting as they stagger and fall to rise no more."[61] Others wrote in a more practical vein and declared that the president's chances for re-election were reduced by the failure to exchange.[62] The same sentiment was expressed in letters to the newspapers.[63]

As a concession to this popular demand, and yet without giving up the principles laid down by Grant, it was planned to effect the release of the sick and wounded prisoners. Butler believed that the South would consent to an exchange of invalids and offered to Ould to exchange all prisoners who would be unfit for active service within sixty days.[64] This proposition was acceptable in the South where citizens were advising the president to parole the prisoners and send them home without equivalents.[65] General Cobb recommended accepting any terms that could be obtained and suggested that the prisoners who were opposed to Lincoln should be paroled and sent home with a statement that the Northern people were being deceived by the assertion that the South would not accept exchange. By this scheme Cobb thought to accomplish three things: the South would be relieved from feeding the prisoners, votes would be cast against Lincoln, and Lincoln would be shown to be refusing an exchange for political reasons. Ould advised sending the disabled men and men whose terms had expired to the extent of the remaining Vicksburg prisoners. To send more than enough to balance the Vicksburg prisoners would weaken the pressure upon Lincoln which Ould hoped would produce an exchange.[66]

Unofficially Ould let it be known that he would accept Butler's proposition and agreed to accept at Fort Pulaski five

[59] New York *Times*, August 23.
[60] *Ibid.*, September 8.
[63] New York *Times*, September 8.
[64] *Official Records*, series 2, VII, 782, 793. Cf. Keiley, *In Vinculis*, 179-81.
[65] *Official Records*, series 2, VII, 783.
[66] *Ibid.*, 796.

[61] *Official Records*, series 2, VII, 767.
[62] *Ibid.*, 787, 816.

hundred sick prisoners. Butler asked that the prisoners be sent him for delivery to the Confederates.[67] On September 18 and 19, five hundred prisoners were sent to City Point to begin the exchange.[68] By September 25, Butler asked for six hundred more to balance the number he expected to receive from Richmond. Unfortunately thirty prisoners had died in one former load, and Butler asked that more care be taken in the selection of prisoners to be sent. He also asked for five thousand for delivery at Fort Pulaski.[69] On the twenty-seventh, Butler, having already learned from Hoffman that there were about twenty-eight hundred prisoners in condition to be delivered, informed the commissary-general that Ould would deliver five thousand sick whether or not he received that many.[70] Hoffman ordered the commanders of the prisons to prepare to send all invalids who would not be fit for service within sixty days.[71] Although arrangements were being made to exchange the sick among the prisoners, there was no intention on the part of the responsible officials of the United States to consider a general exchange. General Lee offered to General Grant an exchange of the prisoners belonging to their respective armies. Grant refused to consider any proposition except for prisoners taken within a few days of the time of the offer. He further asked if Lee intended to include negroes. Lee was willing to exchange negroes not slaves; but Grant, asserting that the United States would protect all its soldiers regardless of color, refused to enter any arrangements.[72] Naval prisoners, however, were exchanged by negotiations between the secretaries of the navy on the two sides. In the delivery of these prisoners no distinction was made between the white and negro sailors.[73] During the month of September Generals Hood and Sherman arranged for an exchange of recent captures, Sherman refusing to accept a proposition which would release to him

[67] Ibid., 818.
[68] Ibid., 858-60. New York Times, September 21.
[69] Official Records, series 2, VII, 872-73.
[70] Ibid., 883.
[71] Ibid., 707.
[72] Ibid., 906-7, 909, 914.
[73] Ibid., 661, 790, 924, 989, 1007. Welles, Diary of Gideon Welles, II, 168-72. Butler, Butler's Book, 60-61.

the prisoners at Andersonville in exchange for soldiers taken from Hood in the Georgia campaign.[74]

Deliveries of the invalid prisoners were carried on without regard to the other questions. Prisoners were delivered in Virginia and ships went to Savannah with others to receive the five thousand from the southernmost camps.[75] Ould agreed that if he did not have five thousand invalids he would make up that number from the well prisoners,[76] and he instructed General Winder to send men whose terms had expired.[77] Mulford, with full equipment of hospital ships and stores, arrived in Savannah November 11, with three or four thousand Confederates, fully prepared to receive a frightful cargo in return.[78] When the deliveries began, he and the Federal commanders were surprised to find the prisoners were not quite in the deplorable condition that the Northern people expected.[79] In the latter part of November the lines between Savannah and Florence were cut,[80] and Mulford moved to Charleston, where he completed filling his ships about the middle of December.[81]

As the prisoners arrived in Savannah and Charleston, newspaper correspondents accompanying Mulford's expedition began to send stories of the prisoners' sufferings to their home papers. The wretched condition of the men became a striking proof of rebel barbarity. Even the daily hospital reports for the month of August in which despairing and overworked physicians at Andersonville vainly petitioned for

[74] *Official Records*, series 2, VII, 784, 791, 799, 808, 817, 837, 822, 846-47, 851-52, 889, 895; series 1 XXXIX, Part ii, 517.

[75] *Ibid.*, series 2, VII, 922, 953-54.

[76] *Ibid.*, 1042.   [77] *Ibid.*, 1090.

[78] *Ibid.*, 1101-2, 1106, 1120.

[79] Foster reported to Halleck that the prisoners received were fully as good as those delivered; they suffered mostly from poor clothing. *Ibid.*, series 1, XLIV, 517. Mulford stated to Butler that their physical condition was better than he had expected but their personal condition was horrible, the prisoners being filthy and ragged. *Ibid.*, series 2, VII, 1149. The commander at Annapolis reported that only part of the prisoners were in bad condition. *Ibid.*, 1162, 1232, 1234. Cf. *National Intelligencer*, November 21, 26.

[80] *Official Records*, series 2, VII, 1169.

[81] *Ibid.*, 1203, 1232.

supplies and assistance, by the magic glasses of war psychosis, were metamorphosed into the gloating of demons over the havoc they were creating. All of the prisoners were reported to hate Captain Wirz for his malicious cruelty.[82] Editors began to demand that the exchange of the sick should be extended until the well also were taken care of and that minor matters like the Vicksburg paroles be set aside.[83] Retaliation was discussed in the papers by correspondents,[84] and the editors advocated adopting a limited form—enough to force the rebels to give up the negro prisoners.[85]

A reaction which was perhaps inevitable occurred in this discussion, and before long Secretary Stanton was receiving all of the blame for the failure of the government to exchange. Walt Whitman declared in a public letter that Stanton's policy was cold-blooded while Butler had made the matter of exchange a means of gratifying his personal vanity and injected into the business his personal pique.[86] The House of Representatives called upon Stanton for a report of developments in the matter of exchange.[87]

This renewed interest in the prisoners and the resulting pressure of the government had the effect of weakening the policy which was being followed. As a preliminary step, about the middle of January, Grant instructed Mulford to accept a proposition which Ould had made in the previous September to exchange all prisoners held on charges and in close confinement for the persons held as hostages for them. Grant, under pressure, discovered that this proposition was "fair and equitable." Any excess was to be made up by the exchange of prisoners not under charges.[88]

[82] New York *Times*, November 21, 26.
[83] *Ibid.*, December 16.
[84] *Ibid.*, December 23, 26.
[85] *Harper's Weekly*, January 7, 1865.
[86] New York *Times*, December 27.
[87] *Official Records*, series 2, VII, 1263, 1276.
[88] *Ibid.*, series 2, VIII, 63. General Hitchcock even ordered the release of two officers who had not been in confinement "but the rebels think they have, and we want to remove every possible objection which might be raised. (*Ibid.*, 74, 87-88, 90, 96, 109, 126, 136, 170-71, 191.)

Even such slight relief as this afforded must have been welcome to the Confederate authorities who were feeling an economic pressure more insistent than the popular demand for exchange in the North. Late in January, General Winder reported that he did not know what to do with his prisoners in Florence; in one direction there was starvation and in the other was the enemy. He repeated his suggestion that the prisoners be paroled and sent across the lines.[89]

Congress took hope from Stanton's report that Grant, now in charge of exchange, had opened negotiations with the South.[90] Grant planned to deliver three thousand a week to the Confederates. He asked Stanton, however, to deliver to him the prisoners from Kentucky, Arkansas, Missouri, Tennessee, and Louisiana, whom the rebels would have difficulty in forcing into the ranks in the east.[91] Mulford was instructed to exchange equal numbers until one party was exhausted.[92]

From the first of February to the end of the war exchanges under this arrangement were carried on. One problem to be faced in the exchange concerned prisoners who did not wish to be sent South but preferred to remain in the Union, taking the oath of allegiance in accordance with the terms of Lincoln's proclamation of amnesty. Only three hundred and thirty-six prisoners from the already conquered states were willing to be sent from Camp Morton, and Stanton ordered that they remain until the oath could be administered.[93] At Camp Douglas it was estimated that one-third of the prisoners would take the oath if they could be given official assurance that they might be released within a reasonable time.[94] Half of the camp at Elmira were reported willing to

[89] *Ibid.*, 96-97.

[90] *Ibid.*, 97-103, January 21. See also Grant to Stanton, *Ibid.*, 98. New York *Times*, January 24.

An added impetus, if one were needed at this time, came from General Butler, who had been removed from command at Fort Monroe. In a speech at Lowell, Massachusetts, Butler defended his conduct of the exchange business and declared that he had all obstacles removed when he was interfered with and exchanges stopped. (Hitchcock to Stanton, *Official Records*, series 2, VIII, 147-51, 162.)

[91] *Official Records*, series 2, VIII, 170-73.   [93] *Ibid.*, 203.

[92] *Ibid.*, 170-71.   [94] *Ibid.*, 210, 219, 220.

become loyal if they could be given the same assurance.[95] Thirteen hundred prisoners at Rock Island refused to be sent in exchange.[96]

Grant opposed the policy of retaining these prisoners. These, he declared, were the very ones to be returned. After they were exchanged, they could desert and take the oath.[97] Halleck thought that the desertion of the prisoners in the camps should receive encouragement and declared that it would be poor policy to force soldiers into the rebel ranks. "It is much cheaper to feed an enemy in prison than to fight him in the field."[98] The South paralleled Grant's policy by delivering the sick, those whose terms had expired, and those who had been kind to the Southern people.[99]

To facilitate deliveries, and overcome the bad conditions of the Confederate railroads, Ould offered to deliver a thousand prisoners a day at Wilmington, North Carolina, as well as in Virginia.[100] Mobile and Wilmington were both accepted as points of delivery.[101] The six hundred Confederate officers held as hostages at Fort Pulaski were delivered by General Foster.[102] Equivalents for all Southern deliveries were to be taken to Richmond.[103] Although the Confederates promised to make deliveries without waiting for equivalents[104] Grant and Mulford took care not to get ahead in their deliveries.[105]

Arrangements were made to exchange the prisoners delivered, Hoffman suggesting that the prisoners received be counted against the thirty-two hundred illegally declared exchanged by Ould.[106] It was agreed to exchange all to March 1,[107] leaving the old account unsettled.[108] It was announced

[95] *Ibid.*, 237, 300.
[96] *Ibid.*, 272.
[97] *Ibid.*, 234.
[98] *Ibid.*, 239, 240, 301.

[99] Ould to Breckenridge, *Ibid.*, 256-57.
[100] *Ibid.*, 206.
[101] *Ibid.*, 238.
[102] *Ibid.*, 218-19.

[103] *Ibid.*, 217. Difficulties developed at Wilmington where the delivery of the prisoners threatened to interfere with the seige of the city. The Federal commander refused to accept the prisoners until he had heard from Grant and had invested the city. *Ibid.*, 268-70, 277, 276, 285-87, 296-98. Cf. also Creelman, *Collections of a Coffee Cooler*, 31.

[104] *Official Records*, series 2, VIII, 235.
[105] *Ibid.*, 309-10, 359, 418.
[106] *Ibid.*, 258-59.

[107] *Ibid.*, 320, 329, 336, 353-54.
[108] *Ibid.*, 375.

that the Confederates had delivered 43,208 while the Federals had sent 35,578 through the lines. The Confederates admitted that there were due nine thousand on the Vicksburg paroles, which made a balance due the United States of 1,350 without having obtained the figures from the west.[109]

On April 2, Grant ordered that no more prisoners be delivered at City Point while the battle then in progress lasted.[110] The next day Hoffman was ordered to City Point with a clerk.[111] On April 9, Ould informed Grant that he was within the Federal lines with the records of the exchange office which were of value to the North.[112] The war was over.

The close of the war left prisoners still in the hands of the United States. Most of these were the prisoners who had offered to take the oath of allegiance and who had therefore not been sent in exchange. May 8, it was decided to allow these prisoners, not above the rank of colonel, to take the desired oath. Hoffman ordered the commanders of camps to release their prisoners as soon as the oath was administered, furnishing them transportation to their homes.[113] Grant advised sending the prisoners as soon as possible for "by going now they may still raise something for their subsistence for the coming year and prevent suffering next winter."[114] On July 5, Hoffman reported that all but a few sick had been released from all the prisons except Johnson's Island, Fort Warren, and Fort Delaware. He recommended that the hundred and fifty officers at Johnson's be removed to one of the other prisons,[115] and on the twentieth orders for the release of all prisoners except these captured with President Davis were given.[116] Early in November, Hoffman was ordered to turn over the records of his office to General Hitchcock and report for duty with his regiment.[117]

[109] Ibid., 504.   [111] Ibid., series 1, XLVI, part iii. 513.
[110] Ibid., 462.   [112] Ibid., series 2, VIII, 482.
[113] Ibid., 538-39. See National Intelligencer, May 25, 1865, for progress of "the inoculation of right and patriotic principles" among the prisoners.
[114] Official Records, series 2, VIII, 556.   [116] Ibid., 709-10.
[115] Ibid., 700-701.   [117] Ibid., 784.

CHAPTER XI

THE AFTERMATH

The close of the war, the surrender of the Confederate forces, the release of the prisoners North and South, did not mark the end of the psychosis which had been engendered in the minds of the people during the conflict. Ready as the people had been to accept the stories of atrocities which came from the battlefield, they were not ready to accept the changed condition of affairs which the downfall of the rebellion had brought about. The war which had ended on the military frontier brought with its close no abatement in each side's hatred of the enemy. This was true of all phases of the war; to each side their generals were the abler, their soldiers the braver, their principles the more correct. To the one side the victory was an evidence of Divine justice, to the other defeat was but an evidence of the temporary dominance of evil. Confederate soldiers paroled by Grant and Sherman or released from Northern prisons returned to devastated farms to begin the work of rehabilitation amid the overwhelming difficulties of a disorganized labor supply and an utter impoverishment. To the homes of the North came the war-worn soldiers to face the peace-time problem of readjusting themselves to a changed economic order. And among them, evidence of the horrors of war but more evidence of the cruelties of their late enemies, came the physical and mental wrecks from the prison stockades of the defunct Confederacy.

To the government and people whose arms had been victorious, the task of preserving the Union, whose existence had been vindicated by force, seemed to have just begun. Out of the confusion of counsels for settling the conflict and insuring the results of the war, one idea seemed to prevail— the leaders of the rebellion must be punished. "Treason must be made odious and traitors punished and impoverished," declared the President of the United States. The trial of the "conspirators" in the assassination of Lincoln revealed the state of the popular mind. Jefferson Davis and his erstwhile cabinet were hunted, captured, and confined to await the vengeance of a nation whose disruption they had sought.

Among the charges which were brought against Davis and his cabinet was that of a deliberate plan to murder the prisoners whom the fortunes of war had placed in their hands. Such charges had been brought by the congressional committee who had visited Annapolis in May, 1864, and in the famous *Report No. 67* they published pictures of the suffering victims of rebel barbarity. The charges had been reiterated with vehemence by the committee of the Sanitary Commission in their *Narrative* a few months later. Senator Foote, who had fled the sinking of the Confederate ship, added proof to conviction by the assertion that the rebel cabinet was conversant with the condition of the prisons in the South and had deliberately advocated the neglect of the prisoners.[1]

But it was not only the political leaders of the Confederacy who were charged with cruelty to the prisoners; the officers in command of the prisons faced similar charges. By Lincoln's proclamation of amnesty, officials charged with cruelty to prisoners were excluded from the benefits of the pardon which he proclaimed.[2] Under this spirit a number of the officers who had been connected with Southern prisons were arrested as the armies of the United States possessed themselves of the country.[3]

In addition to arrests on charges of cruelty to prisoners the arrival of the Federal army in Richmond marked the beginning of a search for money which had been sent to prisoners or which had been taken from them at the time of their capture and which, according to the prevailing belief, had

[1] See the New York *Tribune*, July 10, 1865. Cf. also the denial of these charges made by Secretary of the Navy Mallory to Johnson, *Official Records*, series 2, VIII, 662-64.

[2] Richardson, *Messages and Papers of the Presidents*, VI, 213-15.

[3] *Official Records*, series 2, VIII, 782-83.

been used for the benefit of their captors. Arrests of the officials in charge of the prison accounts began.

In the last days of the Confederacy irregularities in the management of the funds of the prisoners had crept into the prison system. In January, 1865, General Winder gave his approval to the payment of fifteen hundred dollars on the orders of one prisoner at Columbia within one week, and this was in addition to the payment of one hundred dollars a week to the prisoner personally.[4] Such irregularities had not been permitted in the earlier days. In addition, the prison quartermasters purchased from the prisoners, on the order of the quartermaster-general of the Confederacy, greenbacks at a ratio of five to one.[5] When the prisoners from South Carolina were delivered at Wilmington their money failed to follow them.[6] Others from Salisbury also were delivered without their property.[7] The last day of March, Ruggles, commissary-general of prisoners, advised that a board of three officers be appointed to make an accounting of the moneys belonging to Federal prisoners.[8] With the fall of the capital city, Captain Morfit, the quartermaster in charge of these accounts, fled with about about three thousand dollars, which he divided with Major Carrington, former provost marshal of Richmond.[9]

As the Federal officials began to reconstruct the accounts of the defeated government, General Halleck came to the conclusion that Ould and his assistant, Captain Hatch, were responsible for the diversion of funds sent from the North for the relief of prisoners. Without other evidence for such conclusion than the fact that such money was transmitted through the Confederate commissioner, Halleck ordered the arrest of the suspected men. Stanton "cordially approved" this action and added the hope that the men would receive exemplary punishment if guilty. He suggested that Halleck's telegram be published and all people who had transmitted funds to the prisoners be called upon to correspond

[4] *Ibid.*, series 2, VIII, 110.
[5] W. S. Winder to Morfit, *Ibid.*, 172-73.
[6] *Ibid.*, 456-57.
[7] *Ibid.*, 446.
[8] *Ibid.*, 457.
[9] *Ibid.*, 512.

with the investigating board. Halleck, none too sure of his position, however, counseled secrecy, stating that neither Ould nor Hatch, who were confined in Libby prison, had been told the cause of their arrest.[10]

Two weeks later Captain Morfit was captured and sent to Richmond[11] and Halleck ordered a board to make an informal investigation.[12] A month later the board reported that Ould was in no way accountable for the moneys lost and that a reference to his endorsement book showed that he made frequent efforts to have all money and valuables which had been taken from the prisoners returned to them at the time of their exchange. On June 26, Halleck ordered the release of the commissioner of exchange.[13] Major Carrington turned over the money he had received from Morfit and the board found no record of collusion between them.[14] The board declared in a formal report that money taken from arriving prisoners was turned over by Major Turner to Captain Morfit who allowed the prisoners one hundred dollars a month at an exchange rate of seven to one. In only two cases were sums of money confiscated and in those cases the amounts involved were over five thousand dollars and the confiscation was ordered by the secretary of war.[15] Colonel Mulford informed Hitchcock that he could pay from fifty to sixty cents on the dollar to those who claimed to have sent money south.[16]

The findings of this commission were not given a general publicity nor were they of a nature to arouse an intense public interest. The arrests of the men charged with cruelty to the prisoners were of a greater interest. With Johnson's announcement of his intention to issue a proclamation similar in scope to the amnesty proclamation of his martyred predecessor, the public press insistently called upon him to make

[10] *Ibid.*, 529-30. The news of the arrest, however, got to the newspapers. See the *National Intelligencer*, May 6, 1865, and the New York *Times*, May 8. The latter paper added the information that Ould and Hatch had taken $300,000 entrusted to them for the prisoners.

[11] *Ibid.*, 572.   [13] *Ibid.*, 667.   [15] *Ibid.*, 706-7.
[12] *Ibid.*, 636.   [14] *Ibid.*, 671-72.   [16] *Ibid.*, 721-23.

. . . . a special exception of every rebel official who has been concerned, directly or indirectly, in the torturing and murdering of our prisoners. Of all rebel crimes, that was the most devilish, the least capable of extenuation or pardon. If punishment does not strike here it should strike nowhere. . . . The spirit which prompted the maltreatment of national prisoners was essentially fiendish. Nobody, at this day, has the audacity to deny the facts. It is no more certain that this war has taken place than that tens of thousands of national soldiers, who were made prisoners in it were deliberately and wantonly shot to death, as at Fort Pillow, or frozen to death as at Belle Isle, or starved to death as at Andersonville, or sickened to death by swamp malaria, as in South Carolina.[17]

The official attitude was revealed by Stanton's order to Halleck to have a thorough investigation made of the mine under Libby prison at the time of Kilpatrick's raid. Stanton stated that Judge-Advocate-General Holt was desirous of full information.[18] There was no disposition on the part of either the administration or the people to allow the parties responsible for the Southern prisons to escape unscathed.

Early in May a Captain Noyes, on the staff of General Wilson in Georgia, passed through Andersonville where he found Captain Wirz paroling the last of the sick of the prison preparatory to sending them north. Upon arriving in Macon, Noyes reported this to Wilson who ordered him to return to Andersonville and arrest Wirz. On May 7, Noyes executed his orders, taking Wirz from the midst of his family and conducting him under arrest to Macon.[19] Wirz protested, declaring that conditions in the prison were beyond his control and that he should not be held responsible for the acts or omissions of his superiors. Wirz stated that he was a native of Switzerland, and at the outbreak of the war he was a physician in Louisiana. He admitted that he was carried away by the excitement of the times and entered the army as a private. Wounded at the battle of Seven Pines he lost use of his right arm and was assigned to duty with General Winder in Richmond. After the abandonment of the Tuscaloosa prison, which he commanded, he left on a furlough for

[17] New York *Times*, May 28.
[18] *Official Records*, series 2, VIII, 551.
[19] *Trial of Henry Wirz*, 19.

Europe, returning in February, 1864. Upon his return he was ordered to Andersonville. Wirz denied his responsibility and asked General Wilson for safe conduct while he completed his preparations to take his family to Europe.[20] Instead of a safe conduct the adjutant general ordered him brought a prisoner to Washington.[21]

With the arrest of Wirz there came a resurgence of the demand that the perpetrators of cruelties to prisoners be subjected to punishment. The surgeon-general of Pennsylvania obtained information that 12,884 prisoners died in the Georgia prison. Governor Curtin added that "the document reveals a history of cruelty and suffering unparalleled in the annals of warfare."[22] The national government sent an agent to Andersonville to gather evidence of rebel brutality.[23] Against Wirz the hatred of the Northern people accumulated. "The assassins of the president disposed of, the Government will next take in hand the ruffians who tortured to death thousands of Union prisoners. The laws of civilized warfare must be vindicated; and some expiation must be exacted for the most infernal crime of the century. . . . In respect to Captain Werz (sic), for instance . . . it may be shown that he went into his business of wholesale murder, on express instructions by superior authority. . . . It is manifest that this maltreatment must have proceeded from some general design upon the part of the rebel Government. . . . The persons detailed for the charge of the military prisons in the 'Confederacy' were men whose natural disposition especially qualified them for a brutal and base business."[24] The New York *Tribune* adopted a more conservative attitude with the demand that the accused parties be tried by the civil courts rather than by courts-martial. The paper declared that a trial before military commissions when the civil courts were available was an avowal of the weakness of the government's case. This journal also condemned the sensational press for condemning the prisoner before he was tried. In regard to

[20] *Official Records*, series 2, VIII, 537-38.
[21] *Trial of Henry Wirz.*
[22] *National Intelligencer*, June 30.
[23] New York *Times*, July 14.
[24] *Ibid.*, July 26.

"Wertz," "It is very certain that our soldiers in Southern
Military prisons were treated with a degree of inhumanity
and barbarity that finds no parallel in modern civilization.
. . . We desire to see the author of these crimes submitted
to an exemplary punishment," but "it is not the duty of the
newspapers to try him." Pointing to a paragraph in another
paper, the *Tribune* condemned such expressions as "the
Andersonville savage," "the inhuman wretch," "the infamous
captain," "the barbarian" whose crimes go beyond "the wild-
est exaggerations of Jefferson Davis," the "most bloodthirsty
monster which this or any other age has produced."[25] But
the moderation of the *Tribune* was exceptional. The agent
sent by the government to Andersonville recommended that
the prison site be made a permanent reminder of the rebellion
and for this purpose it should be taken over by the government. "The thing most needed since the prostration of the
rebellion is to make it odious and infamous," declared the
New York *Times*. This desideratum was to be obtained by
making the South "face" Andersonville, and the government
was advised that the worst side of the Confederate archives
should be published while loyal men should strive to keep
alive the infamy of the rebellion.[26]

Under such conditions preparations for the trial of Wirz
began. Delays occurred however, in the opening of the
trial,[27] and not until August 21 was Wirz arraigned before
a commission to face the charges against him. Judge James
Hughes, General J. W. Denver, and Attorneys Charles F.
Peck and Louis Schade of the Washington bar appeared as
counsel for the prisoner, but the trial was not destined to
continue. Stanton read the specifications and charges against
Wirz and became enraged at the charge which accused Wirz
of conspiring with General R. E. Lee and Jefferson Davis
to murder the prisoners. The court was dissolved after the
first session.[28] On August 23, the court was reorganized

[25] New York *Tribune*, July 11, August 12, 22.
[26] New York *Times*, August 16.   [27] *National Intelligencer*, July 25.
[28] Chipman, *Horrors of Andersonville Prison*, 16-17. New York *Times*, August
18. *National Intelligencer*, August 17, 18.

under the presidency of General Lew Wallace, with Colonel N. P. Chipman retained as judge-advocate.[29] Under this court the trial proceeded.

Wirz was faced with two charges. The first was of conspiring with Richard B. Winder, Isaiah H. White, W. S. Winder, R. R. Stevens, "and others unknown" to impair the health and destroy the lives of prisoners of war. The term "others unknown" was substituted for the names of Davis, Cobb, R. E. Lee, General Winder, J. A. Seddon and others, after Stanton, according to Chipman, had decided that it was "inexpedient" to bring Davis to Washington from Fort Monroe.[30] Under this charge a single specification set forth that these men conspired to subject prisoners to torture and suffering by putting them in unhealthy and unwholesome quarters, exposing them to the weather, compelling them to use impure water, and furnishing them with insufficient food. Wirz was charged with wilful and malicious neglect "in furtherance of his evil design" in furnishing shelter, refusing to furnish wood, allowing the dead to remain in the prison, countenancing cruel punishments, and ordering the guard to kill prisoners. Ten thousand prisoners were specified as having died of the bad food and water, one thousand died from the "fetid and noxious exhalations" from the decaying bodies of the unremoved dead, one hundred lost their lives as the result of "cruel, unusual, and infamous punishment upon slight, trivial, and fictitious pretenses by fastening large balls of iron to their feet and binding large numbers of prisoners aforesaid closely together with large chains around their necks and feet, so that they walked with the greatest difficulty." Moreover, three hundred prisoners were killed at the "deadline" which "the said Wirz, still wickedly pursuing his evil purpose, did establish and cause to be designated." Finally, Wirz "did keep and use ferocious and bloodthirsty beasts dangerous to human life, called bloodhounds" to hunt escaped prisoners and "to seize, tear, mangle, and

---

[29] *National Intelligencer*, August 20 *et seq. Official Records*, series 2, VIII, 788.
[30] Chipman, *op. cit.*, 16.

maim the bodies and limbs of said fugitives, prisoners of war."

The second charge against Wirz was of murder, "in violation of the laws and customs of war." Under this charge were thirteen specifications. In each case the specification set forth the conditions of the murder, but in no case was the name of the murdered prisoner given. Four of the specifications declared that Wirz shot prisoners with a revolver, in four cases the murder was committed by the guard acting on Wirz's orders. Two prisoners were murdered by being punished in the stocks, one died from the hardships of the "chain gang," while another prisoner, sick and weak, was kicked and stamped upon by the Andersonville commander. One death was caused by Wirz's inciting the bloodhounds to attack an escaped prisoner. Not all of these deaths occurred immediately; two of the prisoners lived one day, two lived six days, one lived five days, and the prisoner who died from the effects of being placed in the stocks lived for ten days. But in no case was the name of the murdered prisoner known to the judge-advocate who drew up the specifications, nor to the witnesses who were summoned by the government to testify against their former jailer.[31]

Arraigned before the commission on these charges, August 23, Wirz was deserted by Hughes and Peck, leaving only Schade to carry on his case. However, the following day a Mr. Baker joined Schade to defend the prisoner. These attorneys entered the pleas that Wirz was protected from arrest by the terms of the convention made by Johnston with Sherman at the time of the former's surrender, that Noyes had promised him at the time of his arrest that he should not be placed in confinement, and that the commission had no jurisdiction as the prisoner had been arraigned on identical charges on August 21, and could not again be brought before a court. The prisoner's counsel also declared that the charges and specifications were too vague and indefinite and did not

---

[31] For the charges and specifications see *Official Records*, series 2, VIII, 785-9. *Trial of Henry Wirz*, 3-8.

CIVIL WAR PRISONS

constitute an offense punishable by the laws of war. These pleas were overruled by Chipman and a plea of not guilty was entered by Wirz.[32]

The trial, thus begun, continued until October 16. During that period one hundred and sixty witnesses informed the court of conditions at Andersonville. Among them several were outstanding. Felix de la Baume, claiming to be a grand-nephew of Lafayette but later recognized as a deserter from a New York regiment and dismissed from a position in the interior department, told of murders. George W. Gray declared that Wirz killed his companion, one Steward, while the two of them were gathering wood. Wirz robbed Steward before killing him. At this testimony Wirz indignantly arose from the couch upon which he reclined all during the trial— his health was bad—and protested. This became proof to the commission that the prisoner was overwhelmed by the direct accusation. Ambrose Spencer, a Unionist residing near Anderson Station, testified that W. S. Winder declared when he built the stockade that he did not intend to furnish shelter as he planned to kill more "damned Yankees than can be destroyed in the front!" Spencer added information of the cruelty of Wirz and General Winder in the use of dogs to kill the prisoners. Kellogg and Davidson, soon to publish in book form accounts of their prison experiences, added stories of cruel treatment. Dr. Calvin Bates told of inhuman treatment of the prisoners in the hospital. In general the testimony bore on specific cruelties only through indirection; the deplorable physical condition of the prison, the bad food, and the murders along the deadline were dwelt upon. The reports of inspector D. T. Chandler and Surgeon Jones, being criticisms of the prison by Confederates—the reports of these men were taken with the archives of the Confederacy—were admitted as confirmatory evidence. Evidence was introduced to prove that Davis and Seddon knew of Chandler's report.[33]

[32] *Official Records*, series 2, VIII, 775-76. *National Intelligencer*, August 23.
[33] Page, *The True Story of Andersonville*, 204-16. *Trial of Henry Wirz*, *National Intelligencer*, and New York *Times*, August 23 to October 16. See *Trial of Henry*

Southern defenders of Wirz have contended that the trial of the Andersonville commander was unfair and the actions of the judge advocate in arbitrarily ruling out evidence and intimidating witnesses revealed a desire to prejudice the court against the prisoner. It seems that Chipman was a victim of the prevailing psychosis to a degree which was surpassed only by his superior, Judge-Advocate-General Holt, and to one not versed in the technique of military law and proceedings the criticism of the Southerners seems justified. On August 28, Baker and Schade deserted the prisoner under conditions which indicated that they could not get fair treatment from the court. They returned to the case only on the earnest solicitations of the friendless prisoner.[34]

Wirz in a letter to the New York *News* attempted to lay his case before a friendly portion of the people, stating that he was not receiving justice from the military tribunal.[35] Wirz's attorney, Schade, in a letter to President Johnson after the verdict of the court had been rendered stated: "Among the 35,000 prisoners were many bounty jumpers and bad characters. Some six of them were hung by their own comrades. If I have the Government's patronage, and the prospect of an office or two (as actually had been the case with some of the witnesses for the prosecution in the Wirz trial) and can give a promise of a safe conduct and perhaps a reward, I do not doubt in the least that among those 500 raiders at Andersonville (as they are styled in the testimony) I shall within four weeks find enough testimony to try, condemn, and hang every member of the Wirz military commission on any charge whatever, provided it is done before such a military commission."[36] Robert Ould, summoned as a witness for Wirz, had his subpoena revoked by Chipman.[37]

Wirz, 282-87, for story of Felix de la Baume, 397-405 for Gray's testimony, 355-62 for Spencer, Kellogg 61-66, Davidson 140-46, Bates 27-43, 662-68, 804-5, 230-32 for proof that Davis knew of conditions in the prison.

[34] New York *Times* and the *National Intelligencer,* August 29, 30.

[35] New York *News,* August 30. New York *Times,* August 31.

[36] *Official Records,* series 2, VIII, 774.

[37] *National Intelligencer,* August 17, 1868.

By October 16, the taking of testimony ended and Baker asked for two weeks extension to prepare his case. This was refused by the court which was willing to allow but one week. Upon the continued protests of the prisoner's counsel the commission extended the time to twelve days, but the attorney refused to accept and withdrew from the case.[38] Four days later Wirz made a plea in his own behalf, setting forth that out of the whole number of witnesses one hundred and forty-five had declared that they had not seen him kill a prisoner, there was no evidence of a conspiracy, and the trial had been conducted unfairly. Colonel Chipman then summarized the evidence against the prisoner.[39]

The findings of the commission were issued as general orders on November 6. On the charge of conspiracy the commission in the light of the evidence added the names of Davis, Seddon, Cobb, General Winder and five others as co-conspirators. The number of deaths resulting from each of the causes—food, water, deadline, and dogs—was omitted. On this charge Wirz was found guilty. Of the thirteen specifications of the second charge Wirz was found guilty of ten. Three other murders not specified by the charges were added to the list, although the court declared that these had not been taken into consideration in arriving at the verdict. Four of the murders charged against the Andersonville commander had been committed in August while Wirz was on sick leave but he was found guilty of these despite adequate proof of his alibi. Wirz was therefore condemned to death by hanging, and President Johnson appointed November 10 as the date of the execution. Despite the fact that Schade petitioned the executive for clemency for the dying man, no clemency was forthcoming.[40] On the appointed day Wirz, accompanied and supported by two priests of the Roman Church, mounted the scaffold in the yard of the Old Capitol prison and was hanged. His body was interred in the "Ar-

---

[38] *Ibid.*, October 16, 1865.
[39] *Official Records*, series 2, VIII, 776.
[40] *Ibid.*, 790-91, 773-74.

senal grounds" by the side of Atzerodt, another victim of war psychosis.[41]

Two stories of an apocryphal character came out of the last days of Wirz. The first of these related that Wirz's wife attempted to poison him during the trial. This story was hailed by the press as evidence that the prisoner was too repulsive a creature to inspire devotion even within his own family circle. The story was added to by accounts of the coldness existing between Wirz and his wife, noticed by the guards during his imprisonment.[42] The second story, revealed later, told of the visit of a secret emissary "from a high cabinet officer" to offer to reprieve the criminal if he would make a confession which would convict President Davis of conspiring to murder prisoners. R. B. Winder and Wirz's confessor are cited as authorities for the story, which is told to reveal the honor and loyalty of the condemned man who indignantly denied contact with the Confederate president.

With one exception Wirz was the only person connected with the Southern prisons to suffer for that connection. Dick Turner, whose notoriety was widespread throughout the North where he was pictured as an inhuman monster and fiend, was held until June, 1866 at the Libby prison and was finally discharged because there could be found no evidence to convict him.[44] Captain R. B. Winder was arrested in August and was held for the revelations of the Wirz trial. Since nothing could be established against him, although he

[41] *Ibid.*, 794. *National Intelligencer*, November 11.

[42] New York *Tribune*, November 11. See Schade's denial of the story in the *National Intelligencer*, November 13.

[43] Page, *op. cit.*, 215 ff. Williamson, *The Old Capitol Prison*, 139-41. Stevenson, *The Southern Side*, 152-53. Davis, "Andersonville and other War Prisons," Belford's *Magazine*, 1890. See R. B. Winder to Davis in Roland, *Jefferson Davis: Constitutionalist.*

[44] For documents relating to Turner, see *Official Records*, series 2, VIII, 764, 783, 911-12, 920, 930, 952, 960-61, 966. Family tradition related that R. B. Winder, confined at the time in the Libby prison with Turner and allowed a freer range of the prison, became friendly with one of the guards, got him intoxicated and destroyed all evidence against the "Rebel Lion." Cf. Turner, "Some War-Time Recollections, the Story of a Confederate Officer Who Was First One of Those in Charge of and Later Captive in Libby Prison," *American Magazine*, LXX (1910) 619-31.

was convicted of conspiring with Wirz to murder prisoners, General Grant ordered his release in December. In March 1866 he was still in prison awaiting the preparation of charges and specifications against him by Ambrose Spencer, the Andersonville Unionist.[45] Colonel Gibbs, commanding at Andersonville before the arrival of General Winder, was arrested soon after Wirz, but was released almost immediately.[46] Major John H. Gee, commander of Salisbury, was brought to trial before a military commission late in August, 1866 on a charge of neglecting to provide wood, water, shelter, and bedding for the prisoners; and on a charge of murder, set forth by seven specifications. The commission, to the disgust of the commander of the military district of South Carolina who had ordered the trial, found the prisoner not guilty on both charges.[47] A single exception to this general rule of immunity was found in the case of a private, James W. Duncan, employed at Andersonville, who was convicted of manslaughter, June 8, 1866, and was sentenced to fifteen years of hard labor at Fort Pulaski. Eleven months later he made his escape.[48]

This failure to convict others of mistreating prisoners was not due to a lack of diligence on the part of the officials of the judge-advocate-general's office. Holt and Chipman bent every effort to obtain evidence against the other prison officials. Philip Cashmyer, formerly sutler at Florence and a favorite of General Winder, corresponded with Chipman to give evidence against not only Wirz but also other officers. He revealed that shelter could have been erected on Belle Isle and cited the extensive hospitals at Richmond as evidence of the plentiful supply of lumber in the city. He accused Dick Turner and a Lieutenant Emack of cruelty and robbery at Libby Prison. Captain Alexander, commanding the polit-

---

[45] For the case of Captain R. B. Winder see *Official Records*, series 2, VIII, 796-98, 815, 817, 819-20, 834. Winder was later dean of the Baltimore Dental College. There is no official record of his release from prison.

[46] *Ibid.*, 552-53.

[47] *Ibid.*, 782-83, 881, 956-60.

[48] *Ibid.*, 926-28, and note.

ical prisoners in Castle Thunder, was accused of harshness, inhumanity, tyranny, and dishonesty. He described the Salisbury prison, and added his observations at Macon, Millen, and Florence. Charges of harshness to prisoners were made against Captain Barrett, Colonel Iverson, and Lieutenant Wilson of the latter prison.[49] General Holt combined this information with that obtained from the Wirz trial and informed Stanton that these men, together with Gee, Duncan, Godwin of Salisbury, Captain John Adams of Memphis, one Peacock who had assisted Wirz at Tuscaloosa, Dr. Nesbit of Salisbury, and Captain Vowles of Millen, should be brought to trial for their "inhuman" crimes.[50] But with the exception of Duncan and Gee none of these men were ever brought to trial. Defenders of the Southern prison system querulously demanded how it was possible for Wirz to conspire by himself or why those who were convicted as co-conspirators by his trial were never forced to face the charges against them.[51] Colonel Chipman in 1891 explained that the other facts brought out by the trial "were buried out of sight by the universal demand that this human monster [Wirz] on trial should not escape punishment; and with his execution the secondary, but really most important, result of the trial, passed out of mind, or was displaced by the rapidly recurring political movements of that eventful period."[52]

But even though the government took no further action, the prison issue was not lost from sight. Prisoners who returned from the South wrote of their experiences to the newspapers, or published accounts of rebel prisons in books, pamphlets, and magazines. The literature of the Civil War prisons is voluminous. During the years 1862-66 fifty-four books and articles were published giving the experiences of prisoners in the South. Twenty-eight of these came off the press in the years 1865 and 1866. During the next five years twenty books and articles saw the light of day, the first flash

[49] *Ibid.*, 764-66. October 12, 1865. See also *Ibid.*, 753.
[50] *Ibid.*, 782-83.
[51] Cf. Rutherford, *Facts and Figures vs. Myths and Misrepresentations.*
[52] Chipman, *Horrors of Andersonville Prison*, 12.

of publication being over. The next five years produced an average of but one book a year. In the years 1871, 1873, 1875, and 1877 no books were published. Twelve books and articles were published from 1878 to 1881 and nineteen in the following five-year period. From 1887 to 1891 there came a resurgence of prison literature and thirty-nine books and articles were published, followed by thirty-two in the ten years from 1892 to 1901. Although the Civil War was fading into the distance and the effects of the passing years were plainly to be seen in the graying hair and faltering footsteps of the veterans who assembled at the annual reunions, fifty-one books and articles were published in the first decade of the twentieth century. Even the complications of the World War did not produce a considerable decline in the number of accounts of prison experiences, and twenty-seven such accounts were published between 1912 and 1921.[53]

This large amount of prison literature came into being for a number of reasons. Foremost among them, especially in later days, stood the desire of old men to relate the experiences of their youth. The writings of the earliest period doubtless sprung from an economic necessity which sought to take advantage of the popular present interest in prisons and prisoners. Whereas these elements were doubtless present to a greater or less degree in every production, most of the books give some other excuse as their *raison d'etre*. Most of them proclaim a patriotic purpose—that the sacrifices which were made to save the Union might not be forgotten.[54] In the

[53] This account of publications is necessarily inadequate, the numbers given are meant to be only representative of the resurgence and decline of interest in the subject. The figures are based upon the number of books copyrighted in the period following the war and the articles are those appearing in magazines listed in periodicals which were indexed in Poole's *Index* and the *Periodical Index*. No attempt had been made to list accounts either in this tabulation or in the bibliography at the end of this study which appeared in newspapers or lesser periodicals. There has been no attempt to distinguish between accounts by Confederates and Federals, and primary and secondary accounts. It is assumed that the number of copyrighted books, and articles appearing in the better class magazines, is indicative of popular interest in the subject of prisons. Order of the Loyal Legion of the United States papers have been counted as "articles."

[54] See for instance, McElroy, *Andersonville*, 645-54 and Urban, *Battlefield and Prison Pen*, preface.

early period the books were written with the avowed purpose of bringing the rebel leaders to judgment. "The magnanimity of our people is beyond question," said one writer, "and our enemies acknowledge it. Our armies have conquered their proud hosts; our kindness must now subdue the enmity of their hearts. We must neither be too lenient nor too severe. To the *leaders* who precipitated us into four years of bloodshed and war, the severest punishment which the law can give; but to the poor misguided masses, that clemency which only noble people are capable of exercising."[55] Another writer gave his account to oppose the subserviency to the "Slave Oligarchy" which he saw in the wholesale issuance of pardons by the national executive. "I send out this book trusting that whatever influence it may exercise will aid in bringing the guilty leaders of Treason to just punishment for their enormous crimes against humanity. . . . Jeff Davis, Robert E. Lee and other rebels high in authority and the monsters whom they placed high in command of the prisons . . . are alone responsible."[56] A prisoner who published an account of his experiences together with a number of accounts of escapes in which negroes aided fugitive prisoners expressed the hope that his book would assist in answering the question "What shall we do with the negro?" which was then (1865) before the national government.[57]

A more potent cause for the publication of prison reminiscences came as a result of the pension legislation of the eighties. Prisoners of war found difficulty in securing sufficient evidence to satisfy the law that they had contracted disability during their prison experiences. The laws required that an officer or two comrades should certify to the origin of any disease upon which a petitioner based his claim for a pension. Ex-prisoners found it difficult to get two comrades whose memories were sufficiently accurate to meet the requirements of the law. Prisoners came to the opinion that

[55] Abbott, *Prison Life in the South*, 206. Same statement in Glazier: *The Capture, the Prison Pen, and Escape*, 348-49.

[56] Roach, *Prisoner of War*, 3-4.

[57] Abbott, *op. cit.*, 7.

the mere fact of having spent the summer of 1864 at Andersonville should be adequate evidence of permanent disability.[58] In 1880 a bill was introduced into the House of Representatives to pay eight dollars a month to all prisoners who were in any Confederate prison for six months, with an additional dollar a month for each month over one year's imprisonment.[59] The National Ex-Prisoners of War Association supported this movement.[60] One writer, inspired by this hope of pensions to write his experiences, declared that

. . . . there are those even here in the North who grew rich through *their* sufferings, who begrudge them the beggarly pittance of a pension of a few dollars to keep them from the poorhouse, when by their heroic fortitude, and their indescribable sufferings, they made it possible for the bonds of the Government to be worth a hundred cents on the dollar. Now they are looked upon as beggars because they ask 10 to 12 dollars a month to assist them in their old age and decrepitude.[61]

Another demanded:

Reader, did these men join the Union army through patriotism? or was it for the $13 a month as it is asserted by some of the renegade editors who justify the pension vetoes and returning the rebel flags?[62]

These narratives of personal experiences revealed a uniformity of testimony which must, by its very mass, have convinced the readers of the truthfulness of the general charges which they brought against the South. In general these accounts begin with the prisoner's capture, immediately after which he was stripped of such serviceable clothing as his captors desired. He was then marched to the nearest prison, usually the Libby, where he was again searched and robbed of any money which he had not, by a display of Yankee ingenuity which most of the writers did not fail to emphasize, hidden in the hollow buttons of his uniform or behind a cud of tobacco in his mouth. Before the establishment of the officer's prison at Macon, the officers were confined in the

[58] Ransom, *Andersonville Diary*, 163.
[59] *Ibid.*, 303-4.
[60] *Ibid.*, 188-92.
[61] Cooper, *In and Out of Rebel Prisons*, 246-47.
[62] Boggs, *Eighteen Months under the Rebel Flag*, 62-63.

Libby prison where the constant tyranny of Dick Turner subjected them to crowded confinement without beds, chairs, or furniture; to poor and inadequate food; to comminations and danger from the watchful guards who shot at every prisoner who looked out the window. The officers' accounts of Macon, Charleston, and Columbia were less filled with horrors, but they too mentioned murders along the deadline, poor food, and inhuman keepers. The privates after the search at Libby were confined in the tobacco warehouses of Richmond where their treatment, though similar, surpassed in wretchedness that of the officers. Those who were sent to Belle Isle remembered it as a place where their numbers were reduced by starvation and disease, while many froze to death during the long shelterless nights. If the privates were sent to Andersonville, and the great majority of these personal narratives were written by survivors of that prison, they were loaded into cattle cars and guarded by inhuman guards, and were insulted by them and by the citizenry of the towns through which they passed. After several days of poor food —the prisoners seldom remember having received rations on these trips—they arrived at Andersonville where they were met by Wirz who cursed them and threatened them with the terrors of the stockade. Entering the stockade, which is described with especial reference to the miasmatic swamp and poor water, the prisoner introduced to his readers the murders along the deadline, the poor, inadequate, and uncooked food, the lack of wood, the raiders, the inhumanity of Wirz and Winder, the sickness, diseases, and deaths in stockade and hospital, and the ferocious dogs that tracked the prisoners who escaped. If the prisoner escaped he was aided by negroes and Unionists until he was recaptured or made his way to the Federal lines.

The consistently harrowing description of Andersonville was followed by stories of lesser tragedies in the prisons at Charleston, Savannah, and Millen or the greater horrors of Florence. Everywhere the typical prisoner met with cruel guards and murderous keepers. To the prisoners who actually or in retrospect suffered these experiences the whole thing was an evidence of a rebel plot to murder or to make unfit for service the soldiers of the enemy. Wirz was pictured as an inhuman monster; General Winder as a fiend who gloated in the deaths of his charges; the commanders of the lesser prisons differed in degree rather than in kind. And at the top stood Jefferson Davis, his cabinet, and sometimes General Lee, as the authors of this diabolic plot.

These stories which almost without variations describe sufferings and lay the blame for them upon the rebel leaders, bear a marked resemblance to the accounts of sufferings given in the Wirz trial. In many cases the evidence of the trial is cited as confirmatory, and in a number of others the borrowing from the published proceedings of the trial is apparent. The books written immediately after the trial are especially open to this criticism. In 1869 a new official source was opened by the publication of a volume on the *Treatment of Prisoners of War by the Rebel Authorities,* published as a committee report by the House of Representatives. This volume was prepared by the committee after the taking of testimony, oral and written, from some three thousand witnesses. The committee explained its purpose in making the investigation by stating that the numerous works might not live for the future, their number was confusing, while "Rebel cruelty demands an enduring truthful record, stamped with the National authority." The preservation of such a record was necessary as a permanent condemnation of the slave system in order that posterity might learn to avoid slavery and its evils. Another reason assigned was that the rebels had infused into the public mind the idea that the Confederacy was driven by destitution to starve their prisoners while the Northern government refused to exchange the dying prisoners. Documents were given to prove the guilt of the rebels and extensive statements were borrowed from Goss, *The Soldier's Story of His Captivity* and from Davidson's *Fourteen Months in Rebel Prisons.* The publication of this volume with "the stamp of the National authority" doubtless accounts for the decline of prison memoirs until the pension agitation of the eighties.[63]

Throughout all of these works, whether stamped by the national authority or merely by the experiences of the prisoners themselves, the evidence of Colonel Chandler and Surgeon Jones was accepted as complete proof of the fiendishness of the rebels. Perhaps the best explanation of Chandler's report is found in his letter to Stanton asking to be released from arrest after the war. Having been arrested in February, 1863 while attempting to cross the Potomac to attend to some private business in Virginia, he was confined in the Old Capitol prison until he was exchanged for the nephew of Andrew Johnson. Being liable to conscription, he took the commission offered in the rebel service and became an inspector and a commander of a quarantine camp. He soon repented his action, however, and resolved to return to his former allegiance at the first favorable opportunity. In such a frame of mind he inspected Andersonville and made the report which was used to such good effect by the prosecution in the Wirz trial, although Chandler complimented the work of Wirz and condemned practically all the other prison officials.[64] Surgeon Jones's orders, which stated that Andersonville was an excellent field for pathological investigation, were taken as evidence of rebel inhumanity and a plot to kill prisoners in order to perform medical experiments. This

[63] This report was published as *House Report No. 85*, 40th Congress, 3rd session (1869). There are exceptions to this summary of prisoners' memoirs. Two such exceptions are notable: Braun, *Andersonville, An Object Lesson on Protection*, published in 1892, and Page, *The True Story of Andersonville*, both defend Wirz. Page denies the truthfulness of the other prisoners who wrote accounts of the prison. Page minimized the sufferings of the prisoners and ascribed those that took place to General Winder. For more typical accounts of the prison reminiscences which follow the summary given above, see Goss, *The Soldier's Story of His Captivity*; Davidson, *Fourteen Months in Rebel Prisons*; Abbott, *Prison Life in the South*; Glazier, *The Capture, the Prison Pen, and the Escape*; Spencer, *A Narrative of Andersonville*; Kellogg, *Life and Death in Rebel Prisons*; McElroy, *Andersonville*; and Urban, *The Battlefield and Prison Pen*. These books are the most complete and seem to have enjoyed the largest circulation. The only differences between them are in the personal incidents; the conviction of a rebel plot is shared by all.

[64] *Official Records*, series 2, VIII, 256-29, May 9, 1865.

order was responsible for the addition of the name of Surgeon-General S. P. Moore to the list of conspirators in the
charges against Wirz.[65] Two other documents served to confirm the charges of a rebel plot. One was a letter from Ould
to Winder telling him to send prisoners for exchange, for
"the arrangement I have made works largely in our favor.
We get rid of a set of miserable wretches, and receive some
of the best material I ever saw." This was evidence that
Ould was in the plot to kill rebel prisoners and destroy their
usefulness, for it was assumed that the statement applied to
military prisoners and in its garbled form it seemed to do so.
But a correct quotation shows that the Confederate commissioner was referring to political prisoners. The date of the
letter, March 17, 1863, changed in Northern hands to August 1, 1864, was at a time when the exchange of any but
private soldiers was suspended.[66] The other document was
an order of General Winder published to the prisoners at the
time of Stoneman's raid against Andersonville. This order
instructed the Florida Battery to open fire upon the stockade
when Stoneman had approached to within seven miles of the
prison. This order was a forgery.[67]

The polemical writers, however, were faced with a problem when they came to an enumeration of deaths to prove
their thesis that the South deliberately murdered prisoners.
The numbers given in the official reports were not sufficiently
large for those who desired to prove deliberate murder.
According to a report made by General Hitchcock to Stanton
and referred by the secretary of war to Congress, 26,436 out
of a total of 220,000 Confederate prisoners died in Northern
prisons while 22,576 prisoners out of a total of 126,950
Union prisoners died in the South. Hitchcock explained that

    [65] Chipman, *The Tragedy of Andersonville*, 413-14.

    [66] The New York *Times*, May 8, 1865. The quotation appears frequently in the
polemical literature of prisons. See *Official Records*, series 2, V, 853 for the correct
version. Cf. also Ould's statement in Jones, *Confederate View*, 210-15.

    [67] See McElroy, *op. cit.*, 564. See Davis, *Escape of a Confederate States Officer*,
for proof of the spurious character of the order. The order does not appear in the
Official Records or in any of the order books of Andersonville preserved in the archives
of the U. S. War Department.

the Southern reports were inadequate and included no statement of deaths at Florence and some other prisons. He also
added that the Christian Commission had discovered six
hundred and seventy-six graves for which no report had ever
been made in those prisons. Stanton failed to mention this
addition in his report to Congress.[68] But writers of prison
experiences looked for more deaths. One writer declared
that there were sixty thousand graves of Union prisoners in
the South—adding, to obtain that number, those whom he
claimed died from the effects of their experiences within a
few weeks of their parole. The Confederate records showed
that they captured 188,145 prisoners, he asserted, and they
had exchanged and paroled 94,073. This left a balance of
94,072 to be accounted for. "Giving them 10,000 for escapes
and enlistments, what became of the remainder, the 84,072?
They perished in those prison hells, or were pursued through
fen and forest by bloodhounds and demons and their mangled
corpses left to the carrion birds."[69] Another declared that

. . . . in all the Southern prisons about 65,000 fell victims to rebel brutality.
The plea of inability to prevent the terrible mortality can avail them
nothing. That thousands died in a land of lumber piles and forests, alone
effectually destroys that defense . . . with such shelter as they could have
furnished, and which the laws of humanity would have required, the mortality would not have been one-tenth of the number. But, allowing even
twenty per cent, which in itself would have been a frightful mortality, and
the fact remains that at least 52,000 hopeless men fell victims of inhuman
treatment.[70]

Different figures were found by Confederate defenders.
Jefferson Davis and Alexander H. Stephens, together with
other Southern writers, added to Stanton's report another
which they alleged came from Surgeon-General Barnes. By
this they arrived at the figure of 270,000 prisoners in Southern prisons while the number of deaths for prisons on both
sides and the number in Northern prisons were unchanged.
By this they were able to prove a twelve per cent mortality

[68] *Official Records,* series 2, VIII, 946-48.
[69] Boggs, *op. cit.,* 59, 61, 63.
[70] Urban, *op. cit.,* Preface.

for the Northern prisons and less than nine per cent for the South. These figures were extensively copied.[71]

The attempt of the Southern writers to juggle figures was an indication of the willingness of the ex-Confederates to carry on the controversy with their Northern accusers on an equal plane. Although fewer prisoners who resided in Northern prisons have attempted to wield the pen after sheathing the sword, they have not been laggards in the virulence of their attack. Northern charges of a plot have been denied, and stories of sufferings have been branded as exaggerations. Such sufferings as are indicated by the thirteen thousand graves of Andersonville have been laid to the poverty of the South, induced largely by the destructive raids of Northern armies. The war is carried into the enemy's camp by charging the Northern government with the entire responsibility for the sufferings in the South because Stanton refused to exchange prisoners. The ex-Confederates forget the proclama-

[71] Davis, *Rise and Fall of the Confederate States*, II, 607. Davis gives no authority for his statement while Stephens in his *War Between the States*, II, 508, cites an editorial in the *National Intelligencer* but without giving a date. Stephens states that Stanton's report did "not set forth the exact number held by each side." The entire problem of numbers of deaths is difficult to solve. According to a letter of Adjutant-General F. C. Ainsworth to Mr. James Ford Rhodes, July 29, 1903, such a report from Barnes cannot be found. General Ainsworth declared that "according to the best information now obtainable, from both Union and Confederate records, it appears that 211,411 Union soldiers were captured during the Civil War, of which number 16,668 were paroled on the field and 30,218 died while in captivity; and that 462,634 Confederate soldiers were captured during the war, of which number 247,769 were paroled on the field and 25,976 died while in captivity." Mr. Rhodes thus concludes: "Thus the mortality was a little over twelve per cent at the North and 15.5 at the South. Taking into account the better hospitals, more skilled physicians, the ample supply of medicines, and the abundance of food at the North and the exceptionally high death rate at Andersonville, Florence, and Salisbury, one might have expected a greater difference, which probably would be the case were all the deaths in the Confederacy known. Still it should be remembered that as the Southern summer bore hardly on the Union prisoners so did the Northern winter increase the mortality of the Confederate as the number of deaths from pneumonia bears witness." Rhodes, *History of the United States from the Compromise of 1850*, V, 506-08. Professor Channing has accepted the figures of Mr. Rhodes (*History of the United States*, VI, 438, 433) and these figures seem to be the most accurate available. Channing adds the suggestion that the prisoners at Andersonville were probably affected with hookworm (p. 422). He declared that the reports of deaths of Union prisoners "give a proportion not far from that of the soldiers in the Union army from disease" (p. 439). See also on the subject of numbers *Publications of the Southern Historical Society*, III, 327, n.

tion of retaliation by their president and the Ould-Meredith controversy over the Vicksburg paroles, and cite Ould's letter of August 10, and Grant's letter in which he declared that an exchange would defeat his and Sherman's armies. Having thus shifted the blame these writers make charges against the Northern prisons. Stories of starvation, of unwholesome food, swamp grounds, dangerous epidemics, and impure vaccine, vie with the revelations of the Wirz trial and the bitter reminiscences of the Northern prisoners. Negro guards—an added indignity—killed Confederate prisoners at deadlines from Fort Delaware to St. Louis; the numbers of prisoners who froze to death are limited only by the imaginative resources of the writer.[72]

Aside from literature, the issue of the prisons has been kept alive by other means. At the execution of Wirz there was formed among the witnesses at the trial the "Andersonville Survivors Association" and there was later a "National Ex-Prisoners of War Association" which backed the pension legislation.[73] In 1893 Libby prison was removed to Chicago for the World's Fair and it has since become a museum for

---

[72] Confederate accounts are fewer in number than those written by prisoners in the South. In literary ability, fertility of imagination, and verbosity, the Southerner falls behind his Northern opponent. Few accounts published outside of periodicals rise above the level of pamphlets. Stevenson, *Andersonville, The Southern Side,* devotes 150 out of 295 pages to stories of Northern prisons and a review of the exchange question. The trial of Wirz is dealt with at length. Keiley, *In Vinculis,* does not come in the class of polemical writings although he criticizes the administration of the Elmira prison. Handy, *United States Bonds* is an account of a political prisoner at Fort Delaware, but contains information about the prisoners of war at that prison. The outstanding Southern defense and counter-attack of any considerable size is Jones, *Confederate View of the Treatment of Prisoners of War,* published in Vol. I of the publications of the Southern Historical Society, and reprinted. Davis and Stephens have sections on prisoners in their histories of the Confederacy. Dunkle (pseudonym, Fuzzlebug), *Prison Life During the Rebellion;* and Murray, *The Immortal Six Hundred,* deal with the Confederate officers confined on Morris Island and contain a few stories of atrocious treatment of prisoners which are not a part of the general fund of horrors from which most of the other writers draw. The association of the survivors of the prisoners who were confined on Morris Island attempted as late as 1914 to obtain damages from Congress for the alleged inhuman treatment to which they were subjected. See Murray, *Claim of Certain Confederate Officers . . . . in support of H. B. 14170.*

[73] See Goss, *op. cit.,* 271 for the A. S. A.; and Ransom, *op. cit.,* 188-92.

Civil War relics.[74]   In 1905 the Georgia Chapter of the
United Daughters of the Confederacy started a fund to erect
a monument to Henry Wirz at Andersonville. The prison site
of Andersonville had been purchased and made into a park
by the Woman's Relief Corps. The graves of the prisoners
who died are in a National cemetery. About the park and
cemetery states have erected monuments to their soldiers
who died in the prison.[75]

Even to this land of the dead the conflict over the prisoners
has been carried. Meeting the eye of the visitor to Andersonville
as he leaves the station is the monument to the former
commander. Upon its sides are Grant's letter refusing to
permit an exchange, and the last dictum of Jefferson Davis
on the subject of prisoners: "When time shall have softened
passion and prejudice, when Reason shall have stripped the
mask from misrepresentation, then Justice, holding evenly
her scales, will require much of past censure and praise to
change places."[76]

[74] See *Libby Chronicle*. This paper, borrowing the title of Beaudry's unpublished
sheet, was the organ of the museum during the fair. Ransom, the author of *Andersonville Diary*, became editor of the revived publication.

[75] See Maile, *Prison Life in Andersonville*, and Chipman, *Tragedy*, for work of
the W. R. C. Cf. also reports of state monument commissions.

[76] Davis, "Andersonville and Other War Prisons," *Belford's Magazine*. For the
work of the monument commission see *Confederate Veteran*, October, 1906; June,
1912; also Rutherford, *True Story of Henry Wirz*.

BIBLIOGRAPHY

I. UNPUBLISHED SOURCES

THE CAMP CHASE LETTERS. These letters, about two hundred and fifty in number, were in the possession of the Ohio Archaeological and Historical Society. The letters were written by prisoners in Camp Chase. Many of the letters are from political prisoners and the majority bear dates of April 20 to 25, 1862. Since being used, a few of these letters have been distributed to relatives—or other claimants.

HISTORY AND TABULAR STATEMENT OF SALISBURY PRISON. A brief account of the prison, evidently made by someone connected with it, giving a brief account of its founding and a list of the commanders. War Department Archives.

HOFFMAN, WM. Letter books of the Commissary-General of Prisoners. The material in these books, some twenty in number, has been printed in the *Official Records of the War of the Rebellion*, with some omissions of minor matters of routine. War Department Archives.

LAWRENCE, WILLIAM R. "That Northwestern Confederacy." An unpublished paper attempting to show the connection between the Confederacy and schemes for the secession of the northwest. Some sidelights on life in Richmond prisons. Library of Congress.

LIBBY PRISON DAY BOOK. List of the prisoners received and sent from Libby prison. War Department Archives.

PAPERS RELATING TO THE SULTANA DISASTER. Affidavits and reports of commanders and inspectors. About three hundred papers unbound and unindexed. War Department Archives.

RUFFIN, EDMUND, Diary. 14 vols. 1856-1865. Ruffin, a Virginian, has some sidelights on the conditions of prisoners in the South. Library of Congress.

II. PUBLIC DOCUMENTS

1. UNITED STATES

BUTLER, BENJAMIN FRANKLIN, *The Exchange Question*. Washington, 1864. Butler's letter to Ould, August 1864, published for circulation in the North.

ELLIOTT, WILLIAM, *List Showing Inscriptions on Headstones for the Confederate Soldiers and Sailors who, while Prisoners of War, Died at Columbus and Camp Dennison, Ohio, and were Buried in Camp Chase Confederate Cemetery, Those Dying at Camp Dennison Having Been Thence Removed*. Washington, 1907.

MURRAY, J. OGDEN, *Claim of Certain Confederate Officers. Statement of Major J. Ogden Murray Before the Committee on War Claims. House of Representatives. 63rd Congress, Second Session, in Support of H. R. 14170 a Bill for the Relief of Certain Officers of the Confederate States Army in the War between the States. March 28, 1914.* Washington, 1914.

United States Quartermaster-General's Office, *The Martyrs Who, for our Country, Gave up their Lives in the Prison Pens in Andersonville, Ga.* Washington, 1866.

The Congressional Globe, 8 vols. 1861-1866.

Senate Executive Document 17. 38th Congress, 1st session. Correspondence in relation to the exchange of prisoners.

Senate Executive Document 24. 38th Congress, 1st session. Relates to captures in Missouri.

House of Representatives, Report 67. 38th Congress, 1st session. Thirty pages devoted to a statement of the condition of returned prisoners at Annapolis. Contains eight pictures of emaciated prisoners. A propaganda pamphlet.

Senate Report 142. 38th Congress, 2nd session. Report of the committee on the conduct of the war. Grant before the committee on matters connected with exchange.

House of Representatives, Executive Documents 20. Exchange of Prisoners of War. Report of Colonel Key on his conversation with General Howell Cobb.

House of Representatives, Executive Documents 32. 38th Congress, 2nd session. Documents relating to the exchange of prisoners.

House of Representatives, Executive Documents 50. 39th Congress, 2nd session. Volume devoted to the trial before a military commission of George St. Legar Grenfel for a plot to release prisoners at Chicago.

2. STATE

New York Andersonville Monument Commission, *A Pilgrimage to the Shrines of Patriotism.* Albany, 1916.

Pennsylvania Andersonville Memorial Commission, *Pennsylvania at Andersonville, Georgia.* Harrisburg, 1901.

PHILLIPS, JOSEPH A., *List of Soldiers (Prisoners of War) Belonging to Pennsylvania Regiments, Who Died at the Military Prisons, at Andersonville, Georgia, from February 26, 1864 to March 24, 1865.* Harrisburg, 1865.

Rhode Island, *Report of the Joint Special Committee on Erection of Monument at Andersonville, Ga.* Providence, 1903.

Virginia, *Acts of the General Assembly of the State of Virginia for Years 1861-1865.*

III. PERSONAL NARRATIVES, PRISONERS' REMINISCENCES, ETC.

1. BOOKS

ABBOTT, A. O., *Prison Life in the South at Richmond, Macon, Savannah, Charleston, Columbia, Charlotte, Raleigh, Goldsborough and Andersonville during the years 1864 and 1865.* New York, 1865.
The Andersonville portion is by another. Also a couple of chapters relating to escapes have been contributed. On the whole it is a simple story of an officer's experiences as a prisoner of war.

BACON, ALVIN Q., *Thrilling Experiences of a Pioneer Boy, while a Prisoner of War.* (No place) 1863 (?).
Pamphlet sold for the benefit of the author's father. Brief captivity and escape from Macon in 1862.

BARBIERE, JOE, *Scraps from the Prison Table at Camp Chase and Johnson's Island.* Doylestown, Pa., 1868.
Experience of a prisoner in the early part of the war.

BATES, RALPH Q., *Billy and Dick from Andersonville Prison to the White House.* Santa Cruz, California, 1910.
This account is utterly inaccurate. The author reverses the usual order of prisons, arriving in Andersonville a year before its establishment.

BATES, WILLIAM C., *The Stars and Stripes in Rebeldom, A series of papers written by Federal prisoners (Privates) in Richmond, Tuscaloosa, New Orleans and Salisbury, N. C.* Boston, 1862.

BEAUDRY, LOUIS N., *"The Libby Chronicle" Devoted to Facts and Fun. A True Story of the Libby Chronicle as written by the Prisoners of Libby in 1863.* Albany, 1889. (Copyright).
Has been considerably edited and even includes a poem on Andersonville which was not written until the next year.

BERRY, CHESTER D., *Loss of the Sultana and Reminiscences of Survivors. History of a Disaster Where Over One Thousand Five Hundred Human Beings Were Lost, Most of Them Being Exchanged Prisoners of War on Their Way Home after Privation and Suffering from One to Twenty-three Months in Cahaba and Andersonville Prisons.* Lansing, Michigan, 1892.

BLISS, GEORGE N., *How I Lost My Sabre in War and Found it in Peace.* Providence, 1903.

BOGGS, S. S., *Eighteen Months a Prisoner under the Rebel Flag. A Condensed Pen Picture of Belle Isle, Danville, Andersonville, Charleston, Florence and Libby Prisons.* Lovingston, Illinois, 1889.
A bitter accusation of the rebel authorities. A German edition, *Achtzehn Monate ein Gefangener unter den Rebellen-Flagge,* was published at the same time.

Booth, B. F., *Dark Days of the Rebellion, or Life in Southern Military Prisons giving a Correct and Thrilling History of Unparalleled Suffering, Narrow Escapes, Heroic Encounters, Bold Achievements, Cold-Blooded Murders, Severe Tests of Loyalty and Patriotism.* Indianola, Iowa, 1897.
Only account of Salisbury by military prisoner, very bitter.

Braun, Herman A., *Andersonville, An Object Lesson on Protection.* Milwaukee, 1892.
A defense of Wirz and the Confederate prison system.

Browne, Junius Henri, *Four Years in Secessia: Adventures within and beyond the Union Lines: Embracing a great variety of Facts, Incidents, and Romance of the War, including the Author's Capture at Vicksburg, May 3, 1863, While Running the Rebel Batteries: His imprisonment at Vicksburg, Jackson, Atlanta, Richmond, and Salisbury: His Escape and Perilous Journey of Four Hundred Miles to the Union Lines at Knoxville.* Hartford, 1865.

Burson, William, *A Race for Liberty: or My Capture, Imprisonment, and Escape.* Wellsville, Ohio, 1867.

Butler, Benjamin F., *Butler's Book.* Boston, 1892.
Important light on the exchange controversy.

Byers, S. H. M., *What I Saw in Dixie, or Sixteen Months in Rebel Prisons.* Danville, N. Y., 1868.
Bitter against the South.
With Fire and Sword. New York, 1911.
Much less so.

Cavada, Frederick Fernandez, *Libby Life: Experiences of a Prisoner of War in Richmond, Va., 1863-64.* Philadelphia, 1865.
A very mild account without the usual atrocity stories.

Cesnola, Louis Palma di, *Ten Months in Libby Prison.* New York, 1865. Reprinted from the U. S. Sanitary Commission *Bulletin*, March, 1865.

Chipman, Norton P., *The Horrors of the Andersonville Rebel Prison. Trial of Henry Wirz, the Andersonville Jailer. Jefferson Davis' Defense of Andersonville Prison Fully Refuted.* San Francisco, 1891.
An account of the Wirz trial by the Judge Advocate. Very bitter.
The Tragedy of Andersonville. The Trial of Captain Henry Wirz. San Francisco, 1911.
A review of the Wirz trial by the Judge Advocate. He lost none of his bitterness in a half century.

Cooper, A., *In and Out of Rebel Prisons.* Oswego, N. Y., 1888.
An officer's imprisonment and escape.

Copley, John M., *A Sketch of the Battle of Franklin, Tenn.; With Reminiscences of Camp Douglas.* Austin, 1893.

CORCORAN, MICHAEL, *The Captivity of General Corcoran, The Only Authentic and Reliable Narrative of the Trials and Sufferings Endured, During His Twelve Months' Imprisonment in Richmond and other Southern Cities, by Brig.-General Michael Corcoran, the Hero of Bull Run.* Philadelphia, 1862.
Evidently written as a recruiting pamphlet.

COX, SAMUEL S., *Eight Years in Congress.* New York, 1865.
Aside from a speech on Negro Troops this work is almost worthless for this study.

CREELMAN, S., *Collections of a Coffee Cooler, Consisting of Daily Prison Scenes in Andersonville, Ga., and Florence, S. C., with Poetic Effusions on Foraging, Army Beans, Army Corn, Soldier's Oration, Soldier's Widow, and the Soldier's Funeral, Silent Sentinels, etc.* Pittsburgh, 1890.

DAHL, O. R., *Key to Southern Prisons of United States Officers.* New York, 1865.

DARBY, GEORGE W., *Incidents and Adventures in Rebeldom, Libby, Belle Isle, Salisbury.* Pittsburgh, 1899.
Very bitter.

DAVIDSON, H. M., *Fourteen Months in Southern Prisons.* Milwaukee, 1865.
Parts of this account were copied by the congressional committee for their report on the treatment of prisoners in the South. It appears also as a part of the book by Isham, Davidson, and Furness.

DAVIS, JEFFERSON, *The Rise and Fall of the Confederate Government.* 2 Vols. New York, 1881.
Chapter xlix on the exchange of prisoners.

DAVIS, SAMUEL B., *Escape of a Confederate Officer from Prison. What He Saw at Andersonville, How He Was Sentenced to Death and Saved by the Interposition of President Abraham Lincoln.* Norfolk, 1892.
Davis was second in command at Andersonville.

DAY, WILLIAM W., *Fifteen Months in Dixie, or My Personal Experience in Rebel Prisons. A Story of the Hardships, Privations and Sufferings of the "Boys in Blue" during the late War of the Rebellion.* Owatonna, Minn., 1889.

DIETRICHSON, PETER G., *En Kortfattet Skildring af det Femtende Wisconsin Regimento Historie og Virksombed under Borgerkrigen sampt Nogle Korte Traek af Fangerness Ophold i Andersonville.* Chicago, 1884.

DOMSCHCKE, BERNHARD, *Zwanzig Monate in Kriegs-Gefangenschaft. Erinnerungen von Bernhard Domschcke.* Milwaukee, 1865.
The usual story of atrocities with some interesting light on the Streight-Dow-Sanderson controversy.

DOUGHERTY, MICHAEL, *Prison Diary of Michael Dougherty while Confined in Pemberton, Libby, Andersonville, and Other Southern Prisons.* Bristol, Pa., 1908.
Extensive borrowings, without credit, from Boggs, *q. v.*

DOWLING, MORGAN E., *Southern Prisons, or Josie, the Heroine of Florence, Four Years of Battle and Imprisonment, Richmond, Atlanta, Belle Isle, Andersonville, and Florence. A Complete History of all Southern Prisons, Embracing a Thrilling Episode of Romance and Love.* Detroit, 1870.

DRAKE, JAMES MADISON, *Narrative of the Capture, Imprisonment, and Escape of J. Madison Drake, Captain Ninth New Jersey Veteran Volunteers.* (No place) 1868.

Fast and Loose in Dixie, An Unprejudiced Narrative of Personal Experience as a Prisoner of War at Libby, Macon, Savannah, and Charleston, with an Account of a Desperate Leap from a Moving Train of Cars, a Weary Tramp of Forty-five Days Through Swamps and Mountains, Places and People Visited, etc. New York, 1880.

A more complete account of experiences containing more details than the above.

DUFF, WM. H., *Terrors and Horrors of Prison Life, or Six Months a Prisoner at Camp Chase, Ohio.* (No place) 1907. (Copyright).

Illiterate.

DUFUR, S. M., *Over the Dead Line, or Tracked by Bloodhounds, Giving the Author's Personal Experience during eleven months that he was confined in Pemberton, Libby, Belle Isle, Andersonville, Ga., and Florence, S. C., as a prisoner of war. Describing plans of escape, arrival of prisoners, his escape and recapture; with numerous and varied incidents and anecdotes of his prison life.* Burlington, Vt., 1902.

DUGANNE, A. J., *Camps and Prisons, Twenty Months in the Department of the Gulf.* New York, 1865.

Accounts of Camps Ford and Groce in Texas, with complete absence of atrocities.

DUNKLE, JOHN J., *Prison Life During the Rebellion, Being a Brief Narrative of the Miseries and Sufferings of Six Hundred Confederate Prisoners sent from Fort Delaware to Morris' Island to be Punished, Written by Fritz Fuzzlebug, one of their number.* Singers Glen, Va., 1869.

Grammar bad, spelling erratic. The work of an illiterate whose mind wanders.

EBY, HENRY H., *Observations of an Illinois Boy in Battle, Camp and Prisons—1861 and 1865.* Mendota, Illinois, 1910.

Written to promote pacifism.

ELY, ALFRED, *Journal of Alfred Ely.* New York, 1862.

Experiences in Richmond of a Congressman taken at Bull Run.

ENNIS, JOHN W., *Adventures in Rebeldom; or Ten Months' Experience of Prison Life.* New York, 1863.

Richmond in 1861. Castle Pinkney and escape.

FERGUSON, JOSEPH, *Life and Struggles in Rebel Prisons. A Record of the Sufferings, Escapes, Adventures, and Starvation of the Union Prisoners. Containing an*

appendix with the names, regiments, and date of death of Pennsylvania soldiers who died at Andersonville. Philadelphia, 1865.
Bitter.

FORBES, EUGENE, *Diary of a Soldier and Prisoner of War in the Rebel Prisons.* Trenton, 1865.
Diary of a prisoner who died February 1, 1865. Very mild.

"Fort La-Fayette Life" 1863-1864, in extracts from the "Right Flankers." A Manuscript Sheet Circulating Among the Southern Prisoners in Fort La-Fayette in 1863-1864. Extra No. 13. *The Magazine of History.* IV (1911) 201-46.

FOSDICK, CHARLES, *Five Hundred Days in Rebel Prisons.* Bethany, Mo., 1887.
Belle Isle and Andersonville. Bitter, inaccurate.

FOX, JAMES D., *A True History of the Reign of Terror in Southern Illinois. A Part of the Campaign in Western Virginia, and Fourteen Months of Prison Life At Richmond, Virginia; Macon, Georgia; Charleston, South Carolina; and Columbia, South Carolina.* Aurora, Illinois, 1864.
Very fair account. Too brief.

FROST, GRIFFIN, *Camp and Prison Journal, embracing Scenes in Camp, on the March, and in Prisons; Springfield, Gratiot Street, St. Louis, and Macon City, Mo.; Fort Delaware, Alton and Camp Douglas, Ill.; Camp Morton, Ind.; and Camp Chase, Ohio. Also scenes and Incidents during a Trip for Exchange from St. Louis, Mo., via Philadelphia, Pa., to City Point, Va.* Quincy, Illinois, 1867.
Counter-attack. Atrocities equal to those of Andersonville are promised in the preface but do not materialize convincingly.

GEER, J. J., *Beyond the Lines, or a Yankee Loose in Dixie.* Philadelphia, Pa., 1863.

GLAZIER, WILLARD W., *The Capture, the Prison Pen and the Escape, Giving a complete History of Prison Life in the South, Principally at Richmond, Danville, Macon, Savannah, Charleston, Columbia, Belle Isle, Millen, Salisbury, and Andersonville, describing the arrival of Prisoners, plans of escape, with numerous and varied incidents of prison life; embracing also the Adventures of the Author's escape from Columbia, S. C. Recaptured, subsequent escape, recapture, trial as spy, and final escape from Sylvania, Georgia.* With illustrations. Hartford, Conn., 1868.
A vituperative account of exaggerated hardships.

GOSS, WARREN LEE, *The Soldier's Story of his Captivity at Andersonville, Belle Isle, and other Rebel Prisons.* Boston, 1869.
Very bitter. Much quoted by the congressional committee.

GRISBY, MELVIN, *The Smoked Yank.* Sioux Falls, S. D., 1888.

HADLEY, JOHN VESTAL, *Seven Months a Prisoner.* New York, 1898.
Macon, Savannah, Charleston, Columbia, and escape.

HAMILTON, ANDREW G., *Story of the Famous Tunnel Escape from Libby Prison.* (No place) 1893 (?)

HANDY, ISAAC W. K., *United States Bonds, or Duress by Federal Authority: A Journal of Current Events during an Imprisonment of Fifteen Months at Fort Delaware.* Baltimore, 1874.
A political prisoner's account of Fort Delaware.

HARRIS, WILLIAM C., *Prison Life in the Tobacco Warehouse at Richmond.* Philadelphia, 1862.

HARROLD, JOHN, *Libby, Andersonville, Florence, The Capture, Imprisonment, Escape, and Rescue of John Harrold. A Union Soldier in the war of the Rebellion. With a description of Prison Life among the Rebels—The Treatment of Union Prisoners, Their Privations and Sufferings.* Philadelphia, 1870.

HASSON, B. F., *Escape from the Confederacy—Overpowering the Guards—Midnight Leap from a Moving Train—Through Swamps and Forest—Bloodhounds— Thrilling Events.* Byron, Ohio, (?) 1900 (Copyright).

HAWES, JESSE, *Cahaba, A Story of Captive Boys in Blue.* New York, 1888 (Copyright).

HITCHCOCK, ETHAN ALLEN, *Fifty Years in Camp and Field.*

HOCKERSMITH, LORENZO DOW, *Morgan's Escape. A Thrilling Story of War Times. A True History of the Raid of General Morgan and His Men Through Kentucky, Indiana, and Ohio; Their Incarceration in the Columbus Penitentiary; Escape Therefrom and Tragic Death of the Intrepid Leader.* Madisonville, Ky., 1903.

HOLSTEIN, MRS. WILLIAM, *Three Years in Field Hospitals of the Army of the Potomac.* Philadelphia, 1867.
Contains some prison sketches.

HOWE, THOMAS H., *Adventures of an Escaped Union Prisoner from Andersonville.* San Francisco, 1886.

HUMPHREYS, CHARLES A., *Field Camp, Hospital, and Prison in the Civil War 1863-1865.* Boston, 1918.
Macon, Charleston, and Columbia.

HUNDLEY, DANIEL ROBINSON, *Prison Echoes of the Great Rebellion.* New York, 1874.
A fair-minded diary with no atrocities.

HYDE, SOLON, *A Captive of War.* New York, 1900.

Incidents in Dixie. Being Ten Months' Experience of a Union Soldier in the Military Prisons of Richmond, New Orleans, and Salisbury. Baltimore, 1864.

ISHAM, ASA B., HENRY M. DAVIDSON, AND HENRY B. FURNESS, *Prisoners of War and Military Prisons, Personal Narrative of Experience in the Prisons of Richmond,*

Danville, Macon, Andersonville, Savannah, Millen, Charleston, and Columbia, With a General account of Prison Life and Prisons in the South during the war of the Rebellion, including Statistical Information pertaining to prisoners of war, together with a list of officers who were Prisoners of War from January 1, 1864. Cincinnati, 1890.

A composite account. Isham treats the officers' prisons, Davidson copies his account as given in his *Fourteen Months*, and Furness adds a general account based on the report of the committee on treatment of prisoners of war.

JAMES, NEWTON MILLER, *The Story of Andersonville and Florence.* Des Moines, Iowa. 1900.

JEFFREY, WILLIAM H., *Richmond Prisons 1861-1862, Compiled from the Original Records kept by the Confederate Government. Journals kept by Union Prisoners of War, Together with the Name, Rank, Company, Regiment, and State of the Four Thousand who were confined there.* St. Johnsburg, Vt., 1893 (Copyright).

JOHNSON, HANNIBAL A., *The Sword of Honor, From Captivity to Freedom.* Providence, 1903.

Good account of adventures among Unionists in the mountains of Tennessee.

The Sword of Honor, Hallowell, Maine, 1906.

A more extensive account than the above.

JOHNSTON, ADAM S., *The Soldier Boy's Diary Book; or, Memorandums of the Alphabetical First Lessons of Military Tactics, Kept by Adam S. Johnston, From September 14, 1861 to October 2, 1864.* Pittsburgh, 1866.

KEILEY, ANTHONY M., *Prisoner of War, or, Five Months Among the Yankees. Being a Narrative of the Crosses, Calamities, and Consolations of a Petersburg Militiaman during an enforced Summer residence North. By A. Rifleman, Esq. Gent.* Richmond, 1865.

This edition was destroyed by fire and later extended in *In Vinculis, Or the Prisoner of War, Being the Experiences of a Rebel in Two Federal Pens. Interspersed with Reminiscences of the Late War, Anecdotes of Southern Generals, etc.* New York, 1866.

The purpose is stated as being a counter-attack on the propaganda of the Federals. The book, however, reveals very little war psychosis.

KELLEY, DANIEL G., *What I Saw and Suffered in Rebel Prisons.* Buffalo, 1866.

KELLOGG, JOHN AZOR, *Capture and Escape, A Narrative of Army and Prison Life.* Wisconsin History Commission, November, 1908.

Lynchburg, Danville, Macon, Charleston, and escape; adventures among the Unionists in Georgia.

KELLOGG, ROBERT H., *Life and Death in Rebel Prisons; Giving a Complete History of the inhuman and barbarous treatment of our suffering and brave soldiers by Rebel Authorities Inflicting terrible suffering and frightful Mortality, Principally*

at Andersonville, Ga., and Florence, S. C., describing plans of escape, arrival of prisoners, with numerous and various anecdotes of prison life, etc. Hartford, 1867.
The author was a prominent witness at the Wirz trial.

KENT, WILL PARMITER, *The Story of Libby Prison, also some Perils and Sufferings of Certain of Its Inmates.* Chicago, 1897.
An account of moving the prison.

KING, JOHN H., *Three Hundred Days in a Yankee Prison, Reminiscences of War, Life, Captivity, Imprisonment at Camp Chase, Ohio.* Atlanta, 1904.

KING, JOHN R., *My Experience in the Confederate Army and in Northern Prisons.* Clarksburg, W. Va., 1917.
Point Lookout and Elmira.

LANGWORTHY, DANIEL AVERY, *Reminiscences of a Prisoner of War and His Escape.* Minneapolis, 1915.

LEONARD, A. C., *The Boys in Blue of 1861-1865, A Condensed History Worth Preserving.* Lancaster, Pa. (No date).
A private's experiences at Belle Isle and Andersonville.

Libby Prison Chronicle. Chicago.
Issues begin with Vol. I, No. VIII, February, 1894, a continuation of Beaudry's *Chronicle*, published at Chicago in Libby Prison after the removal of the building to the World's Fair.

LIGHTCAP, WILLIAM HENRY, *The Horrors of Southern Prisons During the War of the Rebellion.* Lancaster, Wisconsin, 1902 (Copyright).

LONG, LASSEL, *Twelve Months in Andersonville, On the March, In the Battle, In the Rebel Prison Pens, and at Last in God's Country.* Huntington, Indiana, 1886.

LYON, W. F., *In and Out of Andersonville Prison.* Detroit, 1905.

MACCAULEY, CLAY, *Through Chancellorsville, Into and Out of Libby Prison.* Providence, 1904.
Few weeks in Libby in the spring of 1863.

MAILE, JOHN L., *"Prison Life in Andersonville" With Special Reference to the Opening of Providence Spring.* Los Angeles, 1912. (Copyright).
Christian Evidence. The author says that the Spring opened in direct answer to prayers of the prisoners.

MARKS, JAMES J., *The Peninsular Campaign in Virginia, or Incidents and Scenes on the Battlefields and in Richmond.* Philadelphia, 1864.

MAY, WM. HENRY, *The Old Flag, First Published by Union Prisoners at Camp Ford,* Tyler, Texas (No place, no date).

McElroy, John, *Andersonville, A Story of Rebel Military Prisons, Fifteen Months a Guest of the So-called Southern Confederacy, A Private Soldier's Experience in Richmond, Andersonville, Savannah, Millen, Blackshear, and Florence.* Toledo, 1879.
Perhaps the classic account of the sufferings of the prisoners. Written by a journalist. Inaccurate, but interesting.

McCowan, Archibald, *The Prisoners of War. A Reminiscence of the Rebellion.* New York, 1901. (Copyright.)

Merrell, W. H., *Five Months in Rebeldom, or Notes from the Diary of a Bull Run Prisoner, at Richmond.* Rochester, 1862.

Minnich, J. M., *Inside of Rock Island Prison from December, 1863 to June, 1865.* Nashville and Dallas, 1906.

Moran, Frank E., *Bastiles of the Confederacy, A Reply to Jefferson Davis.* Baltimore, 1890.
Replying to Davis' article in *Belford's Magazine.*

Murray, George W., *A History of George W. Murray and His Long Confinement at Andersonville, Georgia.* Hartford, 186-?
"Sold by himself for the benefit of himself and family." The author lost use of his right arm and leg as the result of his confinement. This is a begging pamphlet of 30 pages. There is utterly no internal evidence that the author ever saw a Southern prison.
The Life and Adventure of Serg. G. W. Murray. Minneapolis, 1872.

Murray, J. Ogden, *The Immortal Six Hundred, A Story of Cruelty to Confederate Prisoners of War.* Roanoke, Va., 1911.
Counter-attack by one of the hostages confined on Morris Island.

Newlin, W. H., *An Account of the Escape of Six Federal Soldiers from Prison at Danville, Virginia; Their Travels by Night Through the Enemy's Country to the Union Pickets at Gauley Bridge, West Virginia, in the Winter of 1863-64.* Cincinnati, 1870.

Newsome, Edmund, *Experiences in the War of the Great Rebellion.* Carbondale, Illinois, 1879.
Macon, Savannah, Charleston, Columbia.

Nineteen Months a Prisoner of War in the Hands of the Rebels; Experiences at Belle Isle, Richmond, Danville, and Andersonville, Some Items with Reference to Captain Wirz, with a Map of the Andersonville Prison Camp, called Camp Sumpter. Milwaukee, 1865.

Northrop, John Worrell, *Chronicles from the Diary of a War Prisoner in Andersonville and other Military Prisons of the South in 1864. Experiences, Observa-*

tions, Interviews, and Poems, Written in Prison, with Historical Introduction, An Appendix containing a statement of a Confederate Physician and Officer Relative to Prison Conditions and Management. Wichita, Kansas, 1904.

NOTT, CHARLES C., *Sketches in Prison Camps; A Continuation of Sketches of the War.* New York, 1865.
An account of Camp Groce.

O'HARA, M., *Reminiscences of Andersonville and Other Rebel Prisons. A Story of Suffering, Starvation, and Death.* Lyons, Iowa, 1880.

PAGE, JAMES MADISON, *The True Story of Andersonville Prison, A Defense of Major Henry Wirz in Collaboration with M. J. Haley.* New York and Washington, 1908.
A Federal Prisoner who was befriended by Wirz. Admits sufferings but says Wirz attempted to alleviate them. Not exaggerated.

PIERSON, CHARLES LAWRENCE, *Ball's Bluff, An Episode and Its Consequences to Some of Us.* Salem, Mass., 1913.
Reminiscences of Liggon's Prison.

PIERSON, WILLIAM WHATLEY, Jr., (Ed.) *Diary of Bartlett Yancey Malone.* Chapel Hill, 1919. Experiences of a prisoner at Point Lookout.

PITTENGER, WILLIAM, *Daring and Suffering.* New York, 1887.
Story of the Andrews Railroad raid into Georgia.

POLLARD, EDWARD A., *Observations in the North; Eight Months in Prison and on Parole.* Richmond, 1865.
A political prisoner's account. Little value for this study.

PRUTSMAN, C. M., *A Soldier's Experience in Southern Prisons.* New York, 1901.

PUTNAM, GEORGE HAVEN, *A Prisoner of War in Virginia 1864-5.* New York, 1912.

QUINCY, SAMUEL M., *A Prisoner's Diary* (History of the Second Massachusetts Regiment of Infantry). Boston, 1882.
Short time in Libby in September 1862.

RANSOM, JOHN L., *Andersonville Diary, Escape, and List of Dead.* Auburn, 1881.
In the form of a diary. Gives evidence of having been edited for popular consumption.

RICH, EDWARD R., *Comrades.* Easton, Maryland, 1898.

RICHARDSON, ALBERT D., *The Secret Service, the Field, the Dungeon, and the Escape.* Hartford, 1865.
Superior to the account by Browne, by another *Tribune* correspondent.

ROACH, A. C., *The Prisoner of War and How Treated.* Indianapolis, 1865.
Story of the captivity of Streight's officers. Rabid.

ROE, ALFRED S., *From Monocacy to Danville.* Providence, 1889.

In a Rebel Prison, or Experiences in Danville, Va. Providence, 1891.

Richmond, Annapolis, and Home. Providence, 1892.

The Melvin Memorial. Cambridge, 1910.
Pages 79-133 "Diary of Samuel Melvin" A Prisoner at Andersonville.

ROSE, THOMAS ELLWOOD, Col. *Rose's Story of the Famous Tunnel Escape from Libby Prison.* (No place) 189(?)

ROUSE, J. H., *Horrible Massacre at Guyandotte, Va., and a Journey to the Rebel Capital with a Description of Prison Life in a Tobacco Warehouse at Richmond, Virginia.* (No place.) 1862.
Experiences of a surgeon in Liggon's, 1861.

RUSSELL, D. E., *Seven Months in Prison, or Life in Rebeldom, Details of a Real Prison Life in Richmond and Danville, with a list of Wisconsin men who died in the Andersonville Prison, in a perfect order by Regiments.* Milwaukee, 1866.

SABRE, GILBERT E., *Nineteen Months a Prisoner of War, Narrative of Lieutenant G. E. Sabre, of his Experience in the War Prisons and Stockades of Morton, Mobile, Atlanta, Libby, Belle Isle, Andersonville, Macon, Charleston, and Columbia, and his Escape to the Union Lines, to which is appended a list of Officers confined at Columbia during the Winter of 1864 and 1865.* New York, 1866.

SANDERSON, JAMES M., *My Record in Rebeldom.* New York, 1865.
A defense by an officer who was accused of revealing a plan of escape to the Confederate authorities while a prisoner. Attack on General Neal Dow and Col. Streight.

SCHWARTZ, STEPHAN, *Twenty-two Months a Prisoner of War.* St. Louis, 1892.
The story of confinement in Texas from the beginning of hostilities.

SHEARMAN, SUMNER U., *Battle of the Crater and Experiences of Prison Life.* Providence, 1898.

SHEPHERD, HENRY E., *Narrative of Prison Life at Baltimore and Johnson's Island, Ohio.* Baltimore, 1917.
22 pages. Unimportant.

SHERMAN, GEORGE R., *Assault on Fort Gilmer and Reminiscences of Prison Life.* Providence, 1897.

SHERRILL, MILES O., *A Soldier's Story, Prison Life and Other Incidents in the War of 1861-1865.* (Reprinted from the Newton, N. C., *Enterprise*, 1904.)

SIMPSON, THOMAS, *My Four Months' Experience as a Prisoner of War.* Providence, 1883.

SMEDLEY, CHARLES, *Life in Southern Prisons; from the Diary of Corporal Charles Smedley . . . .* (Fulton, Pa. ?) 1865.

SMITH, CHARLES M., *From Andersonville to Freedom.* Providence, 1894.

SMITH, FRANK W., *Smith's "Knapsack" of Facts and Figures, '61 to '65.* Toledo, 1884.

SMITH, W. B., *On Wheels and How I Came There. A Real Story of Real Boys and Girls. Giving the Personal Experience and Observations of a Fifteen-Year-Old Yankee Boy as a Soldier and Prisoner in the American Civil War.* New York and Cincinnati, 1893.

SPENCER, AMBROSE, *A Narrative of Andersonville, Drawn from the Evidence Elicited on the Trial of Henry Wirz, the Jailer, with the argument of Col. N. P. Chipman, Judge Advocate.* New York, 1866.
Account by a Unionist living near the prison and a witness in the Wirz trial.

SPRAGUE, HOMER B., *Lights and Shadows in Confederate Prisons. A Personal Experience, 1864-5.* New York and London, 1915.
Fairminded account of Libby, Salisbury, and Danville.

STAFFORD, DAVID W., *The Defense of the Flag, A True War Story, Pen Picture of Scenes and Incidents During the Great Rebellion—Thrilling Experiences During Escape from Southern Prisons, etc.* Kalamazoo, 1904.

STEARNS, AMOS E., *Narrative of Amos E. Stearns a Prisoner at Andersonville.* Worcester, 1887.
Libby, Andersonville, Charleston, and Columbia.

STEVENS, LEVERETT C., *A Forlorn Hope.* Providence, 1903.

STEVENSON, R. RANDOLPH, *The Southern Side, or, Andersonville Prison—Together with an Examination of the Wirz Trial—Remarks on the Exchange Bureau, etc.* Baltimore, 1876.

STURGIS, THOMAS, *Prisoners of War 1861-65, A Record of Personal Experiences, and a Study of the Condition and Treatment of Prisoners on Both Sides During the War of the Rebellion.* New York and London, 1912.

TIEMAN, WILLIAM F., *"Prison Life in Dixie."* Brooklyn, 1894.
Typewritten volume in Library of Congress.

TOBIE, EDWARD PARSONS, *A Trip to Richmond as a Prisoner of War.* Providence, 1879.

TUTTLE, F. B., *The History of Camp Douglas,* Chicago, 1865.

URBAN, JOHN W., *My Experiences Mid Shot and Shell and in Rebel Den.* Lancaster, Pa., 1882. (Copyright).
In Defense of the Union or, Through Shot and Shell and Prison Pen.
These two books are identical even to pagination—the only difference being in the binding, in the pictures, and in the title page.

Battlefield and Prison Pen. Lancaster, Pa., 1882.
Urban is widely quoted as an authority on prisons, usually being cited from this book which is identical with the two above.

VAUGHTER, JOHN B., *Prison Life in Dixie, Giving a Short History of the Inhuman and Barbarious Treatment of Our Soldiers by Rebel Authorities. By Sergeant Oats.* Chicago, 1880.

A Voice From Rebel Prisons; Giving an Account of Some of the Horrors of the Stockades at Andersonville, Milan, and other Prisons. By a Returned Prisoner of War. Boston, 1865.

WALKER, JOHN L., *Cahaba Prison and the Sultana Disaster.* Hamilton, Ohio, 1910.

WEISER, GEORGE, *Nine Months in Rebel Prisons.* Philadelphia, 1890.
Andersonville and Florence.

WEST, BECKWITH, *Experience of a Confederate States Prisoner, being an Ephemeris Regularly Kept by an Officer of the Confederate States Army.* Richmond, 1862.
Captive, Old Capitol and Fort Delaware, May 10, to August 5, 1862.

WILLIAMSON, JAMES J., *Prison Life in the Old Capitol.* West Orange, 1911.
A political prisoner's account; chapter on the Wirz trial.

WILLIAMS, SIDNEY S., *From Spottsylvania to Wilmington, N. C , by Way of Andersonville and Florence.* Providence, 1899.

WINSHIP, ALBERT E., *A Fastidious Prisoner, A Reply to "Cold Cheer at Camp Morton," A Work of Fiction in the April Century.* Boston, 1891.
Sarcasm.

2. ARTICLES

ABBOTT, HORACE R., "My Escape from Belle Isle," A Paper read before the Michigan Commandery of the Military Order of the Loyal Legion of the United States. December 5, 1889. Detroit, 1889.

BELL, WILLIAM, "Camp Jackson Prisoners," *Confederate Veteran,* XXXI, 260-61. (1923.)

BERING, JOHN A., "Reminiscences of a Federal Prisoner." *Publications of the Arkansas Historical Association,* III, 372-78 (1911.)

BOATE, EDWARD WILLINGTON, "The True Story of Andersonville, Told by a Federal Prisoner." *Southern Historical Society Papers,* X, 25-32 (1882).

BOWLEY, FREEMAN S., "Seven Months in Confederate Military Prisons." A Paper prepared and read before the California Commandery of the Military Order of the Loyal Legion of the United States. May 2, 1890.

BROOKS, TOM, "In and Out of Prison," *Confederate Veteran,* XXIX, 421-22 (1921).

BURRAGE, HENRY S., "My Capture and What Came of It." *War Papers*. Read before the Commander of the State of Maine, Military Order of the Loyal Legion of the United States, I, 1-20 (1898).

BURROWS, J. L., "Recollection of Libby Prison." *Southern Historical Society Papers*, XI, 83-92 (1883).

CARPENTER, HORACE, "Plain Living at Johnson's Island," *Century*, March, 1891, pp. 705-18.

COX, HENRY C., "Six Months in Andersonville Prison." *The Educational Bi-Monthly*, VIII, 283-97, 406-17 (1914).

CROCKER, JAMES F., "Prison Reminiscences." *Southern Historical Society Papers*, XXXIV, 28-51 (1906).

CROSSLEY, WILLIAM J., "Extracts from My Diary, and From My Experiences while Boarding with Jefferson Davis in Three of his Notorious Hotels. In Richmond, Va., Tuscaloosa, Ala., and Salisbury, N. C., From July 1861 to June 1862." Series 6, No. 4, *Personal Narratives of Events in the War of the Rebellion*, being papers read before the Rhode Island Soldiers and Sailors Historical Society.

DAVIS, JEFFERSON, "Andersonville and other War Prisons," *Belford's Magazine*, January, 1890.

DEVILLEZ, HENRY, "Reminiscences of the Civil War; Andersonville," *Indiana Magazine of History*, XI, 144-47 (1915).

DOBLE, ERASTUS, "Reminiscences of Prison Life and Escape," The *Maine Bugle*, I, 105-15, 214-28, 317-32.

DRAKE J. MADISON, "Adventurous Escape from Prison Life, An Incident of the Late Civil War," *Magazine of American History*, XIV, 404, 406 (1885).

ELLIOTT, JOSEPH TAYLOR, "The Sultana Disaster," *Indiana Historical Society Publications*, V, No. 3. Indianapolis, 1913.

FERNALD, C. O., "Life in Libby," The *Maine Bugle*, I, 232-37.

FORMAN, B. R., "A Confederate Prisoner's Experience." *New Eclectic Magazine*, VI, 420-26 (1870).

FULKERSON, ABRAM, "The Prison Experiences of a Confederate Soldier," *Southern Historical Society Papers*, XXII, 127-46 (1894). (Copied from the *Bristol Courier*, September 8, 1893.)

GEORGE, W. W., "In a Federal Prison," *Southern Historical Society Papers*. XXIX, 1901. (Copied from Richmond *Dispatch*, September 8, 1901.)

HOBERT, HARRISON C., "Libby Prison—The Escape," *War Papers* Read before the Commandery of the State of Wisconsin Military Order of the Loyal Legion of the United States, Milwaukee, 1891.

HOLLOWAY, W. R., "Treatment of Prisoners at Camp Morton. A Reply to 'Cold Cheer at Camp Morton'," *Century Magazine.* September, 1891, pp. 757-70.

HOOPER, I. H., "Twelve Days' 'Absence Without Leave'," *Overland Monthly*, V, 201-13.

HUNT, CHARLES O., "Our Escape from Camp Sorghum." In Military Order of the Loyal Legion of the United States, *War Papers.* (1898). Portland, I, 85-128.

ISHAM, A. B., "Care of Prisoners of War, North and South." A Paper read before the Ohio Commandery of the Military Order of the Loyal Legion of the United States, October 5, 1887. Cincinnati, 1887.

KING, J. T., "On the Andersonville Circuit," *Century*, (1890) November, 100-105.

LEWIS, JOHN W., "Libby." Military Order of the Loyal Legion of the United States Commandery of the District of Columbia, *War Papers No. 61*, read January 3, 1906.

LITTLE, HORACE B., "Reminiscences of the Civil War; Escape from Fort Tyler Prison," *Indiana Magazine of History*, XIII, 42-55 (1917).

MANN, T. H., "A Yankee in Andersonville," *Century* (1890) 447-61, 606-22.

MATTOCKS, CHARLES P., "In Six Prisons." *War Papers*, read before the Commandery of the State of Maine Military Order of the Loyal Legion of the United States, I, 161-81, Dec. 2, 1891 (Published 1898).

McCREERY, WM. B., "My Experience as a Prisoner of War, and Escape from Libby Prison." A Paper read before the Michigan Commandery of the Loyal Legion of the United States, February 6, 1889. Detroit, 1893.

McNARY, OLIVER R., "What I Saw and Did Inside and Outside of Rebel Prisons." A paper read before the Kansas Commandery of the Military Order of the Loyal Legion of the United States (1905).

McRAE, WALTER G., "Confederate Prisoners at Morris Island," *Confederate Veteran*, XXIX, 178-79 (1921).

MEAD, WARREN HEWITT, "Southern Military Prisoners and Escapes." A paper read before the Minnesota Military Order of the Loyal Legion of the United States, November 11, 1890.

MORAN, FRANK E., "Colonel Rose's Tunnel at Libby Prison," *Century*, March, 1888, pp. 770-90.

OAKLEY, J. M., "From Libby to Freedom," *Lippincott's Magazine,* XLI, 812-25 (1888).

OULD, ROBERT, "Captain Irving and the 'Steamer Convoy,' Supplies for Prisoners." *Southern Historical Society Papers,* X, 320-38. (1882).

P——— C———, "Prisoners of War, By a Private Soldier of the U. S. Federal Army," *The Leisure Hour,* XXI, 21-24 (1872).

"Prison Pastimes." *Southern Historical Society Papers,* XIX, 35-47 (1891). Purports to be a Newspaper written by Prisoners at Fort Delaware.

PUTNAM, GEORGE HAVEN, "Prisoners of War: A Soldier's Narrative of Life at Libby and Danville Prisons," *The Outlook,* XCVII, 695-704 (1911).

READ, JOHN, "Texas Prisons and a Comparison of Northern and Southern Prison Camp." In the Military Order of the Loyal Legion New York Commandery. *Personal Recollections of the War of the Rebellion,* 4th series, New York and London, VIII, 1912.

ROBBINS, NATHANIEL A., "Life in Rebel Prisons." Read before the District of Columbia Commandery of the Military Order of the Loyal Legion of the United States. May 2, 1906.

SHEARMAN, MARY A., "A Visit to Andersonville," *Hours of Leisure,* V, 409-15 (1867).

SHELTON, W. H., "A Hard Road to Travel out of Dixie," *Century,* 931-47 (1890).

SMALL, ABNER R., "Personal Observations and Experiences in Rebel Prisons, 1864-1865." *War Papers,* Read before the Commander of the State of Maine of the Military Order of the Loyal Legion of the United States, I, 295-318. (Read December 4, 1895) (Published 1898).

SMITH, GEORGE T., "Prison Experience of a Northern Soldier." *Southern Historical Society Papers,* XI (1883).

STIBBS, JOHN HOWARD, "Andersonville and the Trial of Henry Wirz," *Iowa Journal of History and Politics,* January, 1911.

SWIFT, FREDERIC W., "My Experience as a Prisoner of War." Read before the Michigan Commandery of the Military Order of the Loyal Legion of the United States, December 1, 1886. Detroit, 1888.

SZABAD, LT. COL., "Diary in Libby Prison," *Frazier's Magazine,* LXXVII, 385-406 (March, 1868). Also published in *Every Saturday.*

THOMAS, HENRY G., "Twenty-Two Hours a Prisoner of War in Dixie." *War Papers,* read before the Commandery of the State of Maine Military Order of the Loyal Legion of the United States, I, 29-49, read September 5, 1888. (Published 1898).

WELLS, JAMES M., "Tunneling Out of Libby Prison," *McClure's*, XXII, 317-326 (1903).

WHITE, JOHN CHESTER, "Military Prisons; North and South," *Historical Society of Massachusetts, Civil War and Miscellaneous Papers*, VI (1918) Boston.

WHITENACK, DAVID S., "Reminscences of the Civil War," "Andersonville," *Indiana Magazine of History*, XI, 128-43 (1915).

WYETH, JOHN A., "Cold Cheer at Camp Morton," *Century*, 844-48 (1891).
This article excited a considerable controversy in newspapers and magazines.

IV. MISCELLANEOUS SOURCES

ATWATER, DORENCE, *A List of the Union Soldiers Buried at Andersonville. Copied from the Official Record in the Surgeon's Office at Andersonville.* New York, 1866.

AVERILL, JAMES P., *Andersonville Prison Park, Report of Its Purchase and Improvement.* .Atlanta, 1920.

BLAINE, JAMES G., *Political Discussions, Legislative, Diplomatic, and Popular.* Norwich, Conn., 1887.

BUTLER, BENJAMIN F., *Private and Official Correspondence of General Benjamin F. Butler.* (Copyright by Jessie Ames Marshall). 5 Vols. 1917.

The Demon of Andersonville, or the Trial of Wirz for the Cruel Treatment and Brutal Murder of Helpless Union Prisoners in His Hands. The Most Highly Exciting and Interesting Trial of the Present Century. His Life and Execution Containing Also a History of Andersonville, with Illustrations, Truthfully Representing the Horrible Scenes of Cruelty Perpetrated by Him. Philadelphia, 1865. (Copyright).

HAULY, J. FRANK, *Andersonville.* Cincinnati, 1912.
Report of dedication of Indiana Monument.

HICKS, IRL, *The Prisoner's Farewell to Johnson's Island; or, Valedictory Address to the Young Men's Christian Association of Johnson's Island, Ohio.* A Poem. St. Louis, 1872.

JONES, BUEHRING H., The *Sunny Land; or Prison Prose and Poetry Containing the Production of the Ablest Writers of the South, and Prison Lays of Distinguished Confederate Officers.* Baltimore, 1868.

JONES, J. B., *A Rebel War Clerk's Diary at the Confederate States Capital.* 2 Vols. Philadelphia, 1866.

KRAUSS, WILLIAM H., *The Story of Camp Chase. A History of the Prison and its Cemetery, together with other Cemeteries Where Confederate Prisoners are Buried, etc.* Nashville and Dallas, 1906.

R. E. Lee Camp, No. 1. Confederate Veterans, *Walls that Talk, A Transcript of the Names, Initials and Sentiments Written and Graven on the Walls, Doors and Windows of the Libby Prison at Richmond; by the Prisoners of 1861-65.* Richmond, 1884.

MOORE, FRANK (Editor), *The Rebellion Record,* 11 Vols. 1861-1865.

MOSS, LEMUEL, *Annals of the United States Christian Commission.* Philadelphia, 1868.

O'DEA, THOMAS, *History of O'Dea's Famous Picture of Andersonville Prison, as it appeared August 1st, 1864, when it Contained 35,000 Prisoners of War, Graphic Descriptions of that Famous Locality with Explanation of Key to Prison and Marginal Scenes.* Cohoes, New York, 1887.

ROLAND, DUNBAR (Editor), *Jefferson Davis, Constitutionalist. His Letters, Papers and Speeches.* 10 Vols. Jackson, Miss.

RUFFIN, EDMUND, "Extracts from the Diary of Edmund Ruffin, President Davis and Retaliation," *William and Mary Quarterly,* XXL, 224132.

The Southern Bazaar, Held in St. George Hall, Liverpool, October, 1864. Report of Proceedings. Liverpool.

SUMNER, CHARLES, *His Complete Works,* 20 Vols. (Statesman Edition) 1900. "Retaliation and Treatment of Prisoners of War," XII, 74-96. Speech in Senate. January 24 and 29, 1865.

Union Ex-Prisoners of War Association of Kansas, *Proceedings of the First and Second Annual Re-Unions.* Topeka, 1883.

United Confederate Veterans. United Confederate Association of Chicago, Camp No. 8. *Register of Confederate Soldiers who Died in Camp Douglas 1862-65 and Lie Buried in Oakwood Cemetery.* Chicago, Ill., 1892. Cincinnati, 1891.

United States Christian Commission, *Record of the Federal Dead Buried from Libby, Belle Isle, Danville, and Camp Lawton Prisons, and at City Point, and in the Field before Petersburg and Richmond.* Philadelphia, 1866.

United States Congress, Joint Committee on the Conduct of the War, *Rebel Barbarities, Official Accounts of the Cruelties Inflicted upon Union Prisoners and Refugees.* New York, 1864.

United States Sanitary Commission, *Narrative of Privations and Sufferings of United States Officers and Soldiers while Prisoners of War in the hands of the Rebel Authorities, Being the Report of a Commission of Inquiry. Appointed by the United States Sanitary Commission, with an Appendix, containing the Testimony.* Philadelphia, 1864.
Issued also as Loyal League Pamphlet No. 76. This is the classic document in the propaganda concerning prisoners during the war. A violent and partisan report proving deliberate murder of prisoners by the Confederate authorities.

United States Sanitary Commission. *Extracts from the Quarterly Special Relief Report of the United States Sanitary Commission, Washington, D. C., April, 1865, concerning the Rebel Hospitals at Richmond, and the Provisions made for Their Patients, as Contrasted with the supplies Furnished to Union Prisoners of War in Rebel Hands.* U. S. Sanitary Commission Documents, No. 89, Washington, 1865.

WELLES, GIDEON, *Diary of Gideon Welles.* 3 Vols. Boston and New York, 1911. Unreliable, revised before publication.

V. NEWSPAPERS

Cincinnati *Daily Commercial,* 1861-65.

Columbus *Crisis,* 1861-65.

Harper's Weekly, 1861-65.

New York *Herald,* 1861-64.

New York *News,* 1861.

New York *Times,* 1861-66.

New York *Tribune,* 1861-66.

Richmond *Daily Dispatch,* 1861-65.

Richmond *Daily Enquirer,* 1861-65.

Richmond *Daily Whig,* 1861-65.

St. Louis *Missouri Republican,* 1861-65.

Washington *Daily National Intelligencer,* 1861-66.

VI. SECONDARY WORKS

1. BOOKS

BARTLETT, JOHN RUSSELL, *The Barbarities of the Rebels, as shown in their cruelty to the Federal Wounded and Prisoners; in Their Outrages upon Union Men; In the Murder of Negroes, and in their unmanly conduct throughout the Rebellion, by Col. Percy Howard, late of the Royal Horse Guards.* Providence, 1863.

BLISS, GEORGE N., *Prison Life of Lieut. James M. Fales.* Providence, 1882.

BRISTOL, FRANK MILTON, *The Life of Chaplain McCabe, Bishop of the Methodist Episcopal Church.* New York (copyright), 1908.

BROSS, WILLIAM, *Biographical Sketch of the Late Gen. B. J. Sweet, History of Camp Douglas. A Paper read before the Chicago Historical Society, Tuesday Evening, June 18, 1878.* Chicago, 1876.

BULLARD, K. C., *Over the Dead Line or who Killed "Poll Parrot."* New York and Washington, 1909.

CARNAHAN, JAMES R., *Camp Morton, A Reply to Dr. J. A. Wyeth.* Indianapolis, 1892.

FAIRCHILD, CHARLES B., *History of the 27th Regiment N. Y. Vols. Being a record of its more than two years of service in the War for the Union, from May 21st, 1861, to May 31st, 1863. With a complete Roster, and short sketches of Commanding Officers. Also a record of experience and suffering of some of the comrades in Libby and other Rebel Prisons.* Binghamton, New York, 1888.

Famous Adventures and Prison Escapes of the Civil War. New York, 1893.

GODFREY, C. E., *Sketch of Major Henry Washington Sawyer, First Regiment Cavalry, New Jersey Volunteers. A Union Soldier and Prisoner of War in Libby Prison under Sentence of Death.* Trenton, N. J., 1907.

HAMLIN, AUGUSTUS C., *Martyria: or Andersonville Prison.* Boston, 1868.

HOLMES, CLAYTON WOOD, *The Elmira Prison Camp. A History of the Military Prison at Elmira, New York, July 6, 1864 to July 10, 1865.* New York, 1912.

JONES, J. WILLIAM, *Confederate View of the Treatment of Prisoners completed from Official Records and other Documents.* Richmond, 1876.

The Military History of Ohio, etc. New York, Toledo, and Chicago, 1886.

RUTHERFORD, MILDRED LEWIS, *Facts and Figures vs. Myths and Misrepresentations, Henry Wirz and the Andersonville Prison.* Athens, Georgia, 1923.

SHANKS, J. P. C., *Speech of General J. P. C. Shanks, of Indiana, On Treatment of Prisoners of War. Delivered before the Grand Army of the Republic, Washington, D. C., March 19, 1870.*

WILSON, THOMAS L., *Sufferings Endured for a Free Government; or, a History of the Cruelties and Atrocities of the Rebellion.* Washington, 1864.

WYMAN, LILLIE BUFFUM CHASE, *A Grand Army Man of Rhode Island.* Newton, 1925.

2. ARTICLES

ANDERSON, C. C., "Who was Responsible for Andersonville?" *Confederate Veteran,* XXIX, 168 (1921).

ANDREWS, MATTHEW PAGE, "Treatment of Prisoners in Confederacy." In the *Gray Book* published by the Sons of the Confederate Veterans, 1920. Also *Confederate Veteran,* XXVI, 147-50 (1918).

ASHE, SARAH W., "The Trial of Henry Wirz." *N. C. Booklet,* XVII, 154-56. (Jan. 1919).

CHRISTIAN, GEORGE L., and others, "Treatment and Exchange of Prisoners." *Southern Historical Society Papers,* XXX, 77-104 (1902).

Duckworth, W. A., "Escape of Iowa Soldier from Confederate Prison." *Annals of Iowa*, IX, 337-59 (April).

Gratz, John, "The Andersonville Prison Park," *Confederate Veteran*, XXIX, 91-92 (1921).

"Dr. Jones Report on Andersonville." *New Eclectic*, VI, 176-86 (1870).

Keady, William G., "Incidents of Prison Life at Camp Douglas, Experience of Corporal J. G. Blanchard." *Southern Historical Society Papers*, VII, 269-73 (1884).

Mangum, Adolphus Williamson, "History of the Salisbury, N. C., Confederate Prison." Reprinted from the Charlotte, N. C., *Observer*. *Southern Historical Association Publications*, 1899.

Peeke, Hewson L., "Johnson's Island," *Ohio Archaeological and Historical Quarterly*, XXVI, 470-76 (1917).

Potts, Charles P., "A First Defender in Rebel Prison Pens." *Schuylkill County Historical Society Publications*, IV, No. 4, 341-52.

Richardson, Rufus B., "Andersonville," *The New Englander*, III, 729-73 (1880). With the exception of the chapter in Rhodes' *History of the United States*, VI, this is the only attempt to approach the subject of prisons and prisoners in a scientific spirit.

Rutherford, Mildred Lewis, "Henry Wirz, the True Story of Andersonville Prison." *Miss Rutherford's Scrap Book*, Vol. II, June, 1924. Athens, Georgia.

Shepard, Frederic J., "The Johnson's Island Plot." *Publications of the Buffalo Historical Society*, IX, 1-51.

Southern Historical Society, Papers, XVIII, 327-33, 333-40 (1890). XVII, 378-81 (1889). (Article relating to the treatment of prisoners in the North, resulting from the publication of Wyeth's "Cold Cheer at Camp Morton.")

Turner, William Dandridge, "Some War-Time Recollections. The Story of a Confederate Officer who was at First one of those in Charge of and Later a Captive in Libby Prison," *American Magazine*, LXX, 619-31 (1910).

Tyler, Lyon G., "Judicial Murder of Major Henry Wirz," *Confederate Veteran*, XXVII, 178-80 (March, 1919).
"Major Henry Wirz," *Wm. and Mary Quarterly*, XXVII, 145-51 (January, 1919).

Wyeth, John A., "Prisoners North and South," *Southern Historical Society Papers*, XIX, 47-51 (1891).

VII. FICTION

"At Andersonville," *Atlantic Monthly*, XV, 285-96 (1865).

COLLINGWOOD, HERBERT W., *Andersonville Violets. A Story of Northern and Southern Life.* Boston, 1889.

RUSSEL, CHARLES WALCOTT, *The Prisoner of Andersonville. A Military Drama in Four Acts.* New York, 1903.

TOMILSON, EVERETT TITSWORTH, *Prisoners of War. A Story of Andersonville.* Boston and New York, 1915.

INDEX